JANE'S DELICIOUS
URBAN
GARDENING

JANE'S DELICIOUS
URBAN
GARDENING

Jane Griffiths

Photography by Keith Knowlton and Jane Griffiths

SUNBIRD PUBLISHERS

SUNBIRD PUBLISHERS

First published in 2015

Sunbird Publishers
The illustrated imprint of Jonathan Ball Publishers
A division of Media24 Ltd
P O Box 6836, Roggebaai 8012
Cape Town, South Africa

www.sunbirdpublishers.co.za

www.janesdeliciousgarden.com

Design and typesetting by MR Design; Cover design by MR Design
Editing, project management and index by Michelle Marlin
Proofreading by Kathleen Sutton
Photographs by Jane Griffiths and Keith Knowlton

Reproduction by Resolution Colour, Cape Town
Printed and bound by Imago Productions (FE) Pte Ltd, Singapore

ISBN 978-1-920289-87-4

"The ultimate goal of farming is not the growing of crops, but the cultivation and perfection of human beings."
Masanobu Fukuoka, *The One-Straw Revolution*

For all the passionate and dedicated urban farmers who are making a difference

Thanks to
My Garden Angels who guide me;
Ceri, Michelle and Marius for believing in Beautiful Books;
and most of all to Keith, my urban farming partner

CONTENTS

INTRODUCTION

We live in an old double-storey house covered with green creeper – literally a 'green house'. When we moved in, there was a classic English-style garden with lawns, roses and a large swimming pool. In the 22 years that we have lived here, much has changed. Most of the lawn has given way to a vegetable garden or beds planted with herbs and water-wise plants. The roses intermingle with fruit trees and the pool is now filtered by a wetland with fish, frogs and water plants. Under the bay tree live Itchy and Scratchy, my two egg- and manure-producing hens. A vertical strawberry garden wraps the rainwater harvesting tank and succulents cover the grey-water tank. Outside the back door, containers and pots overflow with edibles and herbs. In every available space are fruit trees, including ones in pots and espaliered against sunny walls. At last count our urban orchard included 24 fruit trees and ten different types of berries and vines – and we live in the middle of the largest city in South Africa: Johannesburg.

When I wrote my first book, *Jane's Delicious Garden*, I knew hardly anyone who grew their own food. That has changed. Growing organic vegetables, once a fringe activity, is now mainstream. When people begin growing their own food, it changes them. Awareness of the environment increases as resources such as water, space and nutrients become important. Once the vegetable gardening bug bites, people begin growing herbs and then fruit. They become avid recyclers and junk collectors. When eating out they want to know the origin of their food and whether it has been farmed ethically. Dinner conversations include heirloom seeds and composting tips. These small changes multiply and make a big difference.

I have been both a participant and a beneficiary of this expansion. I have learned (and continue to learn) so much more about growing food and sustainable living since I wrote my first book seven years ago. I've been lucky enough to meet many inspirational, passionate and knowledgeable food gardeners. Urbanites, with no desire to move to a farm or smallholding, are finding innovative and productive ways of growing healthy organic food in limited city spaces. From people in the queue at the supermarket, who proudly show me cell phone photographs of their vegetable gardens, to women in townships who are growing food for AIDS orphans, from roof tops to converted bowling greens, public alleyways to pavement gardens, there is a growing green revolution spreading throughout South Africa. With predictions that by 2050, up to 70 per cent of our population will be living in cities, and food production will need to double to feed an increasingly affluent population, urban farming will supply the food of our future.

However much I like the idea of living off the grid, becoming completely self-sufficient while living in the city is a rather daunting idea. Instead, I aim to create an environment that is as eco-friendly as possible. *Jane's Delicious Urban Gardening* is about exploring and sharing ways that urbanites can live a more connected and sustainable life in the city. How, even with our demanding schedules, we can become a *part of* nature instead of living *apart from* nature. Whether it's growing vegetables or harvesting rainwater, contributing kitchen waste to a community farm's compost heap or converting a chemical pool to a natural one, all urban dwellers would benefit if each of us took a few steps towards becoming more environmentally aware urban farmers. As our gardens transform slowly into urban oases, they improve the quality of our lives and reduce our impact on the environment. By creating an interconnected ecosystem we lessen our reliance on increasingly unstable urban supply systems.

In our Twenty-first century of absolute convenience and consumerism, we have become disconnected from nature. We somehow believe that not only can we live separately from nature, but that we can also take as much as we want without giving anything back. And that is not how a successful relationship works. We are a part of nature and if we continue to live as if we are a privileged and separate species, we risk losing everything. The multitude of problems facing us as human beings on this planet can be overwhelming and daunting. But one thing each and every one of us can do is to take personal responsibility to cultivate a better relationship with the piece of planet on which we live.

URBAN
VEGETABLE
GARDENING

GARDENING IN THE CITY

When I first began growing vegetables in my urban garden two decades ago, I had no idea it was going to be the beginning of one of the most important relationships in my life. I wasn't really interested in growing anything; I just wanted some unusual varieties of chillies for my kitchen. But after that first chilli season I was hooked – hooked on the seemingly simple process of taking a handful of seeds, sowing them, nurturing the plants and making the most of the abundant harvest.

I suppose it was fitting that my 'fling' with growing vegetables began with chillies. They are hot, spicy, beautiful to look at and, like any good affair, they left me wanting more. So I dug up more lawn. And sowed more seeds. The chillies were joined by lettuces, tomatoes, eggplants and beans. And as my garden grew, my fling slowly developed into a fully-fledged relationship.

As with any relationship, it required all those familiar elements: commitment, love, generosity, tolerance, trust, communication, respect – and let's not forget compromise. Before I knew it, those lazy Saturday afternoons, hanging in a hammock lost in a novel, were instead being spent, sweatily and joyfully, in my vegetable patch. In those days there was no Google. And I didn't know anyone else who was growing vegetables. I bought books and subscribed to magazines. But almost all of these were American or British, as there was little information in South Africa on growing organic vegetables in an urban garden. I had to either ignore much of it or adapt it to my environment. So I learned from my garden itself, experimenting, observing, documenting and growing. And as my garden expanded, so did my knowledge and understanding of the plants, the soil and the cycles. I learned how to replenish my soil, listen to my plants and observe the insects. I stopped worrying about it being perfect and just let it be. I received its gifts of abundant harvests with gratitude and learned from the failures.

I soon realised that the most essential tool you can have in a garden is knowledge. The more you know about your plants and their environment, the better off you and your garden will be. And this comes from spending time in your garden, not just slaving away but observing the details, absorbing the energy. The cycles of nature that I observe in my garden are timeless and boundless. They connect me to a deeply rooted order that is natural and universal. They are evidence that nature will continue to do what she has always done. And my relationship with my garden is only part of it.

There are endless other relationships existing within it. I have observed the harmony of different insects and their 'time share' of favourite flowers – you never get traffic jams on insect highways as they come out at different times of the day. Mulch, layered on the surface, soon decomposes into rich food for multiple organisms. In this intricate balance of life, death and decay, nothing is wasted and everything is recycled and reused.

Growing your own food might seem a mundane and prosaic activity. For me, however, there is something far more spiritual and magical about it. My garden is not just for feeding my body, it is also a haven that nourishes my soul. In the city, living my busy life with pressures and deadlines, it is easy to lose touch with nature. Gardening changes that as I become far more aware of seasons, cycles and the intricate natural balance that surrounds me. If there is one thing I have learned from my garden it is this: by putting Mother Nature in the central position, by learning from her every move, I have not only become a more successful gardener, but a far more contented person.

BENEFITS OF URBAN FARMING

Increasing the amount of food grown in our cities will do more than provide fresh, affordable, organic vegetables, fruit and herbs on our doorstep. Urban food gardens create greener spaces in our cities, reducing food miles and recycling waste that would have gone to landfill sites. City areas are heat-creating islands of concrete, tarmac and glass, with increased air pollution from traffic and industry. Greener spaces within the city lessen air pollution, as plants clean and filter the air. Vegetation absorbs heat and insulates buildings, reducing the need for energy-hungry air conditioners and heaters. Stormwater, instead of running off flat roofs, walls and pavements and out of the city, is slowed by plants and their growing media. Green spaces attract and provide habitat for birds and insects, reconnecting city dwellers with nature and relaxing green havens.

Urban farms give urbanites an increased appreciation of our food and its origins. People, particularly children, who are involved in growing their own food, are more likely to want to eat it, leading to better eating habits and a healthier society. Gardening opens eyes to the importance of recycling and conserving precious resources. A city farm is an effective way to teach children practical aspects of science and biology and how the world around us works. This increased knowledge leads to opportunities for job creation and entrepreneurs. And finally, green havens simply look and feel good, improving the quality of our lives.

Whether you are growing vegetables in your own back garden, a patio or on a large city rooftop, a basic understanding of soil, plants and how to grow them is the first step to success.

GROUNDWORK

What does the term 'organic' mean for those of us wanting to grow our own food? Organic gardening is nothing new; in fact it is a very old way of gardening. It is the way all farming and gardening was done before the advent of chemical fertilisers and pesticides. You might think that gardening organically just means replacing chemical pesticides and fertilisers with organic ones. In my view, there is much more to it than that. Organic gardening is an all-encompassing holistic approach to gardening and our environment. It is about acknowledging that we are inextricably connected to natural cycles that are far greater than we are.

Our aim in an organic garden is to minimise and replenish all the resources that we and our gardens consume. Organic gardeners will rather recycle an old fence to create raised beds than buy new material. They are usually avid junk collectors, always having a stash of things that 'might have a use one day'. And all organic gardeners understand that a healthy garden begins with the soil.

SOIL

One of the first things we need to understand about plants is that they are co-conspirators in the vegetable plot: they want to grow. All we need to do is create the optimum environment that will invite Mother Nature in to do what she does best. And this begins with creating and maintaining healthy soil.

Healthy nutrient-rich soil = healthy strong plants = healthy humans. Just as a healthy body is more resistant to infections, so healthy soil builds up a plant's resistance to attacks. The first step to controlling diseases and insects is to cultivate healthy soil.

So what is healthy soil and how do we achieve it? 'Healthy soil' means soil full of humus – the broken-down organic matter that is the 'life force' of the soil. Humus-rich, healthy soil encourages a dynamic thriving ecosystem with billions of organisms such as fungi, bacteria, algae, insects and worms. In one teaspoon of healthy soil there are more than six billion microscopic organisms. These are the workhorses of the soil, performing a multitude of beneficial functions ranging from:

- Breaking down organic matter and improving soil structure. This increases soil fertility, aids seed germination and creates healthier seedlings and plants with stronger roots.
- Enriching the soil. Earthworms, for example, leave the earth eight times richer after being digested through their intestines.
- Nutrient exchange. Certain bacteria form symbiotic relationships with legumes, such as peas and beans, and convert nitrogen gas into a usable form for the plants. In exchange the bacteria receive minerals and sugars.
- Cleansing the soil. Pathogens such as *E.coli* and salmonella are destroyed in an earthworm's intestine.
- Communicating information. Scientists have recently discovered large underground fungal networks that enable plants to communicate with one another. If a tomato is attacked by a disease it will leave a marker in the fungal network. Any other tomato plant that sinks its roots into the same network (that can spread kilometres underground in undisturbed soil) will pick up and 'read' the message. This enables it to build up its defences against the disease.

HUMUS

Vegetable gardens need as much humus in the soil as possible:

- Humus acts as an extremely high-absorption sponge, sucking up and retaining water.
- Chemically, humus has numerous active surfaces, which bind to the nutrients. Hence a humus-rich soil is a nutrient-rich soil.
- It improves the physical structure of soil, making it moist, crumbly and aerated, providing the ideal home for roots and beneficial bacteria.

NO-DIG GARDENING

The first step to creating humus-rich soil is to disturb the soil as little as possible. Early on in my gardening journey I discovered the joys and benefits of no-dig gardening. In many gardens it is a tradition to dig up the soil regularly, beating the earth with a fork to break up the clods and loosen the soil. The good news is – you can say goodbye to all that work because digging up and turning over the earth is more harmful than beneficial to the soil.

Every time you dig, you are destroying billions of beneficial soil organisms, their homes and their networks. Instead of being of assistance in the soil, they now have to spend time rebuilding. Earthworms, for example, breed only when undisturbed.

Digging causes moisture loss, as pockets of moisture trapped in the soil are exposed to air. And nutrients dissolved in this moisture are also lost.

Digging also upsets the balance of beneficial organisms. Aerobic organisms (that need air to function) prefer to live closer to the surface, while anaerobic ones (that don't need air) function better at the lower levels. And, finally, digging causes dormant weed seeds to surface and germinate.

Digging results in less moisture, less nutrients, no beneficial organisms helping you and a thriving crop of weeds. So stop digging! Whenever I speak to garden clubs, this comment inevitably provokes a rumble of comments from the audience. "But I need to dig; if I don't dig the soil will become compacted. That's *why* I dig . . ."

So there are a few No-dig Rules. Firstly – never, ever stand on your soil. It is our weight pressing down on the soil that leads to it being compacted in the first place. Therefore a second sensible rule is to make your garden beds just wide enough so you can reach the middle easily. (A good sized bed is the size of an average door, 2 m by 1 m.) This removes the need to stand on the soil. If your existing beds are bigger than this, simply place stepping stones at a comfortable distance apart.

If you have sufficient humus in your soil it won't become compacted. To maintain high levels of humus, add organic matter – compost, well-rotted manure and organic mulch – regularly to the surface of beds. Nature is designed to incorporate material from the surface into the lower layers. Earthworms come up at night and pull it into the soil, rain and heat break it down and in no time it will be converted into humus for your plants' roots.

With no-dig gardening it helps to have an edging around the beds, just high enough to retain the enriched soil inside the beds. It is also a good idea to have pathways between the beds. Ensure that your main pathways are wide enough for a wheelbarrow; allow at least 90 cm. Side pathways for walking can be narrower; about 60 cm. Pathways can be created from a variety of materials: bricks, planks, paving stones, railway sleepers or simply earth mulched with gravel, straw or bark. If budget allows, it is preferable to create permanent pathways as a simple mulched path will, over time, become muddy and weeds will grow through it. Line permanent pathways with a good-quality weed cloth before laying the path on top. This will save you plenty of weeding later.

The only time you need to dig deep in your garden is to remove an unwanted perennial, to harvest roots of a plant, or when preparing a new bed.

GARDENING, THE HAPPY DRUG

We gardeners have always known that spending time in our gardens makes us happy. Now it has been proved scientifically. Researchers recently discovered a strain of bacteria in the soil that triggers serotonin, the feel-good chemical in our brains. When we garden, we breathe in this bacteria and it enters our bodies through tiny cuts on our fingers. It acts as a natural anti-depressant, increases cognitive ability and reduces anxiety. All the more reason to head outdoors and start growing.

LOCATION

Most vegetables need full sun – which means at least eight hours of sunlight a day. The best location for a vegetable garden is north-facing, as this is the sunniest aspect. However, if you don't have the ideal position you can still work around it by getting to know your microclimate and your plants. For example, a south-facing wall will throw a solid shadow south of it for at least three months in mid-winter. So this is not a good spot for a winter garden. However, it is an ideal spot for lettuces and rocket in summer. If you don't have the perfect aspect, there are several solutions suggested for a shady garden on page 153.

PREPARING BEDS

Intensive methods of gardening work best in rich, fertile soil. The first time beds are prepared, enrich them with manure and compost. Once you've dug and prepared your beds, you never need to do it again.

Sunken Beds

In very sandy soil, especially in hot arid regions, creating a sunken bed will help retain moisture and keep the beds cooler. When preparing the beds for the first time, before enriching the soil, remove some of the lower subsoil layer and use it to create hills between the beds. This creates a trench for the vegetables with the pathway on the hills above them.

- Working in small sections, remove the topsoil layer and dig a trench about half a metre deep.
- Loosen the subsoil layer – don't turn it over, just aerate it by sticking a fork in and wiggling it back and forth.
- Add a thick layer (20 to 30 cm deep) of well-rotted manure and compost.
- Fill in the trench, adding the topsoil last. After adding the topsoil, the surface will be higher than the surrounding path. This is why adding an edge to the beds is necessary to retain the enriched soil inside the beds.

This method works well on soil that needs to be improved. To create a quick vegetable garden on relatively fertile soil, see page 248.

AMENDING SOIL

For a plant to function properly, its roots need access to air, water and nutrients. Many factors can compromise these three simple needs: poor aeration from compacted soil; inadequate or too much moisture; pH levels that are too high or low; or soil that drains too slowly or quickly.

Soil amendments are added to address these problems and create the optimum environment for roots. These amendments are not fertilisers, although some do add fertility to the soil. They should be incorporated when the beds are first prepared. Here are some of the most common soil problems and recommended amendments.

Sandy soil has large particles and pores between them, which tend to drain fast and don't hold nutrients. To increase the moisture- and nutrient-holding capacity, use the following amendments: all organic material including peat, leaves, straw, sawdust, wood chips and compost. Mix them into the top 15 to 20 cm. These will break down quickly. Replenish by adding more organic matter to the surface.

Clay soil has tiny particles and pores, does not drain well and can become waterlogged quickly. Roots cannot take up nutrients without air and so begin to rot. To increase porosity, amendments are added to encourage the small particles to clump together into bigger ones. Again the remedy is to incorporate organic matter, such as sawdust, leaves, compost and straw, into the top 15 to 20 cm. Sawdust is particularly good to encourage clumping.

Incorrect pH balance. Soil might contain all the nutrients a plant requires, but if the pH balance of the soil is incorrect, they can't dissolve and are therefore unavailable to the plants, leading to deficiencies. Most nutrients required by plants dissolve in a soil solution with a pH between 6 and 7.5. Below pH 6 calcium, magnesium, nitrogen, phosphorus and potassium are reduced. Above pH 7.5 boron, copper, iron, manganese and zinc are less available. With some nutrients, such as iron and manganese, lower pH results in excessive amounts being available, leading to toxicity. To test soil, use a soil meter available from most nurseries.

To amend slightly acidic soil, add a sprinkling of agricultural lime to the surface only. Lime will take a few months to change the pH and it is best added in autumn.

To amend highly acidic soil (below pH 5) incorporate agricultural lime into the top 15 to 20 cm. Test after a few months and repeat as needed until it reaches a neutral pH of 7. Be careful of adding too much lime as it is difficult to undo. Once the pH is correct, test annually and if it drops add lime to the surface.

To amend alkaline soil (above pH 8) incorporate peat moss, decomposed oak leaves, pine needles or flowers of sulphur to the soil until it gradually becomes more acidic. It is a slower process to bring an alkaline soil back to neutral pH and may take up to a year to achieve.

ENRICHING THE SOIL

After preparing the beds the first time, you will never need to dig them again. By adding compost, manure and mulch regularly to the surface of the beds, you emulate the natural process, providing your plants with a steady supply of nutrients.

Compost, made from recycling all your garden and kitchen waste, can be enriched by adding plants such as alfalfa, comfrey and yarrow. Manure also increases the nutrient content, but it must be well-rotted before being added to the beds. Green manure – growing nutrient-rich plants in the beds and then chopping them down – also adds a variety of nutrients. See pages 62 to 70 for more on compost, green manure and nutrients.

NITROGEN THEFT

When incorporating any carbon-rich organic matter into the soil, such as sawdust, dry leaves or straw, add a nitrogen-rich fertiliser at the same time. (Avoid sawdust from pressure-treated or painted wood as it can contain harmful chemicals.)

Organisms that break down organic matter use carbon as energy and nitrogen to build cells. When a carbon-rich material is added to the soil, the organisms are stimulated to break it down but they don't have sufficient nitrogen. So they pull it out of the soil, in the process robbing surrounding plants of their nitrogen. However, when mulching with a carbon-rich material, you don't need to add extra nitrogen, as decomposition takes place more slowly on the surface.

PLANTING

Once you have prepared your beds and enriched the soil, the next step is to begin planting. You can choose seeds or seedlings, and there are advantages to both. Buying seedlings from a nursery is definitely a quicker option, giving you an almost instant garden. However, it is more expensive and the choice of nursery seedlings doesn't come close to the variety of seeds available.

The number of heirloom and organic seed suppliers in South Africa has increased dramatically over the last few years, providing home growers with a far wider choice of interesting vegetables and herbs. (See page 46 for more.) I can lose myself on seed websites for hours, browsing and salivating over the delicious choices. It is easy to be fooled into thinking that with one click of the mouse, the digital vegetable on the screen will manifest in my garden. Unfortunately there are a few more steps required between click and harvest. Although sowing from seed can be daunting for a beginner, there are advantages. It is far cheaper to grow vegetables from seed and there is a much wider choice available. Successive sowings are simpler using seed rather than seedlings.

In my garden I use a combination of purchased seedlings and seeds. I plan my garden, so I grow mostly from seeds. But there are times when I am super busy or have been away and haven't sown a successive crop of lettuces, and by the time I see my lettuces going to seed, it is too late. And that is when bought seedlings come to the rescue.

Don't sabotage your sowing by using old seeds. Seeds have varying life spans and viability. Some, like chilli seeds, can last for years, while most herb seeds last only about 12 to 16 months. To store seeds, keep them in a cool dark spot. Don't store them in plastic otherwise they can go mouldy. Freezing seeds is a good way to extend their life span. (For more on seeds, see page 40.)

SOWING SEEDS DIRECTLY

Many vegetable seeds (such as beans, leafy greens, lettuce and squash) are best sown directly into the garden so that they don't suffer the trauma and setback of transplanting, resulting in fast-growing, strong plants. One of the problems when sowing small seeds (such as lettuce) *in situ* is clumping: uneven clusters of seedlings next to bare patches of earth. To prevent this:

- Remove all stones, weeds, or clods and rake the soil smooth. What looks like a little dip to us is a deep valley to a seed. Water will flow to the lowest points, taking seeds with it.
- Cover with a smooth layer of seedbed mix (see opposite). Press down firmly and evenly with a flat piece of wood.
- Mist the surface, wetting it without disturbing it.
- Sprinkle small amounts of seeds, alternating a north-south with an overlapping east-west pattern, until the seeds are evenly distributed. (Interestingly the word 'broadcast', which we associate today with television and radio, is derived from the gardening term 'to broadcast', meaning to scatter seed evenly.)
- Cover with a layer of seedbed mix so the seeds are covered just double their size and mist gently to moisten.
- Sometimes despite your best efforts, uneven patches result. Simply fill these gaps with seeds a few weeks later.

For medium seeds, such as beetroot, radish and Swiss chard, prepare the area as for small seeds. Make shallow furrows or poke evenly spaced holes (also known as drills) in the ground to a depth of double the size of the seed. Drop seeds into the holes or into the furrows, evenly spaced according to the final size of the plant. Cover and press down firmly.

Large seeds, such as beans and squash, are the easiest. Simply poke a hole in the ground double the depth of the seed, drop the seed in, cover and press down firmly.

Keep seeds moist, but not waterlogged, until you see green leaves starting to emerge. Once they germinate, reduce watering to encourage seedlings to develop strong roots. Seed germination rates vary and sowing two or three seeds per hole will guarantee at least one seedling but this is a waste when using expensive seed. With these, rather sow one and if it doesn't germinate fill in the gaps later, resulting in a successive harvest.

If seeds are sown too thickly, leave them until they are about 7 cm high. Thin by snipping them at the base with small scissors. (This is better than pulling them out, which disturbs the remaining roots.) Don't waste edible thinned seedlings – add them to a salad as microgreens. (For more on microgreens, see page 146.)

SOWING SEEDS IN SEED TRAYS

With some seeds it is worth taking the time and effort to sow them in seed trays first and then to transplant the seedlings. There are several advantages to this.

- Seeds (such as brassica) that take a long time to germinate and reach transplanting size, are best sown in seed trays. In the time it takes for them to reach transplanting size, a quicker crop can be direct sown and harvested in the beds.

MAKE YOUR OWN MIXES

Seedbed and transplanting mix
- 4 parts sieved compost
- 1 part vermicompost
- 1 part Talborne Organics seedling food
- You can add 1 part well-rotted leaf mould (comfrey leaf mould is very nutrient-rich)

Seedling soil mix
- 2 parts sieved compost
- 2 parts coco peat
- 1 part pre-wet vermiculite
- 1 part well-rotted leaf mould

- Even the most careful direct seeding can result in uneven plant spacing. Broadcasted seed falls in a random pattern and not all seeds germinate. This results in a concentration of plants in one area and bare gaps in others. When transplanting seedlings, however, they can be placed in the best pattern for optimum growth.
- Sowing seeds in seed trays means getting a head start on the season in cold weather. Summer seeds, such as tomatoes and chillies, can be sown in seed trays under cover in mid-July. By the time the weather has warmed up enough towards the end of August they will be a healthy size and ready to be transplanted. (For a seedling soil mix, see page 25.)

TRANSPLANTING SEEDLINGS

Before buying seedlings from a nursery, inspect them thoroughly. Don't buy plants with yellow leaves, thin spindly stems or any signs of disease. Choose strong ones with sturdy stems. And bigger is not necessarily better. A larger seedling will have developed more roots, which become cramped in a seedling tray, resulting in stress and increased risk of transplanting shock. Check the soil for weeds before selecting your trays.

When you get seedlings home, don't transplant them straight away. They have spent their short lives as pampered and protected babies and will benefit from being exposed to the open gradually. This is called hardening off. Place them in a sheltered spot and over a few days gradually expose them to more sunlight and wind. Give them enough water while they wait to be transplanted, but don't over water because the soil in the seedling module will become muddy and loose, making it difficult to transplant. You want the whole block of soil to come out easily without damaging the roots. Preferably plant your seedlings late in the afternoon, especially if it is hot. This will give them the whole night to settle in before facing the heat of the day.

Start by measuring and digging the required number of holes first, before taking the seedlings out of their containers. This enables you to create a pattern with equidistant spacing (see page 38 for more on spacing). It also gets you into a rhythm of first digging and then transplanting. Dig the holes slightly deeper than the seedlings and add a small handful of transplanting mix (see page 25) and mix it into the soil at the bottom. This ensures that the roots receive all the nutrients they need. Don't make the mistake of over watering them in the days that follow. By encouraging them to hunt a little for water, you will help them develop strong roots.

If you have extra seedlings don't try to squeeze them into limited space. Rather repot them into a larger container and put them in a sheltered spot where you will remember to water them. These can be used as replacement plants if any of the ones in beds succumb to disease, hail damage or get eaten. They can also be used as a successive crop (see page 36). By transplanting them a few weeks later, they will mature later than the first ones.

GROWING

As home farmers, we have inherited many methods from commercial farmers, but our requirements are very different. Commercial farmers want their harvest to be uniform, so that it fits in boxes that can be packed on a truck and driven to the market. But a home grower doesn't want uniformity. We want to grow as much variety as possible, to provide us with a wide range of herbs and vegetables. We want green beans *and* purple beans *and* yellow beans.

A commercial grower wants the produce to look as good as possible, so buyers are tempted to pick it from the supermarket shelf. They are not too concerned with the fact that once that red tomato is sliced open at home it is often pale and tasteless inside. When we grow our own food, we are aiming to grow the best possible tasting vegetables, packed with nutrients. It doesn't matter if there is a blemish or a bug bite – what matters is how it tastes.

A commercial grower wants everything to ripen at once, so it can all be harvested efficiently at the same time. The last thing a home grower wants is for everything to ripen all at once. We want our vegetable garden to provide us with a steady bounty throughout the year.

So we can throw many of the rules of commercial farming out of the window – particularly monoculture, the practice of planting just one crop in one field (or bed). Even on a small scale in our urban gardens this is an invitation for pests and disease: a cabbage moth flying over a bed planted only with cabbages will see a bug buffet laid out before it. Realising that there is way more than it can eat, it will invite all its buddies in for a feast. If a fungal disease starts on one side of a bed filled with squash, it will quickly spread and infect the entire bed. If, however, our beds contain a medley of different plants, this is prevented.

GETTING THE MOST OUT OF YOUR GARDEN

When I first began growing vegetables I quickly ran out of room. I also experienced bouts of overwhelming abundance – often far too much for us to eat – followed by periods when nothing was coming out of the garden. I began experimenting with using vertical spaces and planting more intensively and I began to plan more carefully what I was planting where.

By combining the following planting methods I have an intensively planted garden full of natural diversity and variety: interplanting; companion, succession, vertical and intensive planting; and crop rotation. This not only helps prevent insect infestation and disease, it also provides the maximum harvest from a small space without depleting the soil. And it solves the feast or famine problem, by providing a steady supply of food year round.

Interplanting

This method of planting (also known as intercropping) mixes different varieties of plants together to avoid monoculture. Most interplanting is done using plants that don't compete with one another for sun or root space, such as lettuces and onions. Be aware of both the above-ground and below-ground space. Lettuces and onions are examples of good bedfellows. Above the ground the lettuce is round and frilly, while the onion leaves are contrastingly tall and skinny. Below ground, the lettuce root is quite neat and compact, allowing room for the onion to grow a fat bulb. Interplanting also combines slow- and fast-growing crops, maximising the amount of harvest from one bed.

By interplanting four or five different varieties of vegetables and herbs, we reduce insect damage as the diversity doesn't provide the one-stop shop that insects like. It confuses them and even if one or two bugs do stop for a nibble, an infestation is unlikely. The diversity also helps prevent the spread of diseases, as these often affect the same type of plant. By interplanting different varieties we provide a 'firebreak' to prevent the disease from spreading.

Horseradish flowers (top) and pansies (bottom) are edible and attract beneficial insects into the garden.

Companion Planting

This takes interplanting one step further by combining herbs, vegetables and flowers that have a mutually beneficial effect on one another. These can range from attracting beneficial insects, deterring pests, storing and transferring nutrients or camouflaging plants.

Attracting beneficial insects into our garden is one of the first advantages of companion planting. (For more information on beneficial insects see page 50.) But what about the insects we don't want? Most strong-smelling herbs will repel harmful insects such as aphids and whitefly. Artemisia, feverfew, lavender, rosemary, scented pelargonium and tansy are all good examples. These can be planted at the ends of beds or in containers so they can be moved around the garden. Many of these herbs like being cut back and the trimmings can be used as an insect-repelling mulch. They can also be used to make insect sprays (see page 60). Some plants can be used as trap crops, attracting harmful insects to come to them instead of infesting our vegetables. For example, nasturtiums attract aphids, and shield bugs just love amaranth.

Alfalfa and comfrey are good examples of herbs that supply nutrients to our vegetables. Their roots extend many metres deep, accessing nutrients that the roots of our vegetables cannot reach. Comfrey leaves, for example, contain more potassium than kraal manure. Another nutrient powerhouse is yarrow. The leaves of these plants can be chopped and added to the surface of the beds or to the compost pile. They can also be used to make a nutritious fertiliser (see pages 68 to 69).

Other nutritious companions are members of the legume family, such as alfalfa, clover, fenugreek and soy beans. These plants have a symbiotic relationship with bacteria in the soil. The bacteria take nitrogen gas from the air in the soil and feed it to the legumes. In exchange the plants provide carbohydrates to the bacteria. When the crops are used for compost or turned under as a green manure, this nitrogen is returned to the soil in a usable form for other plants. Because of this, legumes are called 'nitrogen fixing' plants.

A further benefit of companion planting is to use what I call shape-shifting plants. A cabbage moth, for example, is programmed to recognise the distinctive shape of a cabbage. However, if you plant a nasturtium to ramble around the cabbages, its large, saucer-shaped leaves will hide the cabbages' easily recognisable, round shapes. A cabbage moth flying over your garden will not spot your cabbages and will instead head on over to your neighbour's garden – where the cabbages are planted in large blocks without any companions camouflaging them from the enemy.

USEFUL COMPANIONS

PLANT	USES	COMPANIONS	GROWING
Alfalfa	• Breaks up soil • Nitrogen fixer • Deep roots accumulate iron, magnesium, phosphorus and potassium • Flowers attract beneficial insects • Use trimmings as mulch or in compost	All round good companion but particularly good for asparagus and mielies	• Full sun • Hardy (roots hardy, tops die down in frost) • Perennial • Drought-resistant • Likes being trimmed regularly
Amaranth	• Accumulates nutrients • Creates useful shade in midsummer • Trap crop for shield bugs	All round good companion but particularly good for beetroot, eggplant, mielies, onions, potatoes and tomatoes	• Full sun • Semi-hardy • Annual • Self-seeds • Drought-resistant
Artemisia (African wormwood)	• Repels harmful insects, beetles and caterpillars • Use trimmings as mulch, sprinkled onto cabbages and to confuse birds on newly seeded areas • Can be made into insect-repelling spray* • Repels mites in hens' bedding	All round good companion	• Full sun • Hardy • Perennial • Drought-resistant • Cut back in spring to prevent becoming shaggy • Preferably plant it away from the vegetable garden but near enough to pick leaves
Basil	• Repels flies, mosquitoes, sap-sucking insects, tomato hornworm • Flowers attract beneficial insects	Fruit trees, peppers and tomatoes. Helps prevent mildew on cucurbits	• Full sun • Annual (tender) • Perennial (semi-hardy) • Self-seeds • Needs regular moisture
Bay	• Repels insects • Sprinkle leaves around garden • Leaves can be used as insect-repelling mulch • Use leaves in stored grains, flour and seeds to prevent weevils	All round good companion	• Full sun • Hardy • Perennial • Drought-resistant • Likes being pruned • Can shade vegetables • Prune or plant it outside vegetable garden

*See page 60 for recipe

PLANT	USES	COMPANIONS	GROWING
Borage	• Soil and compost improver • Accumulates silica and potassium • Attracts bees, butterflies and wasps • Repels squash bugs and tomato hornworms • Use as nutritious liquid fertiliser*	All round good companion but particularly good for beans, brassicas, fruit trees, squash, strawberries and tomatoes	• Full sun to semi shade • Hardy • Annual • Self-seeds
Buckwheat	• Accumulates calcium and phosphorus • Attracts insects, particularly bees, butterflies, hoverflies and tachinid flies • Good green manure and cover crop	All round good companion	• Full sun • Tender • Annual • Self-seeds
Calendula	• Flowers attract bees, butterflies, crab spiders and hoverfly	Tomatoes and brassicas	• Full sun to semi shade • Hardy • Annual • Self-seeds
California poppy	• Flowers attract bees and crab spiders	All round good companion	• Full sun • Hardy • Annual • Self-seeds
Catnip	• Leaves repel leaf-eating and sap-sucking insects • Flowers attract beneficial insects • Can be made into an insect-repelling spray** • Use trimmings as mulch and to confuse birds on newly seeded areas • Repels mites in hens' bedding	Beans, brassicas, cucumber, eggplant, squash and tomatoes	• Full sun to semi shade • Hardy • Perennial • Spreads easily
Chives	• Prevents mildew, repels aphids and other sap-suckers and leaf-eating beetles • Accumulates calcium and sulphur • Improves disease resistance of nearby plants • Flowers attract beneficial insects	Carrot, cucumbers, eggplant, fruit trees, parsley, squash and tomato	• Full sun to semi shade • Hardy • Perennial • Divide every three years
Clover	• Fixes nitrogen • Accumulates potassium, phosphorus and nitrogen • Good green manure and cover crop • Flowers attract beneficial insects	All round good companion	• Full sun to semi shade • Hardy • Annual and perennial • Likes regular trimming

*See pages 66 to 68 for more on fertiliser plants | **See page 60 for recipe

PLANT	USES	COMPANIONS	GROWING
Comfrey	• Accumulates calcium, iron, magnesium, nitrogen and potassium from deep in the soil • Use as nutritious liquid fertiliser* • Compost activator • Flowers attract beneficial insects • Hens love it • Use leaves in potato planting holes	Particularly good fertiliser plant for eggplant, fruit trees, potatoes and tomatoes	• Full sun to semi shade • Hardy (roots hardy, tops die down in frost) • Perennial • Can spread so keep it in its own bed • Divide every few years
Echinacea	• Flowers attract beneficial insects, especially bees and butterflies • Disguises shapes of plants around it	Generally beneficial plant	• Full sun to light shade • Hardy (roots hardy, tops die down in frost) • Perennial • Self-seeds • Drought-resistant • Divide every few years once established
Fenugreek	• Good green manure and cover crop • Fixes nitrogen	Asian greens, beans, cucumber, lettuce, squash and tomatoes	• Full sun • Semi-hardy • Annual
Feverfew	• Flowers attract beneficial insects • Leaves repel harmful insects • Repels mites in hens' bedding • Can be made into an insect-repelling spray**	All round good companion	• Full sun to light shade • Tender • Short-lived perennial • Self-seeds
Lavender	• Strong-smelling leaves repel harmful insects and rodents • Flowers attract bees, butterflies and other pollinators • Use trimmings as mulch and to confuse birds on newly seeded areas	All round good companion	• Full sun • Hardy • Perennial • Prune in early spring
Marigold	• Repels asparagus beetle, chafer beetle, nematodes, potato beetle, sap-sucking insects, tomato hornworms, whiteflies • Flowers attract beneficial insects, especially bees and hoverflies	Asparagus, beans, cabbage, cucumber, dill, eggplant, fruit trees, potatoes and tomatoes	• Full sun • Hardy • Annual • Self-seeds

*See pages 66 to 68 for more on fertiliser plants | **See page 60 for recipe

PLANT	USES	COMPANIONS	GROWING
Mint	• Repels ants, aphids and moths • Use trimmings as mulch to keep insects away from seedlings or newly seeded areas • Accumulates magnesium and potassium	Cabbages and tomatoes	• Full sun to semi shade • Hardy (roots hardy, tops die down in frost) • Perennial • Will spread and can become invasive
Nasturtium	• Disguises shapes of plants around it • Attracts beneficial insects • Repels cucumber, potato and squash beetles, and tomato hornworms • Good trap crop for aphids • Good cover crop	All round good companion	• Full sun to semi shade • Tender • Annual • Self-seeds
Oregano	• Repels sap-sucking insects	Generally beneficial to all plants, particularly broccoli, eggplant and squash	• Full sun • Hardy • Perennial
Pansy	• Flowers attract beneficial insects	All round good companion	• Full sun to semi shade • Hardy • Annual
Parsley	• Accumulates calcium, iron, magnesium and potassium • Flowers attract beneficial insects	Asparagus, carrots, chives, mielies and tomatoes	• Full sun to semi shade • Hardy • Biannual
Pelargoniums (scented)	• Strong scent repels leaf-eating insects • Flowers attract beneficial insects	Brassicas	• Full sun • Semi hardy • Perennial
Radishes	• Best as a companion when left to flower • Flowers attract beneficial insects • Repels beetles	Beetroot, bush beans, pole beans, carrots, cucumber, lettuce, parsnip, peas and squash	• Full sun • Hardy • Annual • Needs plenty of moisture
Rosemary	• Flowers attract beneficial insects • Pungent leaves repel leaf-eating insects • Twigs good to protect young seedlings from cutworms, insects and sun	Beans, brassicas and carrots	• Full sun • Hardy • Perennial • Drought-resistant • Benefits from being cut, so harvest regularly

OPPOSITE: Pansies, echinacea and borage are all excellent companion plants in the garden.

PLANT	USES	COMPANIONS	GROWING
Sage	• Use trimmings as mulch, and to confuse birds and repel insects on newly seeded areas • Flowers attract beneficial insects • Pungent leaves repel leaf-eating insects	Beans, brassicas and carrots	• Full sun • Hardy • Perennial • Prune in early spring • Divide every three to four years
Tansy	• Accumulates potassium • Leaves repel ants, flies, leaf-eating insects and mice • Ladybirds love tansy and will breed on it • Can be made into an insect-repelling spray**	Good companion to most plants	• Full sun • Hardy (roots hardy, tops die down in frost) • Perennial • Can spread and become invasive • Can be fatal to grazing animals
Thyme	• Useful groundcover • Leaves repel harmful insects	Generally beneficial to other plants, particularly brassicas and all leafy greens	• Full sun • Hardy • Perennial • Drought-resistant • Divide every three years
Yarrow	• Accumulates calcium, copper, magnesium, phosphorus, potassium and sulphur • Compost activator • Use as nutritious liquid fertiliser** • Leaves repel harmful insects • Flowers attract many beneficial insects	General all round good companion that increases the health of plants near it	• Full sun • Hardy (roots hardy, tops die down in frost) • Can spread

*See page 60 for recipe | **See pages 66 to 68 for more on fertiliser plants

STAGGERING YOUR HARVEST

Another useful way of staggering the harvest is to take advantage of the patterns of sun and shade in your garden. I discovered this by accident when transplanting cauliflower seedlings one year. I ran out of room in the sunnier beds and transplanted four or five into a bed that received about three hours less sun. These seedlings took much longer to reach maturity and form heads, supplying me with a later harvest, after those in the sunnier beds were finished. This is yet another benefit of getting to know the patterns of your own garden.

Succession Planting

Succession planting of the same vegetable or herb is a method of ensuring a continuous and steady supply of food. It can be very overwhelming to suddenly have twenty cauliflowers forming heads at once, or ten bush bean plants all bearing at the same time. This can lead to wastage. There are some herbs and vegetables that go to seed more quickly than others, particularly in hot weather. Lettuce, coriander and rocket, for example, will all produce flowers far more quickly in midsummer than during the cold winter months. By staggering the plantings of these vegetables and herbs – spacing the plantings every two to four weeks – a new crop will start to bear as the first one fades or goes to seed.

Succession planting also helps prevent pest infestations. Plants that have been bearing for a while will begin to tire, becoming vulnerable to insect attacks and disease. With successive sowing, as a new crop starts to bear, the older, more susceptible one can be removed. Some pests are more prolific at different times of the year than others. Staggered plantings can take advantage of this. A later sowing of squash for example, will ripen in early autumn when there aren't as many shield bugs around.

Vertical Planting

One of the most successful methods of increasing the yield from a small space is using the vertical space – I call it 3D gardening. When I realised I didn't have quite enough space to grow real-estate-hungry plants such as gem squash and butternut, I began experimenting with training them to grow up tripods. And it worked. They grew happily up their tall support, allowing me to grow many more vegetables in my limited space. (See pages 138 to 145 for more information on vertical gardening.)

INTENSIVE PLANTING TIPS

- Combine short- and long-maturing plants, such as Asian greens and rocket planted with broccoli.
- Use bigger plants as sun protection for those needing it, for example lettuce planted under squash leaves in midsummer.
- Include some edible flowers and herbs in the mix.
- Plan ahead by sowing seeds under plants that will shortly be harvested and removed. Their leaves will provide protection and help retain moisture for germinating seedlings.

Intensive Planting

Most seed packets give spacing recommendations based on the traditional method of planting in rows, leaving wide spaces between each row for walking. We have also inherited planting methods from England, where the climate is very different to ours. There, plants are spaced to maximise the amount of sun they receive. Here we have so much sun we sometimes need to protect our plants from it.

By practising no-dig gardening and using smaller raised beds, we don't need to leave large spaces in between for walking as we will not be standing on our soil. We can space the vegetables much closer together, so when they grow to full size, their leaves just touch one another, maximising the amount of ground available. The plants of the resultant mass each have just enough room and, when fully grown, create a living umbrella, keeping the soil below them moist and also crowding out weeds.

An additional advantage of intensive planting is that beneficial organisms in the soil are most prolific in the rhizosphere – the root zone. The more plants you can fit in, the more roots there are, therefore increasing the number of beneficial organisms in the soil. Intensive planting works best when plants are spaced using a hexagonal pattern. This results in each seedling having six seedlings equidistant from it. By interplanting different varieties we ensure that a balance is maintained.

Crop Rotation

Crop rotation minimises disease and maximises fertility. Each crop has different requirements of the soil and deposits different residues. Growing one type of plant on the same piece of land year after year depletes the soil and leads to a build-up of diseases. Rotating crops prevents this. I use crop rotation principles as a rough guide. By using green manures (see page 66), no-dig gardening, interplanting, companion and intensive planting, my soil remains healthy and fertile. Over the years I have experienced few problems with disease or decreased soil fertility. However, it helps to have an understanding of crop rotation and use it as a guideline when planting.

1.

As a general rule, individual vegetables from the same family do not follow one another year after year. You can also organise your rotations by roughly dividing them into four groups according to the nutrients they require: leaf, fruit, root and legume.

1. Leaf

Nitrogen is the most easily soluble of all nutrients making it the hardest for the soil to retain, so begin with plants from the leaf group that use lots of it to build strong stems and crispy leaves. Leafy plants include broccoli, cauliflowers, greens, herbs, kale, lettuce, spinach and mielies (not a leaf crop, but it is a heavy user of nitrogen – young mielies will provide necessary shade for summer lettuces).

2.

2. Fruit

Follow leafy plants with a member from the fruit group. These all use potassium to set blossoms and develop fruit. If these plants are grown in a soil that is too rich in nitrogen, they will develop beautiful leaves but not as many flowers and fruit. By following a nitrogen-hungry crop, the nitrogen is reduced. Cucumbers, eggplants, melons, peppers, squash and tomatoes all fall into this group.

3.

3. Root

Next come the root crops, which need plenty of phosphorus and even less nitrogen than fruit crops. There will be very little nitrogen left in the beds but the phosphorus will be ready and waiting for the root crops. Beetroot, carrots, garlic, leeks, onions, parsnips, radishes and turnips are all root crops. Potatoes are also root crops, but to prevent disease they should not follow other members of the nightshade family such as tomatoes and eggplant.

4.

4. Legume

And finally, plant a legume to put the nitrogen back into the soil, ready to begin the rotation again. These are all the beans and peas.

SEEDS

When buying seeds to plant in your garden, there is a wide choice available. There are organic seeds and hybrid seeds, heirlooms and open-pollinated seeds. And more recently genetically modified or engineered seeds. So what do all these terms mean?

Organic seed

An organically certified seed means it was produced by a certified organic grower and hasn't been exposed to any chemicals throughout growth, harvest or packaging. To be certified organic is an expensive process, involving annual renewals and inspections. This is beyond the reach of many of the emerging organic seed companies in South Africa – so when they say they are selling us organic seed, we sometimes have to go on faith and reputation.

Open-pollinated seed

These are varieties where the harvested seed can be saved and when planted will be the same as the parent plant. All heirloom seeds are open-pollinated – but not all open-pollinated seeds are heirlooms, as new varieties are too young to qualify.

Genetically modified seed (GM)

Although this term is often used interchangeably with GE (below), they don't have the same meaning. GMO refers to an organism that's had its DNA manipulated, either by hybridising or through genetic engineering.

Genetically engineered seed (GE)

Seed that's had one or more extra genes added to its DNA from another species is GE. Although they have been developed using high-tech methods, these are imprecise and have unpredictable and potentially disastrous results. Luckily for now, home gardeners won't be encountering many GE seeds, as these are patented seeds for large-scale agriculture by multinational agri-businesses, with profit as their main motivator. They include canola, cotton, mielies and soy beans. Organic rules prohibit the use of GE seeds. However, pollen from GE crops can unintentionally cross-pollinate nearby organic ones, particularly mielies.

Hybrid seeds

These are produced in a controlled environment by cross-pollinating different strains to produce seed that will result in a plant with specific characteristics, such as disease resistance, improved yield or quicker ripening. Seed saved from these will not come true to the parent plant. A hybrid seed can be organic.

Heirloom seed

An heirloom is a treasured item that has been passed down through the generations. And that is exactly what heirloom seeds are – they have been handed down from one generation to the next. These seeds were saved and replanted because they had the best flavour and yield in home gardens. Definitions vary, with some saying that to qualify as an heirloom it has to go back at least 50 years. Some of these seeds have a history going back 300 years or more. An heirloom seed is not necessarily produced organically, but most are.

THE SECRET OF SEEDS

When we leave vegetables unharvested, they flower and produce seeds. Seeds are complex and magical – encapsulated in one tiny seed, are all the nutrients and information needed for the embryonic plant to burst into life. As seeds ripen, the plant moves nutrients away from leaves and towards the seed. Leaves become much smaller and sparser. Once the seeds have bulked up to full size, they begin to dry out. In a self-sown garden, seeds left to dry naturally on the plant will have longer viability.

Plants use different mechanisms to distribute and protect their seeds. Some produce seed cases, which become brittle as they dry and then explode, scattering the seeds away from the mother plant. Some, like carrots and other members of the Umbelliferae family, coat their seed with germination-inhibiting chemicals as they ripen during late summer and autumn. This ensures the seed won't fall and germinate immediately under the parent plant, competing with it for space and nutrients that have already been pulled from the soil. Rainwater washes the seeds steadily away from the plant, slowly removing the chemicals. By then, winter is over and spring has warmed up the soil, ready for germination.

Commercial seed companies flush seeds with chemicals and growth hormones to counteract these inhibitors. When we save these seeds, or buy organic seeds, they will still have the inhibitors intact, slowing down germination. So for carrot, caraway, celery, coriander, dill, fennel, lovage, parsley and parsnip seeds, lay them on wet tissue paper and rinse with water twice a day for three days before sowing. This will replicate the natural process of rainwater washing the chemicals off and speed up germination. I discovered this gem of information and much more in *The Secret Life of the Garden* by Chris Beardshaw.

A SELF-SEEDING, SUSTAINABLE GARDEN

Imagine walking through a luscious vegetable garden, brimming with edible plants. Now imagine that somehow, magically, this vision had planted itself. Sounds like a dream? Well it doesn't have to be. Many herbs and vegetables produce seeds enthusiastically (as long as you leave them to flower) and, with only a little bit of help from us, will continue to plant themselves, providing us with free plants season after season. Or instead of leaving them to self-seed, we can save the seeds, to be sown where we want them to grow.

Leaving vegetables and herbs to go to seed will create a self-sustaining garden, attract beneficial insects and allow the planting ecosystem to complete its natural cycle. Self-sown vegetables save money and time. They most often produce stronger, healthier plants that germinate and grow in places that are best suited for optimum growth. As the seasons pass, these evolve and adapt to the local climate and pests. The hardest part of growing a self-sown garden is learning to recognise the young seedlings so you don't weed them out!

Select the strongest and most vigorous plants and leave them unharvested to flower and go to seed. If you are happy for the plant to self-seed where it is, then leave it to do its thing. If you want plants to grow in another place, pick the seed bearing stems, break them up and scatter them where you want them to grow. The leaves and stems will provide mulch and protection for the emerging seedlings. It helps to press the branches into the ground a little.

When we sow a bed of mustard from a seed packet, we might use about 40 seeds. When nature sows seeds, she does it in the thousands. Many of these won't survive; they will be eaten, washed away or rot. But plenty remain to populate our self-sown vegetable gardens. Sometimes there are too many and then they become a weed. Examples of enthusiastic self-seeders are amaranth, borage, evening primrose, fennel, feverfew, sorrel and tansy. Manage these by cutting the flowers off before seeds form, thereby controlling how many you allow to seed themselves.

Plants such as tomatoes and gooseberries can also self-seed vigorously. They can be controlled by harvesting fruit regularly and by not placing the fruit in the compost (or making sure the compost reaches high enough temperatures to kill the seed). If a plant seeds itself too vigorously, leave the seedlings to grow to about 10 to 15 cm high, then slash them down and chop up the leaves and stems. These rot down, adding nutrients back to the soil. Or with edible ones such as amaranth, eat them as nutritious and colourful microgreens. (For more on microgreens, see page 146.)

With certain plants you need to keep an eye on disease. Self-sown tomatoes, for example, can carry disease from the previous season. If you have had problems with disease, transplant the volunteers to containers out of the garden so the disease isn't perpetuated.

Self-seeding Vegetables, Herbs and Companion Plants

PLANT	SEEDS
Amaranth	Forms a red fuzzy seed head that can be left or picked when the seeds begin to fall off it
Asian greens (bok choy, mizuna, mustard, tat soi)	Produce yellow flowers followed by long seed pods containing beige, brown or black round seeds
Basil	Makes long spires of purple and white flowers, with tiny dark brown seeds
Calendula	The bright orange and yellow flowers mature into a seed ball with crescent-shaped seeds
California poppies	Form long seed pods containing tiny round seeds. They self-seed sunnily without ever becoming a problem
Cherry tomatoes	Leave fruit to ripen and fall. They can become weeds, so learn to recognise the babies
Coriander	Creates umbels of delicate white flowers, followed by robust-flavoured round green seeds, which ripen to brown. Green coriander seeds are a gourmet secret for home gardeners, tasting of a delicious mixture of fresh coriander leaves and the more earthy flavour of coriander seeds. Self-sown coriander plants tend not to bolt as quickly as transplanted seedlings
Dill and fennel	Form yellow umbels (much loved by ladybirds), followed by crescent-shaped seeds, which ripen to brown
Gooseberry	Self-seeds prolifically and can become a nuisance. Keep it under control by harvesting regularly and keeping the fruit out of your compost
Lettuce	Goes to seed by growing a tall central spire, with small groups of wispy flowers that produce minute seeds
Nasturtium	Flowers mature into small clusters of green seed, which gradually dry to beige. The fresh green seed has a spicy flavour and is good pickled
Radish	Grows into a tall plant with pink and white flowers, followed by round dark seeds that need to be pushed into the ground
Rocket	Is a great self-seeder, with white or yellow flowers forming thin seed pods
Spinach	Produces a central spire with clusters of small white flowers nestled on the stem. These are followed by clusters of green seeds that ripen to brown
Spring onions	Form a ball-shaped white or pinkish flower (which butterflies love) followed by small black seeds. Will self-sow near the mother plant or you can sprinkle seeds where required
Sunflowers	Leave the flowering head to dry before saving or scattering seed
Swiss chard and beetroot	Produce a long central spire with clusters of angular-shaped seed

SEED SAVING

The next step to creating a sustainable garden is to save seed from your own vegetables and herbs. There are many reasons for doing this. You might start because of budget restrictions – saving seeds will save money. Or perhaps the seed has sentimental value: it evokes memories of a particular place or it is from a plant given to you by your Granny. Another reason is simply to keep a strain of seed alive. Many people don't realise that a seed variety can go extinct very quickly. If you have a special tomato that was brought out from Europe by your great-grandfather and has been in the family garden for generations, someone needs to collect its seeds every year and replant them, otherwise it will die out.

A further motivator to save seeds is to maintain the genetic diversity of seeds. The food plants we eat today bear little resemblance to their ancient ancestors. Over many hundreds – and sometimes thousands – of years, farmers have nurtured and developed new strains, by saving seeds from plants with the traits that they liked and that grew best in their environment. The Nineteenth and Twentieth centuries saw an increased understanding of how plants and DNA function and with this knowledge came new techniques of hybridising. This complicated process of cross-breeding and inbreeding, with very careful record-keeping, became the domain of large seed companies. The advantages of hybrids are many as these seeds have been bred with specific traits, such as increased yields, disease-resistant qualities, or hardier plants. Tempted by these, farmers and gardeners soon stopped growing and saving seed from their own locally adapted plants, resulting in a steady decrease in the gene pool.

As seeds have become an increasingly commercialised business, so the choice has been reduced to a relatively few highly developed varieties. If a seed doesn't sell, it is dropped off the production line. We have permanently lost many of the varieties that we once had, with a further reduction in the gene pool available to us and to plant breeders. And genetic diversity is our insurance that we will have new sources to turn to if and when the seeds we are using become susceptible to disease. Towards the end of the Twentieth century, the entire rice crop in India – a staple crop in that country – was decimated by blight with dire consequences. It was only after extensive searches that agronomists found an obscure variety that was resistant to the disease.

With the advent of genetic engineering (see page 40) in the late 1990s and the increasing threat from multinational companies intent on controlling the food supply through patents, the need to save seed is paramount. By saving seeds we keep the food supply in our hands.

Whatever your reason for seed saving, you will soon find that crops from seeds that you have saved and re-sown in your garden will, more often than not, grow better than ones purchased elsewhere.

Seed Saving Techniques

When saving seeds, choose open-pollinated varieties (see page 40) as plants grown from these seeds will resemble the parent plant. If you save seed from a hybrid, the plants will grow with an unpredictable mixture of characteristics, often inferior to the hybrid.

Plants can be self-pollinated, wind-pollinated or insect-pollinated. It is easiest to save seeds from the first group because there is a lower chance of cross-pollination. These plants include beans, broccoli, lettuce, tomatoes and peas. Biennial self-seeders such as beetroot and carrots need a bit more patience as they will only set seed in their second season.

It is more complicated to save pure seed from wind-pollinated and insect-pollinated plants, as they can quickly cross-pollinate, with wind or insects spreading pollen from one plant to another. These include most cucumbers, chillies, melons, mielies, peppers, pumpkins and squash. If you want to save seed from these you need to keep them separated from one other.

Save seeds from the healthiest and strongest plants. Or if you want to develop a particular trait, such as heat tolerance, select the seed from the plant that was the last to bolt. Seeds contained inside a husk should be left to dry on the plant, until just before it splits open and releases the seeds. The whole plant can be picked and hung upside down with the seed pods in a brown paper bag (labelled so you know what it is). Vegetables that contain their seed inside the fruit, such as cucumbers, peppers, squash and tomatoes, should be left to become overripe before they are collected. Separate the seeds from the flesh by scraping them into a bowl of water and rubbing all the flesh off the seed. Most of the pulp will rise and viable seed will sink to the bottom. Rinse and repeat until the seeds are clean. Spread out on a flat surface to dry. (See right for more tips on seed saving.)

SEED SAVING TIPS

- Start with one or two easy-to-save varieties, such as beans or pumpkins.
- Kids love to be part of the watermelon seed saving process as they need to spit the seed into a bowl.
- When harvesting for seed saving, always harvest over-mature fruits, when the fruit is past eating but the seed is at its best.
- Do a little research on keeping varieties pure. For instance, not all pumpkins will cross-pollinate. There are four different species, and you can plant at least two side-by-side and they will not cross, thus keeping your seed pure. Also, many chilli species and sweet peppers will not cross, but then again others will. So a little research and judicious planting will go a long way in keeping your own seed pure.
- Finally, one of the most important aspects of saving seed is sharing seed. Giving your own home-saved seed as a gift is the best way to keep heirloom seed alive and available to all.

Sean Freeman, Livingseeds

SOUTH AFRICAN SEED SUPPLIERS

A few years ago the variety of vegetable seed available in South Africa was very limited. If gardeners wanted more interesting seeds than those on offer by large seed companies, they would have to bring seed in illegally from overseas. Luckily this is changing rapidly with the emergence of a number of local seed companies specialising in organic and heirloom seeds. Now we can grow purple cauliflower, black tomatoes, yellow zucchini and white carrots without resorting to seed smuggling.

Reel Gardening

When Claire Reid was 16, her Dad set her a summer holiday project to grow vegetables for the family. She was allocated a budget and a small space in the garden. The first hurdle was the amount of wastage. Her small garden needed only a few handfuls of fertiliser, but the smallest bag she could buy was 2 kg. Likewise with seeds; the packets contained thousands more than she could sow in her small garden. And then sowing the seeds was problematic. As she had never grown anything before, she battled to sow the correct amount of seed at the right depth and distance apart.

Claire realised that if she was battling, others would also be. So she came up with a practical solution – she created strips of 'seed tape' with newspaper. Using a paste made from flour and liquid fertiliser she encased the seeds at the correct depth and distance apart. After being entered in a local expo, Claire's invention went on to win the International Stockholm Junior Water Prize, as well as a number of other prestigious awards.

On her return, she put it in a drawer and forgot about it – until 2009 when, as a qualified architect, a corporate client needed a vegetable garden included in a design. Claire secured funding to develop her concept into a commercially viable product, and Reel Gardening was born. Her invention is a simple approach to vegetable gardening. Seeds and fertiliser are encased in a biodegradable strip of paper at the correct distance apart and the correct depth. The strip is buried and watered daily until the seeds germinate. The top of the strip sticks above the soil, letting you see exactly where the seeds are, thus reducing water wastage. The paper keeps the seeds moist and targets the fertiliser where it is needed; at the roots. Her innovative creation is now a successful commercial product and it is integral to Claire's non-profit company Reel Life, which focuses on the implementation of sustainable community gardens throughout South Africa.

Seeds for Africa

Grant Muller's online seed company Seeds for Africa, began as a hobby. He had always been interested in gardening and started selling seeds on bidorbuy. The response was phenomenal and he soon left the corporate world to run his seed business full time. Seeds for Africa now employs seven people and offers over 2 600 indigenous African and exotic plant varieties.

It seems that seeds are hot business with Seeds for Africa proudly stocking the largest range of chilli pepper seeds in Africa – as well as an impressive array of vegetables and herbs, including a certified organic range and many heirlooms. They don't grow their own seed, but source it globally, having developed relationships with trusted seed suppliers to ensure good-quality seeds, with a germination rate tested at above 80 per cent. They do not sell any genetically engineered seeds, although they do stock some hybrids, such as the English cucumber, which you can't get as an open-pollinated seed.

Part of their success is due to them responding to what their market wants. If they don't have a requested seed in stock, they will source it.

Sought After Seedlings

When Linda Galvad began growing her own organic vegetables she became frustrated at the lack of interesting varieties available in South Africa. Her business brain saw an opportunity to provide local gardeners with far more exciting options. After extensive research, she decided to import Franchi Sementi heirloom seeds, produced by an Italian family-owned business that has been growing and selling heirloom seeds for over 200 years.

Sought After Seedlings has made its mark on the heirloom seed landscape, providing a range of rare and interesting vegetable seeds, with a high germination rate, ideal for urban vegetable gardens. Linda believes that heirloom seeds are the real answer to food security and a solution to ending poverty and starvation as they produce strong, healthy plants with excellent-tasting fruit and vegetables. The seeds of these plants can be harvested each season and saved for planting at the next season, without cost to the gardener other than keeping them dry and cool.

The Gravel Garden

Shannon Draper of The Gravel Garden specialises in growing and saving heirloom vegetable seeds. Her Somerset West garden is more like a farm, with rambling vegetable beds, chickens and a large greenhouse, which her husband constructed for her. As an avid vegetable gardener for ten years, she was constantly on the lookout for 'new' varieties, but discovered to her surprise that the 'old' varieties were the most flavoursome.

The Gravel Garden offers a wide variety of fascinating heirloom vegetable seeds, from the Turk's turban pumpkin to strawberry popcorn. But it is Shannon's tomato collection that truly shines. As she explains, the tomatoes that we have become accustomed to are generally picked green for shipping and gassed with ethylene to speed up ripening. They can sit in cold storage for a long period and make it to your salad looking perky and ripe, as if they were just plucked from the vine. But the taste has fallen by the wayside. Older,

tastier varieties are just not marketable. They don't travel or store well. Their shapes are far from uniform and don't fit into polystyrene punnets. So the flavour has been compromised for convenience, and we have forgotten how good that flavour should be. Shannon's array of heritage seeds brings the tastes and colours of history into our gardens and kitchens.

Shannon is as passionate about the stories behind heirloom seeds as she is about the seeds themselves. She tells of treasures that have been smuggled over borders and seas in times of war and unrest, often sewn into hemlines and jackets, as immigrants from all over the world travelled with seed that had traits they found desirable. In keeping with this tradition, she believes that collecting and swapping seed is a craft that can be passed on to the next generation to teach them the fundamentals of life on our Earth.

Livingseeds

Sean Freeman and his wife Nicola live on a farm south of Johannesburg, where they try to live a self-sustainable lifestyle that includes producing everything from grain to protein and vegetables. Sean started collecting indigenous seed when he was ten years old, but with the arrival of their first daughter 17 years ago, his focus

changed to vegetable seed. A passion for the unusual, rare and hard-to-find vegetable followed naturally.

Livingseeds was born out of a desire to share their small but fast-growing collection of seed. Sean started sharing seed on a 'what have you got to swap' basis and out of that grew South Africa's premier supplier of locally grown heirloom vegetable seed. Well over 600 varieties are grown on the Livingseeds Farm every year, and many new varieties are trialled for release in their catalogue. Their aim is to enable gardeners and farmers alike to be self-sustainable in their planting methods, ensuring a seed-secure future.

Sean believes heirloom seed is critical for the continued food security of the world. Heirloom seed enables home gardeners, subsistence farmers, small-scale farmers and speciality farms to grow and save their own seed in a cost-effective manner, without the need to pay royalties to large corporations. He encourages as many people as possible to save and propagate their own seed. "As much as we would like to, seed houses like Livingseeds and many other specialist heirloom seed companies are unable to save every variety available. It's up to home gardeners and small farmers to keep these unique varieties alive and available to all."

"I'm a firm believer in many small, individual seed banks maintained and curated by ordinary people who have a passion for seed. This way all our seed is not held in one or two large baskets, but is kept in the hands of numerous interested people. If thousands of home gardeners were able to save just one or two unique varieties each, the world would always have a viable seed resource to draw from."
Sean Freeman, Livingseeds

PROTECTING OUR PLANTS

All the successful organic gardeners I have met have one thing in common – they are constantly active and busy in their gardens. They inspect their gardens often and believe that the best time to do something is now. They know their plants intimately and love being in their gardens. However, with busy city living this is sometimes difficult to do. Try to make the time to do at least a daily walk through your garden, to see what is going on and to make notes of what you need to do as soon as you do have a moment. Observation and quick action are the first steps to successful plant protection.

PROTECTING SEEDS AND SEEDLINGS

Nothing is more disheartening than spending hours preparing beds, sowing seeds, nurturing them as they germinate and then finding them all mowed down by birds or insects. Seedlings need some mollycoddling until they are well established. Birds will notice a newly prepared area and target it. Even if they are not seed-eating birds, they will cause damage by digging and scratching for worms in the freshly exposed soil. Seedlings, used to being in semi shade, will wilt quickly in full sun. Cutworms lie in wait under the soil, ready to devour the tender transplants, leaving you with nothing more than a stalk. And slugs and snails like nothing more than a meal of tasty seedlings.

Luckily there is a solution that protects against many of these. Artemisia, feverfew, rosemary, sage, scented pelargonium and tansy are all strong-smelling plants that can be used to provide multiple protection. Break off a selection of twigs from any of these bushes and strip off the bottom leaves. Scatter these leaves as a mulch in amongst the seedlings or over the newly seeded area. This hides a newly prepared area from birds and helps deter slugs and snails. Push the base of the twig right into the ground next to the stem of the seedling. This protects the vulnerable stem from cutworms. Bend or break the top bushy bit of the twig and position it to block the hot afternoon sun from the seedling. By the time the leaves of the protective twig have completely withered, the seedlings should be strong enough to withstand the heat.

In many areas of the country, a late frost will kill off tender vegetable and herb seedlings. The growing season can be extended by using tunnels or greenhouses. (See pages 133 to 137 for more on growing under cover.) If you don't want to go to the trouble of doing this but want to ensure your spring tomato or eggplant seedlings are not knocked out by a late frost (or early hail), cover tender seedlings with cheap plastic laundry baskets. These can quickly be covered with frost cloth or hay if a late frost threatens. These baskets also prevent birds from snacking on the seedlings. They are quicker and easier to use than erecting bird netting over the entire bed. Choose ones with perforated bases to allow rain to pass through.

A cloche is good for protecting seedlings from birds, cutworms, slugs, snails and wind, and it creates a moist microclimate. Make your own by cutting the bottom off a two-litre plastic bottle and placing it over the seedling, pushing the rim firmly into the soil to stop cutworms. Take the lid off first so that the plant can breathe. Once the seedling is big enough, remove the cloche. Toilet rolls or pieces of PVC piping (see opposite) pushed into the ground over the seedling will also provide protection from cutworms.

1.

2.

3.

1. Brass scouring wool makes an effective snail barrier (see page 53 for more)

2. Plastic laundry baskets protect seedlings from hail and birds

3. A simple cloche made from a plastic bottle

CREATING A BALANCED ENVIRONMENT

Once our seedlings have grown up, they are still vulnerable and the anticipated harvest can never be counted until it is on the kitchen table. A healthy harvest can go from luscious to annihilated in the space of a day or two.

So how do we protect our crops from being eaten – by something other than ourselves? In an organic garden we are aiming for a balanced ecosystem, where there's never enough of one pest to cause too much damage, because we have a balance of beneficial insects to keep them in check. While I was writing my first book *Jane's Delicious Garden*, some aphids appeared on my honeysuckle. Normally I would have sprayed them with a good blast of water, as that is the easiest way to disperse aphids. But I was writing the book and I needed photographs of the bad guys too. So I left them. Within a few weeks I started seeing ladybirds. Not just one or two, but dozens of ladybirds gobbling up aphids. They were so happy they began breeding and soon there were tiny yellow geometric dots of ladybird eggs next to the aphids. These hatched into spiky tractor-like aphid-eating machines. Within a month I had no aphids left and I had a healthy population of ladybirds who still inhabit my garden today. It was a good lesson to me about learning through observation and letting things be.

Organic gardening might begin with the soil but it doesn't end there. Our aim is to create a balanced environment, which involves many factors – soil, water, climate, plants and a plethora of living organisms. In a vegetable garden we are creating a food chain, with us at the top eating the vegetables. Which means there have to be some bugs at the bottom busy nibbling at something. So don't panic at the first sight of insect damage or pests. They provide food for the beneficial insects we want in our garden.

BENEFICIAL INSECTS

When I walk into my vegetable garden it is alive with activity. A simple walk through my garden can turn into a game-viewing expedition (albeit with a macro lens instead of a telephoto one). I spend hours watching and photographing the intricate and endless life of insects. Bees nestle into chive flowers or disappear nose first into the purple fuzz of artichokes. Hoverflies, glistening in the sun, flit above their favourite fennel flowers. Dragonflies and damselflies dart above the water of my wetland pool. Butterflies, colourful and delicate, drop in to sip nectar from calendula. Robust carpenter bees hover like humming birds, and a wasp, sitting on a leaf, gives itself a good clean. A bright yellow crab spider is a delight to discover, camouflaged amongst the petals of a yellow nasturtium.

I have come to recognise their habits, as certain insects visit only at specific times, happily time-sharing their favourite flowers with others. Some choose their plants, like the citrus butterfly, which lays eggs only on citrus leaves. We want as many of these in our gardens as possible, carrying out their multitude

Beneficial Insects

- The all-important pollinators – bees, bee flies and butterflies.
- The predators – assassin bugs, damselflies, dragonflies, hoverflies, lacewings, ladybirds, praying mantises, spiders and wasps.
- The parasites – tachinid flies and wasps that lay their eggs on the host's body (most often a troublesome caterpillar). When the larva hatches out, the caterpillar becomes its food. This is the type of 'insecticide' I want in my garden.

of functions and reducing the amount of work we need to do. The more beneficial insects we have, the healthier and happier our gardens will be.

There is much we can do to invite these beneficial insects into our gardens and encourage them to stay:

- Create as much diversity and variety as possible, by choosing plants with varying heights and interplanting different varieties.
- Interplant herbs amongst your vegetables. Many of these have flowers that pollinating insects love. Others simply attract certain insects, such as tansy, which is a magnet for ladybirds.
- Leave some vegetables to go to flower. Many vegetables have beautiful, and edible, flowers that attract a range of insects. Bees love the yellow flowers of broccoli and mustard. Hoverflies are attracted to the smaller flowers of carrots, fennel and lettuces. (An additional advantage of leaving vegetables to go to flower is that many will seed themselves – reducing the cost of buying new seedlings or seeds. See page 42 for more on self-seeding.)
- Include edible flowers, such as California poppy, cornflowers, nasturtiums and violas. These all attract beneficial insects.
- Provide insect-sized water sources, such as small bowls. When I first thought about this I put a dog bowl in the garden filled with water. A few days later, I walked into my garden to find a dead butterfly floating in the bowl. What I had thought was an insect-sized water source was a huge dam to an insect. Now I always add a stone or a log to water sources, as a landing pad for thirsty visitors. To be a successful organic gardener you have to start thinking like an insect.

COMMON PESTS AND DISEASES

It is beyond the scope of this book to cover all the nasties that can make a gardener's life a misery. The first step to pest prevention is knowing the enemy. I find Google images invaluable when trying to identify an insect or disease. Once you know what you are dealing with, you can use the correct prevention or cure. Below are a few of the more common pests and diseases.

Birds

For the first ten or so years of growing vegetables I didn't have too much of a problem with birds eating my crops. There would be a few nibbled leaves and I didn't mind sharing. Then one year, almost all my brassicas were stripped of their leaves in one afternoon by a marauding flock of louries. I tried shiny reflecting CDs and twirly scarecrows, and I tried smelly seaweed spray but nothing prevented hungry mid-winter birds once they had discovered my garden. And they retained the memory. The following winter, the louries were back, this time they were joined by mouse birds. So I went out and bought bird netting and battened down the hatches. In summer, the birds will target fruit before they eat the greens and netting helps protect these harvests too.

Snails and slugs

One of the most common questions I am asked is, "How do I stop snails eating my plants?" I haven't had a snail or slug problem since I began keeping chickens. They eat every single one in my garden. (See pages 206 to 214 for more on keeping hens.) And if they miss any, the frogs that inhabit my wetland pool will get them. (See pages 228 to 239 for more on wetland pools.) But if you don't have hens (or frogs) then the next best thing is to keep the snails out. Brass scouring wool (found in the cleaning section at the supermarket) rolled into long sausages

and pinned in place around beds, forms an extremely effective razor wire barrier. Snails and slugs won't cross it, as it will cut their 'feet' to shreds.

A good organic snail bait is Biogrow Ferramol. Its active ingredient is iron phosphate. After eating the pellets, snails and slugs lose their appetite and die.

Insects and mites

There are unfortunately many *goggas* that can become pests in our garden, eating plants, spreading disease and reducing our yield. They can be divided loosely into two categories: sap-suckers and leaf-eaters. Common sap-suckers are aphids, fruit flies, leaf hoppers, mealybugs, pumpkin flies, red spider mites, scale insects, thrips and whiteflies. Leaf-eaters include beetles, caterpillars, cutworms, grasshoppers and locusts. (For solutions to garden pests, see pages 55 to 60.)

Larger creatures

Monkeys, baboons, buck, porcupines and other creatures can destroy a garden in minutes. (See page 137 for a garden that will keep your vegetables secure.)

Common diseases

Plants can be attacked by viral, fungal and bacterial disease, but the most common are fungal. Again, Google images is the best resource to help you identify the disease you are dealing with. Luckily there are some effective natural solutions.

Snails, shield bugs and tomato hornworm are unwelcome visitors in the vegetable garden.

BIRD NETTING

One of the great pleasures of my garden is the beauty it provides. Almost every morning I find something new to photograph or look at in wonder. The bird netting bothers me aesthetically because it is a barrier, albeit a delicate green one, between me and the visual smorgasbord of the plants. So it was with mixed feelings that I covered up my luscious brassica beds with netting, but it had simply become a choice of netting or no harvest.

I am quite a scavenger and my husband is an even better one. If he sees an abandoned wooden crate or some pallets on the side of the road, he goes back with the Kombi to pick them up. A tree being cut down in the neighbourhood means firewood to be collected for our pile. And we throw very little away. Old wooden fence slats, bamboo poles and tyres are piled behind my shed, and inside the shed are stashes of shade cloth, hessian, chicken wire and pots, all used and reused again and again. Many things are collected without a specific purpose – like the stack of worn-down brooms and rakes in the corner.

When I put up bird netting for the first time, I hunted through the junk treasure trove to find something to support the netting – and spied the brooms. We use grass brooms with wooden handles and they have turned out to be the perfect bird netting support. The wooden handles are pushed firmly into the ground and the remaining bristles on the top hold the netting in place. Now, during winter, my garden looks as if a coven of witches is visiting. I peg the edges of the netting into the ground using rosemary twigs – which are easily pulled out if I need to gain access under the netting. The only thing I had to buy was the netting – which is reused year after year. As I am forced to put up a barrier between me and my vegetables, at least it is one that is recycled, reused and reinvented as much as possible.

ORGANIC SOLUTIONS TO PESTS AND DISEASE

If a pest infestation or disease develops, the first step is to observe your garden to see why it is happening. Do you have enough variety? Are you attracting enough beneficial insects? Are your plants too crowded? An insect infestation is often caused by an imbalance – too much of one variety perhaps. Or an excess of liquid fertiliser results in fast growth spurts, which in turn attract insects. Moderation, variety and balance are what we are aiming for.

As much as we try to create a balanced environment, sometimes things go out of kilter and pests descend. If this happens, don't be tempted to grab the pesticide 'just this once'. Apart from being toxic and adding poisons to plants and soil, chemical pesticides kill indiscriminately, killing both the bad and the good insects. If you spray an aphid infestation with a toxic pesticide, you will also kill off any ladybirds that might be eating them. The problem is what happens next. Bad guys, unfortunately, tend to breed much faster than the good guys. Once you've killed off the aphids with a pesticide, they will start breeding again. And very quickly. However, the pesticide also killed all the ladybirds. And their breeding cycle is much longer. The result? A massive aphid infestation and not nearly enough ladybirds to keep them in check.

If you do see a small amount of insect damage – don't panic. Very often a plant will recover from a bit of a nibble and this can make it stronger. I walked into my garden one morning to find a runner bean turned into confetti by beetles. I didn't think it would survive. However, a few weeks later it was winding its way happily up a support and produced a great harvest; better than its counterpart that had not been eaten. We need a balance of the good guys and bad guys. However, you should do regular patrols to check that the bad guys aren't gaining the upper hand. Many of these only come out at night and a head torch is useful for evening inspections.

The first step to successful pest control is diligence and early action. Many pest infestations can be prevented if they are spotted and dealt with quickly.

Insect infestations, such as shield bugs (left) and aphids (right) are more easily controlled when spotted early.

Hand removal of the first shield bugs or beetles will prevent them breeding and becoming a problem. Deterring pests by using repellents such as garlic, neem and oil will prevent them colonising a plant. These are applied as a foliar spray and to be effective must cover both the top and underside of the leaves. They will also wash off after rain and need to be applied regularly.

There are numerous organic solutions on the market, as well as many homemade options (see page 60). When using these, always go for the least toxic option first. Here are a few of the more commonly used options.

Borax

(Find it in the cleaning section of the supermarket.) This naturally occurring mineral is toxic to ants. Mix borax with sugar and place it in jars with holes punched in the lid. Position this close to the ants' nest. It is slow-acting but will get rid of them.

Copper soap

(Biogrow's Copper Soap; Margaret Roberts Organic Fungicide) A fungicide that utilises copper and fatty acids to make a soap that effectively controls many fungal diseases, such as powdery and downy mildew, rust and blight. Good coverage of the entire plant is essential. It works best as a preventative. If you see signs of the disease, remove all infected leaves and then spray the rest of the plant thoroughly.

Diatomaceous earth (DE)

(Talborne Organics) A powder made from fossilised crustaceans called diatoms. Its sharp edges cut into insects' bodies, causing them to die of dehydration. It is effective against soft-bodied insects, such as aphids, as well as larger pests including beetles, slugs and snails. It does not harm beneficial soil organisms. Make sure you buy 'food grade' DE. It is most effective when puffed directly onto the insects or onto dry soil where slugs, snails and ants will crawl and beetles hatch out. Bees coming into contact with DE can be killed. They are smart and will avoid it if they can.

To prevent harming them, avoid dusting unnecessarily or too thickly, and don't dust open flowers. Rather dust after the bees have gone to bed. Wear a mask when applying as it is dangerous if inhaled.

Neem

(Biogrow's Bioneem; powder from an Asian spice shop or oil from a health shop) An oil and powder derived from an Asian evergreen tree, it both repels insects and is a natural steroid, causing insects to lose their appetite and stop laying eggs, hence breaking the breeding cycle. It is effective against a wide range of insects, particularly those that grow quickly and breed rapidly, such as shield bugs and many beetles. It is best used preventatively, before an infestation sets in. It is relatively harmless to beneficial insects as it has to be ingested to be effective, but I recommend using it late in the afternoon after they have gone to bed.

Organic insecticidal oil

(Biogrow's Vegol; Margaret Roberts Organic Insecticide; or try one of the homemade sprays on page 60) Oil works by interfering with respiration, causing the insect to suffocate. It controls all soft-bodied insects and immature beetles. Because it works on all stages of insect, it can be used on dormant fruit trees, sprayed into bark crevices and drenched into the ground below to control pests that overwinter there.

Organic insecticidal soap spray

(Biogrow's Neudosan; or try one of the homemade sprays on page 60) Effective on mites and soft-bodied insects such as aphids, mealybugs, scale and whitefly. It can also be used on the larvae of larger insects, such as shield bugs, grasshoppers and leafhoppers. It has no residual effect and kills only when sprayed directly onto the insect. Thoroughly wet both sides of leaves and all crevices. Repeat every 5 to 7 days.

Pyrethrum

(Ludwig's Insect Spray; Biogrow's Pyrol) Made from the flowers of a white daisy (*Tanacetum cinerariifolium*), pyrethrum paralyses insects almost instantly. It is effective against ants, beetles, caterpillars and all soft-bodied insects. To prevent harm to beneficial insects, use after sunset.

Traps

Traps can be made using recycled plastic bottles. A bait placed inside the bottle attracts insects and they can't get out. These are effective against chafer beetles, shield bugs, pumpkin flies, whiteflies and fruit fly. (See page 110 for how to make a trap.)

GROWING YOUR OWN PESTICIDES AND FUNGICIDES

Growing pest-repelling plants among your vegetables is the first step towards providing good protection. Use trimmings from these plants as a protective mulch or, to take it one step further, use them to whip up an inexpensive homemade spray. (See page 60 for the recipes.) The most effective plants to use are African wormwood, elderflower, feverfew, rhubarb, tansy and tomato.

There are many other pest-repelling plants that are easy to grow in your garden. Basil, catnip, lavender, lemon grass, mint, oregano, rosemary, sage and thyme are all strong-smelling herbs that help deter insects. They can be planted in amongst vegetables, where low-growing ones such as thyme and oregano form insect-repelling groundcovers. Or they can be planted in pots and moved to where they are needed. Many of these herbs benefit from regular trimming and the leaves can be used as mulch or added to a homemade spray.

USEFUL INSECT-REPELLING PLANTS

PLANT	GROWING	USES (IN ADDITION TO SPRAY)	USED FOR
African wormwood (Artemisia)	• Indigenous, up to 2 m tall • Bushy drought-resistant shrub • Grows easily from seedlings or cuttings • Unfussy about soil • Full sun • Cut back by two thirds in early spring to encourage new growth	• Very strong-smelling leaves that few insects can withstand • Scatter between leaves of vulnerable plants to repel leaf-eating caterpillars • Use leaves as insect-repelling mulch • Scatter over newly-seeded areas or in amongst seedlings	Ants, aphids, caterpillars, moths, slugs, snails, whitefly
Elder	• Large deciduous shrub • Propagate from cuttings or buy a young tree • Likes well-drained soil • Full sun	• Leaves repel numerous insects • Use leaves as insect-repelling mulch • Dry leaves to use as ant or flea repellent • Helpful tree near a compost heap, as wide-spreading roots assist in breaking down compost	Ants, aphids, beetles, fleas, moths, whitefly
Feverfew	• Member of daisy family • Grows easily from seed • Will self-seed in places it grows best • Likes well-drained soil • Full sun • Deadhead flowers often to keep it in bloom • Dies back in winter in colder areas but re-emerges in spring	• Contains pyrethrum, a natural insecticide • Plant in vegetable beds • Good under fruit trees • Flowers can be dried and ground into an insect-repelling powder	Aphids, caterpillars, flies, fruit fly, moths, whitefly

PLANT	GROWING	USES (IN ADDITION TO SPRAY)	USED FOR
Rhubarb	• Perennial, can be grown from seed or small plants • Full sun • Don't harvest in first year to allow underground crown to establish • Divide every four years	• Has toxic leaves containing high levels of oxalic acid • Leaves help deter insects and prevent disease in other plants (particularly club root, a fungal disease affecting brassicas) • Use only as spray or soil drench • Used as a spray (see page 60), it is an all-purpose natural insecticide • Use as a soil drench before sowing seeds or transplanting brassica seedlings	General insecticide
Tansy	• Pretty yellow-flowered bush • Develops into a straggly plant by sending out rhizomes • Likes well-drained soil • Full sun • Can be invasive • Keep in check by cutting back continually and pulling out new growth around the edges	• Excellent insect-repelling properties • Plant in vegetable beds or plant in pots and place where needed • Good under fruit trees • Use trimmings as insect-repelling mulch	Ants, beetles, flies, fruit fly, moths, whitefly
Tomato	• Likes well-drained soil • Full sun • Frost tender • Indeterminate (rambling) varieties need support	• Insect-repelling leaves contain solanine • Has an inhibiting effect on fungal infections, particularly black spot • Use only as spray or soil drench	Fungal spray

Some of the most effective insect-repelling plants are African wormwood (opposite), tansy, rhubarb and fewerfew.

Homemade Insect-repelling Recipes

When dealing with pests and fungal infections, a simple solution is often the best. Homemade sprays and drenches can be whipped up using ingredients you already have in your kitchen, and are as effective as many purchased organic insecticides. Adding dishwashing soap to a spray will help it stick to the leaves.

SENSIBLE SPRAYING

Whenever I spray my plants with anything – be it a purchased fungicide or a simple homemade garlic and oil spray, I always mix in some liquid foliar feed. If a plant is battling a pest or disease, a good feed will help it along. Plus, if you are going through the mission of spraying you may as well gain double the value for your labour.

BASIC PEST-REPELLING SPRAY

- ½ bucket leaves and stems of strong-smelling herbs
- just-boiled water
- 2 tablespoons dishwashing liquid

Half fill a bucket with leaves and stems of strong-smelling herbs, such as African wormwood, elder, feverfew, tansy and tomato leaves (see the chart on pages 58 to 59 for more details on each plant).

Add the just-boiled water, stir and leave to stand for two days. Strain out the leaves and stems and add them to your compost heap. Add the dishwashing liquid and mix. The spray will keep for up to a month.

To increase the efficacy of the basic spray, include some garlic, onion and chilli. Chop up finely and add to the plants with the boiling water.

To use: Spray affected plants every few days as the insecticide breaks down quickly. Spray underneath the leaves as well as on top.

Effective as a general insect repellent.

INSECTICIDE SOAP SPRAY

- 2 teaspoons pure soap
- 1 litre boiling water

Mix the soap and water together and stir until dissolved. Store in a jar.

To help it stick, add 1 teaspoon of canola or sunflower oil. To make it more effective, add half a teaspoon of ground garlic or chilli (or both).

To use: Mix 1 teaspoon of the concentrated soap solution with 1 litre of water and spray directly onto the insects. (Be sure to use pure soap, otherwise you will be spraying unwanted chemicals and oils onto your plants.)

Effective on all soft-bodied insects.

RHUBARB SPRAY

- 500 g rhubarb leaves, chopped
- 1 litre water
- 1 tablespoon dishwashing liquid

Boil the leaves in water for 30 minutes. Cool, strain and mix with the soap.

To use: Spray directly on insects and onto leaves, covering both sides. If spraying on edible leaves, wash before eating. This spray can keep in the fridge for up to two weeks but is most effective when used within 24 hours. The mixture breaks down in sunlight, so spray on a cloudy day or in the evening.

Effective as a general insecticide. Use on all soft-bodied insects and beetles.

GARLIC INSECTICIDAL OIL

- 1 head garlic (peeled)
- 4 onions
- 1 tablespoon chopped hot chillies
- 2 tablespoons canola oil
- 2 tablespoons dishwashing liquid

Finely blend the garlic, onion and chillies with the oil and dishwashing liquid. Cover and leave for 24 hours. Strain, seal and refrigerate.

To use: Mix 1 tablespoon of prepared oil per 1 litre of water and spray directly on insects and onto leaves, covering both sides.

Effective on all soft-bodied insects (such as aphids and whitefly), mites and small beetles.

ANTI-FUNGAL SPRAY

- 1 litre milk
- 1 litre water

Mix together well and use immediately.

To use: Spray top and bottom of leaves. It is most effective if repeated weekly.

Helps prevent fungal diseases such as powdery mildew and rust. It also increases the plant's health and yield.

NUTRITION

As organic gardeners we try to emulate nature, but in many ways we work against nature. In a natural environment a carrot would store its nutrients in a fat root and when it dies these nutrients would slowly be returned to the soil. But we harvest the carrots we grow and those nutrients are lost to the soil. So, to maintain the fertility of the soil, we need to replace the nutrients we remove.

FEEDING WITH ORGANIC FERTILISERS

Vegetables require plenty of nutrients – especially when we are gardening intensively and trying to grow the maximum amount of vegetables in a small space. This is where organic fertilisers come in.

Interestingly, plants do not recognise the difference between organic and inorganic fertilisers. A plant can only absorb nutrients once they have broken down completely to their elemental form. And there is no difference between an element that has come from your organic compost pile and one that has come from a chemical fertiliser factory. So why should we use organic fertilisers rather than chemical ones? Well, there are a number of reasons and it helps to look at the history of chemical fertilisers.

After the Second World War, the USA was left with surplus ammonium nitrate, the main ingredient for explosives. As it happens, it is also an excellent source of nitrogen for plants, and so redundant munitions plants were turned into fertiliser factories. The chemical fertiliser industry was born. Added to this was the growth of pesticides and herbicides, many of which are based on poison gases developed by the military. So in the space of a few decades, simple farming very quickly grew into a massive agri-business, increasingly dominated by a powerful chemical industry.

Research showed three main elements were needed to improve plant growth: nitrogen (N), phosphorus (P) and potassium (K). So this is what the fertiliser manufacturers concentrated on. They led farmers and gardeners to believe they too need only focus on N, P and K. However, further research has shown that there are more than 60 trace elements found in plants. And of these, 16 are essential for growth. Plants were pulling these out of the soil, but they were not being replaced by the fertilisers. With increased use of chemical fertilisers that contained only the 'big three', the soil in our gardens and farms was steadily stripped of micronutrients.

These trace elements are equally important for humans and if the plants don't contain them then the people eating the plants don't acquire them either. It is no coincidence that there has been a concurrent increase in the manufacture and sale of bottled vitamins as the use of chemical fertilisers has increased. An apple a day keeps the doctor away right? That phrase was coined in 1914. Today, we would have to eat 26 apples to get the same

USING FERTILISERS

Luckily for South African gardeners, there has been a substantial increase of commercial organic fertilisers over the last 15 years. A leading example is Talborne Organics, a South African family-run business that manufactures and distributes a range of internationally certified organic fertilisers. They have been pioneers at the forefront of the growth of organic production in South Africa. Organic fertilisers are derived from living things such as blood, manure, seaweed and bone meal, containing all 16 essential elements, plus many more.

Organic fertilisers come in liquid and solid forms. Liquid ones, made from seaweed, fish emulsions or beet, are concentrated and must be diluted before being applied. It is better to feed weak solutions more often than a rich feed infrequently. They can be applied directly to the soil as a drench or used as foliar spray. This is a quick solution to help a plant that is battling or to give newly transplanted seedlings a boost.

Solid organic fertilisers release nutrients slowly, providing a long-term rich source of fertility. They are large organic compounds which, when added to the soil, are slowly broken down into their inorganic components. They emulate the natural process by providing a slow and steady supply of nutrients. If you have good soil, a well-balanced fertiliser needs to be applied only once every four to six months, either by sprinkling on the surface of the beds (called top dressing) or incorporating it into the top layer of soil. Fertiliser can also be placed into the planting holes before transplanting, providing a food source directly where the roots will grow. Always water fertilisers in well after applying.

amount of nutrients that an apple in 1914 supplied. That is what we have done to our soil by using chemical fertilisers. So stop using them.

And there are further reasons not to use chemical fertilisers. Chemical fertilisers are manufactured in a highly concentrated, water-soluble form. This means the plants are forced to take up the nutrients – whether they need them or not – because they are dissolved in the soil water. Plants are designed to absorb just the right amount of nutrients for optimum growth. When they absorb too many, it results in an unnatural growth spurt with extra amino acids being packed into the leaves. All you will see is luscious leafy growth, but insects will see a bug banquet. Far too much for them to eat. They will invite all their friends to join them and soon you will have a pest infestation.

Because chemical fertilisers are water soluble, they are often washed away below where our plants can reach. This is a waste. Plus it has a knock-on effect when the excess nutrients are washed downriver to the sea. In the Gulf of Mexico there is a dead area of sea the size of Swaziland. The land mass that drains into this area is the agricultural heartland of America, amongst the heaviest users of synthetic fertilisers in the world. Excess nitrogen and phosphorus collects in the gulf, feeding oxygen-hungry algae, which effectively smother all other life in the area. The Great Barrier Reef, the largest life form on the planet, is also under threat from the very same thing. All the more reason to stop using chemical fertilisers.

THE NUTRIENTS PLANTS NEED

Different vegetables require and use up different nutrients. Leafy vegetables use plenty of nitrogen to produce luscious leaves, but if you feed a high-nitrogen fertiliser to tomatoes, they will produce masses of leaves but not much fruit. The following is a guideline for balanced feeding.

Bud-forming greens (broccoli, Brussels sprouts, cauliflower) need phosphorus and calcium to develop strong roots and then plenty of nitrogen to develop large leaves. Plant with Vita-Grow 2:3:2 and top dress with Vita-Veg 6:3:4.

Flowering and fruiting crops (chilli, cucumber, eggplant, melon, pepper, tomato, and summer and winter squash) need phosphorus and calcium to develop strong roots and potassium for flowers and fruit. Plant with Vita-Grow 2:3:2 and before flowers start forming top dress with Vita Fruit & Flower 3:1:5.

Leafy greens (Asian greens, cabbage, herbs, kale, lettuce and spinach) need nitrogen for green growth and potassium for strong cells. Plant and top dress with Vita-Veg 6:3:4.

Roots and bulbs (beetroot, carrot, garlic, onion, parsnip, potato, sweet potato and turnip) need phosphorus to develop strong roots and bulbs, and nitrogen for their leaves. Add Vita-Grow 2:3:2 when planting. Top dress with Vita-Green 5:1:5. Top dress potatoes with Vita Fruit & Flower 3:1:5 before flowers form.

Seeds, pods and legumes (beans, broad beans, mielies and peas) need phosphorus and some nitrogen to develop into sturdy plants, then potassium to encourage flowers, pods and seeds. Plant with Vita-Grow 2:3:2 and top dress with Vita Fruit & Flower 3:1:5 before flowers develop.

HOMEMADE FERTILISERS

One of the more expensive inputs into a garden is fertiliser. This cost can be reduced and even eliminated by growing nutritious fertiliser plants and recycling all your kitchen waste. Different plants gather and accumulate different nutrients from the soil – some more than others. Comfrey, for example, contains more nutrients than kraal manure, as its roots go metres deep, allowing it to pull nutrients from way below the reach of our vegetables' roots. These nutrient-rich plants can be added to compost, grown as a green manure or made into a fertiliser.

Compost

Making your own compost is the cheapest and simplest way of providing nutrients for your plants, and conditioning your soil. Like so many other aspects of organic gardening, making compost is about using common sense.

Building a compost pile is a bit like making a lasagne, with alternating layers. It is preferable to position it on bare earth, allowing worms and other beneficial organisms to enter. Place a bottom layer of thin branches or hay for drainage, and gradually build up the pile layer by layer.

The compost ingredients can be divided into two categories: carbon-rich (brown) and nitrogen-rich (green). Green ingredients include fresh grass clippings, garden cuttings and all the scraps from your kitchen (except dairy, meat and grain as these will attract rats. Rather add these to a bokashi bin first – see page 69). Brown ingredients are ash, dry leaves, hay, sawdust, sticks and straw. To create a good balance, the brown layers should be about a third thicker than the green. Manure can be added in between the layers to help speed up the process.

The pile should be kept moist but not sodden. In rainy weather covering it up with an old tarp or piece of wood will prevent it from becoming too wet. Covering it also helps retain moisture and heat, which are the two essentials for successful compost making. Leave it to sit for six weeks and then turn it, moving the outsides to the centre. Repeat this process until it is uniformly broken down. Sieve it to remove any larger sticks and then bag it.

SMALL SPACE COMPOSTING

Composting bags made from recycled advertising billboards are ideal for tidy composting in small spaces.

They are strong and can produce half a cube of compost. The top zips shut, preventing rats and pets from foraging, which is often a problem with city compost piles. The bags can be rolled to mix and aerate the compost easily. They are manufactured for Earth Probiotic by Waste2Wow, a non-profit company focusing on uplifting disadvantaged women.

Benefits of Green Manure

- Retains and adds nutrients to the soil.
- Adds organic matter to the soil.
- When combined with crop rotation (page 39) it increases yield.
- Provides a living mulch, protecting the soil from drying out, compacting or washing away.
- Increases the amount of roots in the soil, thereby increasing the rhizosphere (the area around a plant's roots where beneficial organisms are most active). This greater concentration of biological activity improves the health of the soil.
- Increases humus content, improving the structure of the soil, preventing compaction and creating a crumbly texture that holds more water and nutrients.
- Suppresses weeds.
- Attracts beneficial insects if left to flower.

Green Manure

When I first heard the term 'green manure' I was a bit put off – it didn't sound like something I wanted in my garden. I then discovered that green manure is simply a fast-growing cover crop, which is chopped down and incorporated into the top layer of soil. All the nutrients the crop has accumulated from the soil are broken down and added back to the soil. Growing a green manure is just one of the ways we can use plants to create our own fertilisers efficiently and cost-effectively.

To grow a green manure crop, sow a mixture of green manure seeds quite thickly into a bed that has been raked smooth. Press it down well, cover lightly with compost, and water. Once the green manure crop has grown to the point when it is lush and leafy, chop it down, leaving the roots in the soil to decompose. Cut up the leaves and stems quite finely and leave them to wilt for a few days before incorporating into the soil. If the ground is wet, just scatter the chopped plants on top of the soil. If it is dry, dig half of them into the top layer of soil and then scatter the rest over the top and water well. Don't let a cover crop become too woody before cutting it, as it can take too long to break down. Most green manures should be cut before they start flowering, as the nitrogen is lost to the flower and seed head. However, alfalfa and perennial clovers are the exception as they can be grown over a few seasons.

Although using green manure was a technique developed for large farms, it can be adapted to smaller vegetable gardens and even container gardens.

- Grow a low-growing green manure, such as clover, under taller plants.
- Fill any bare patches and interplant perennials with a fast-growing annual green manure, such as buckwheat.
- Grow green manures, such as alfalfa, in a separate bed and trim them regularly. Use the trimmings as nutrient-rich mulch in perennial beds.
- Grow a green manure, such as cow peas, vetch and ryegrass, in a container. When it is ready to be cut, scatter the chopped plant matter and the contents of the container on the surface of a perennial bed, or add to other containers.

A variety of crops can be used as green manure. Plants from the legume family (such as alfalfa, clover, cow peas, fenugreek, serradella, soya beans and vetch) have the additional benefit of fixing nitrogen in the soil. Other non-legumes that can be used are buckwheat, millet, mustard, ryegrass and wheat. These all add bulky organic matter to the soil. There are a few specialist seed companies that sell green manure seeds (see page 46).

Green manures such as vetch (above) alfalfa, buckwheat and mustard (opposite) are effective natural fertilisers.

Green Manure Crops

PLANT	DESCRIPTION	WHEN TO PLANT
Alfalfa	Very deep-rooting, hardy perennial Nutrient-rich legume Can be cut back often	Spring, before leaf crops
Buckwheat	Tender quick-growing annual with extensive root system Smothers weeds Does not like very hot, dry weather	Spring, after roots, before legumes
Clover	Hardy shallow-rooted annual and perennial A rambling legume, it smothers weeds	Spring and autumn, before leaf crops
Fenugreek	Tender annual, similar to clover Drought-tolerant legume	Spring and autumn, before leaf crops
Mustard	Hardy quick-growing annual Adds fibrous organic matter to the soil Can help cleanse soil of pathogens and disease	Spring, before tomatoes and peppers Autumn, before root crops
Ryegrass	Hardy grass with extensive root system Suppresses weeds and adds organic matter to the soil	Autumn, before root crops
Serradella	Semi hardy, bushy legume with deep roots Drought-tolerant and suppresses weeds	Autumn, before leaf crops
Vetch	Hardy annual Rambling legume with edible purple flowers	Autumn, before leaf crops
Wheat	Hardy annual Discourages disease and nematodes	In autumn and over winter, before tomatoes and peppers

Other Fertiliser Plants

There are many other herbs and plants that accumulate nutrients and can be used as fertiliser-creating plants. Some of these are considered weeds by many gardeners – stinging nettle (1), yarrow (2) or chickweed (3). But before you pull them out and toss them away, have a look at the chart below to see the valuable nutrients these so-called weeds accumulate. To get the benefit of the nutrients, use the leaves as mulch, add the leaves (or whole plant) to the compost pile or brew a fertiliser tea (see recipe opposite).

FERTILISER PLANT CROPS

PLANT	DESCRIPTION	ACCUMULATES
Borage	Hardy annual with long tap root	Potassium and silica
Chickweed	Fast-growing, spreading, tender annual	Copper, iron, manganese, phosphorus and potassium
Comfrey	A hardy perennial, with a very deep root system Can be invasive Dies back in winter	Contains higher levels of potassium than kraal manure Also accumulates calcium, iron, magnesium, nitrogen and silica
Dandelion	Hardy annual with long tap root	Calcium, copper, iron, magnesium, phosphorus, potassium, silica and sodium
Stinging nettle	Hardy perennial Can be invasive, so plant in containers	Calcium, copper, iron, potassium, silica, sodium and sulphur
Watercress	Hardy, short-lived perennial	Calcium, iron, fluorine, magnesium, phosphorus, potassium, sodium and sulphur
Yarrow	Hardy perennial Dies back in winter	Calcium, copper, magnesium, phosphorus, potassium and sulphur

1.

2.

3.

This tea is a nutritious feed for hungry plants. Half fill a bucket with nutrient-accumulating plants (see charts on pages 67 and 68). Cover the plants with boiling water and let them rot for about a month, stirring every now and then.

Dilute one part tea to ten parts water, and use as a soil drench or foliar spray.

If you use a bucket with a tap on the side, you can top up the brew and pour it off whenever you need it. (Put the plants in a sack first to prevent them from blocking the tap.)

This tea can be applied every one to two weeks.

Bokashi

I first heard about bokashi from a gardener in Cape Town who showed me the difference between a bed fertilised with bokashi compost and one without. The bokashi bed was much healthier and more productive. I soon had a bokashi bin fermenting away in my kitchen. Bokashi differs from normal composting by enabling gardeners to recycle all food waste, including starch, bones, fat, meat and dairy. These normally can't be added to compost. Apart from the horrible smell created while they decompose, they attract vermin and flies. Bokashi (the Japanese word for 'fermented organic matter') ferments food waste in an airtight bin, pickling it rather than rotting it. The process is straightforward:

- You need an airtight bin and a bag of bokashi (wheat bran brewed with beneficial micro-organisms and then fermented).
- Collect food waste and empty daily into the bin.
- Sprinkle a generous handful of bokashi on top to get the fermentation process started.
- Continue layering food waste and bokashi until the bin is full.
- Leave it to sit for two weeks to ferment fully.

Because the fermenting organisms are anaerobic, the layers should be pressed down firmly to eliminate air pockets. A potato masher is a good tool for this. It is also worth having two bins, as you will need the second for filling while the first is brewing.

"Food waste is one of the most detrimental streams in a landfill, contributing to greenhouse gases as it rots and contaminating underground water. The methane gas produced from rotting organic waste is 25 per cent more harmful to the environment than carbon monoxide."
Earth Probiotic

Once fermented, the contents of the bin can be added to compost. It works best if you dig a hole in your compost and mix it into the lower layers. Fermented food waste decomposes very quickly due to the increased microbial activity and it will speed up the decomposing time of the entire compost pile. It can also be added to a worm farm, but it needs to be introduced slowly so the worms can get used to the higher pH of the fermented waste. Once they start munching, they will process it very quickly as it is already pre-digested by the fermentation bacteria. Bokashi can also be buried under a new vegetable bed, but don't plant anything there for at least two weeks in order to allow it to break down to a rich fertiliser.

Worm Farms

Whether you grow herbs on a windowsill garden or manage a large community garden, a worm farm can be used to convert kitchen scraps into super-nutritious fertiliser. Vermicompost (the proper name for worm poo) not only adds fertility to the soil, it also increases germination, improves soil structure and its ability to retain moisture, and ultimately results in improved yield.

There are many commercial worm farms on the market, ranging from large ones for catering kitchens to small units for home use. A homemade bin is relatively simple to make with numerous plans and choices on the web. The designs differ but the principle is the same. Earthworms are housed in a container (with air holes) and fed vegetable kitchen scraps. Most earthworm farms consist of stacked trays, making it easy to access the composted material.

The worms used in farms are red wigglers, which are not the same as the deep-diving earthworms in our gardens. Red wigglers live in the top 10 to 15 cm of soil and are very efficient at composting organic material. They have the ability to convert their body weight a day into nutritious castings.

Food earthworms love includes: kitchen greens, fruit, peelings, ground-up egg shells, paper and cardboard (shredded and soaked beforehand), cereals, grains (in moderation), bread, tea bags and coffee grounds. It will speed up the process if you chop larger pieces in a blender and soften any hard foods by soaking them first. Worms love horse or cow manure and this will increase the nutrient content of the vermicompost. Don't feed worms citrus, onions, garlic, pineapple, fats or oil, salty food, spoiled canned food, cut grass or fresh sawdust.

If you are going away add a layer of soft scraps, such as bananas or moist bread, to the top of your worm farm. Cut a butternut in half lengthways and place both pieces on top of the scraps. Cover everything with shredded, damp paper and place it in a cool, dry spot.

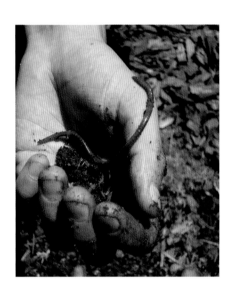

Worm Wee

Most worm farms have a tap for emptying the liquid that collects at the bottom of the bin. It is not actually worm wee (as it is commonly called) but rather a liquid by-product of decomposition that seeps through the vermicompost. This leachate can be beneficial to plants but if a worm farm is slightly out of balance, it can contain unwanted microbes that could harm your plants. If it smells at all foul don't use it. A mature, well-balanced farm will produce nutritious leachate. It should be diluted ten parts water to one part leachate, and can be used as a weekly foliar spray or drench.

WATER

My awareness of water conservation began at a very young age. I have many fond memories of visiting my grandfather's farm as a child. But one thing I never looked forward to was bath time. I remember that there always seemed to be 'A Drought' and this resulted in many conversations about 'The Weather'. It also resulted in having to bath in water that was only a few centimetres deep. And as I was the youngest I usually bathed last, after my grubby boy cousins had already used the precious few centimetres and left it not only dirty, but ice cold.

My father continued my water education. He was one of the first grey water recyclers I knew. When my parents built their house in the early Sixties, he rigged up the plumbing leading from their en suite bathroom so the bath water flowed out into the garden. The main recipient of the water was a large kumquat tree and for many years this gratefully produced masses of fat kumquats. Many family conversations still revolve around 'The Weather', a topic to be chewed over endlessly. So today, water conservation is second nature to me.

South Africa is a semi-arid country with an average annual rainfall of 450mm, well below the global average of 860mm. Therefore we have to take water conservation seriously, particularly as the population is exploding while the amount of water available has been constant since time began. The average family of four uses between 300 and 350 litres of water daily and almost 90 per cent of that water leaves the home as wastewater. That means 115000 litres of fresh, drinkable water are simply being washed down the drain every year. It is time to start thinking about our water supply and how we can save, harvest and recycle as much as we can.

WATER-WISE VEGETABLE GARDENING

Water does more than provide liquid for our plants to drink. It breaks organic matter in the soil into soluble nutrients. Water carries these through the soil, to the roots and into the plant where they are put to use. Healthy soil will allow water to soak into it (rather than run off immediately), holding onto some but allowing the excess to drain away. This leaves both moisture and air in the soil pores. No-dig gardening and increasing the amount of organic matter and humus in the soil, will improve its water retention ability.

An additional advantage of using small intensively planted beds is that they use less water. Water loss from exposed soil is reduced as the leaves form a protective canopy, preventing the soil from drying out. Mulching (see page 80) is another method that reduces the amount of watering required. However, even when using these methods, if there is no rain, we need to water.

Watering Systems

Drip irrigation is the most water-wise and efficient method of watering a vegetable garden. When you sow seeds or transplant seedlings next to the drip irrigation pipes, you provide water right where the plant is. This is the most effective way to deliver water directly to the roots, without any wastage or loss from evaporation. It also means fewer weeds. Drip irrigation can be connected to a timer to ensure regular watering.

These systems are easy to install and change, with the parts available at most hardware stores. Water is fed to the plants using soaker hoses, drip irrigation pipes or sprinkler hoses. I have found soaker hoses – also called porous piping – to be very effective. (See photo on page 78.) These are spongy and permeable, allowing the water to slowly seep out, soaking the soil 30 to 50 cm either side. They are either placed on the surface of beds or just below the mulch or topsoil, delivering water right where it is needed most, to the roots. They are flexible and can be placed in loops so the whole bed is covered. Plants needing extra water can be given an additional loop. They use standard irrigation connections and the only maintenance required is to flush them out once or twice a year. Avoid uneven water distribution by setting up separate zones with no more than 30 metres of hose each. They work best within a specified pressure range and if yours is above this, a pressure regulator will ensure even distribution.

Drip irrigation pipes are slightly more complicated to set up. Water is fed to the beds using pipes and sub-pipes, connected with elbows and tees. Using a punch tool, small holes are made in the pipes, spaced at intervals to target the water directly where it is needed. If a plant is really thirsty, several holes can be made. Although it is more expensive than soaker hose, drip irrigation piping is more precise.

Sprinkler hoses – flat perforated hoses – emit a fine spray of water into the air. They are laid out on beds in much the same way as soaker hoses, but they aren't as easy to curve. They can be turned over to create a drip irrigation

WATERING TIPS

- Group plants with similar watering requirements together.
- Rather water deeply and less often than shallowly, often.
- On a slope, create terraces along contours to retain water.
- During frosty winters, water in the morning.
- During hot weather water either early in the morning or after the sun has set to reduce loss of water through evaporation.
- If plants are drooping during a hot day, don't worry, they are just closing stomata (minute openings in their leaves used for respiration) to retain water. If they are still drooping when it has cooled, it is time to water.

effect, so the spray goes directly into the ground. This reduces loss due to evaporation. You can make your own sprinkler hose by piercing holes in an old garden hose using a punch or a heated needle. Place a stopper at one end.

Overhead watering – especially during summer – can increase the chances of spreading disease such as mildew. However, there are times when plants benefit from increased moisture in the air from overhead watering. During hot, dry weather, increased humidity will encourage vegetables such as chillies and tomatoes to flower. Many winter vegetables, such as cauliflower and cabbage, are designed to catch and hold water in their leaves, which can only happen with overhead watering.

Easy Watering System

A simple and effective watering system can be created using a bucket or drum attached to sprinkler hose. If you are gardening in a public area or on a rooftop with limited access to water, this is a good option. It is also a time saver as you can fill the buckets, turn on the taps and then get on with other jobs while the water drips into the garden. The buckets will also collect rainwater. Ideally set up one bucket system per bed. You will need:

- A strong bucket (if you can buy one with a tap on the side all the better)
- A plastic tap
- Lengths of sprinkler hose
- A stopper for the end of the hose
- Bricks or something to raise the bucket

Drill a hole in the side of the bucket and, using a sharp knife, enlarge it bit by bit until the tap can be squeezed into it. Place the bucket on a raised support next to the bed. Attach the hose to the tap and lay it evenly across the surface of the bed. Plug the end of the hose with the stopper. Fill the bucket with water and turn the tap on.

RAINWATER HARVESTING

An increasing number of urbanites are investing in rainwater tanks as more people become aware of the fragility of our natural resources. Rod Cairns, managing director of JoJo Tanks says, "At this stage the cost of water in South Africa is not that high, so we tend to be wasteful. Urban dwellers in particular tend to take water for granted. The reality is that water will become more and more expensive and there may simply not be enough water to meet the country's future requirements, so the need to save water will be forced upon us."

Four years ago we installed JoJo Tanks to collect and store all the rainwater from our roof – 1mm of rain on 1m² delivers 1 litre of water into the tanks. We have a large roof and so all those litres, which were previously washing away down the stormwater drain, are now saved into the tanks and we use them to water the garden, wash the car or top up the wetland swimming pool. In summer, when the tanks start overflowing from all the rain, we empty them into the swimming pool. There is a tap installed to the side of the tanks and when opened, it turns on a pressure-activated pump. This is handy as all my regular hose and tap fittings, and irrigation can be used.

I had always viewed JoJo Tanks as rather ugly, garishly-coloured things, but I was pleasantly surprised to find a range of colours and shapes to choose from and the sandstone 'Slimline' ones look quite elegant in our driveway. I have used one of them to create a vertical garden with strawberries and herbs (see pages 142 to 144). Another has a creeper from the house winding its way around it. In a couple of years it will be completely covered – a truly green tank!

Installing a Rainwater Tank

Even though rainwater tanks are harvesting rainwater from the roof, they don't have to be situated right next to the house – or even above the ground. Above-ground tanks are less expensive to install, while underground tanks are specifically designed to withstand the pressures of an underground installation. An underground tank can be placed under paved light-weight traffic areas, driveways, garden beds or lawns, providing a large storage area that is aesthetically pleasing. Although they can be retro-fitted, underground systems are more cost-effective when installed during construction of a house. Another solution to creating underground storage area for rainwater is to convert an unused swimming pool into a tank covered with a deck.

"Underground tanks are the answer when space and accessibility are an issue, especially in an urban environment."
Rod Cairns, JoJo Tanks

1.

3.

2.

HOW TO INSTALL AN ABOVE-GROUND TANK

1. Create a solid, level concrete or brick foundation – the tank will be heavy once it is full of water.

2. You don't have to make any changes to your existing gutters. Simply extend a pipe from the gutter and put it through a hole in the lid of the tank.

3. To keep your water clean a first-flush diverter helps. This diverts the first flow of water from the roof away from the tank. This is the dirtiest water as the rain washes debris off the roof. The diverter prevents this from flowing into the tank. To further improve water quality, a Leaf Eater can be fitted to the pipe above the tank. This is a barrier that deflects leaves and debris away from the flow of water and prevents them from entering the tank. Check this regularly and clean out any leaves that are stuck in it, otherwise it can block water from flowing into the tank. You can also fit a mesh screen into the tank opening to prevent leaves from going into the water. The final step is to connect an overflow pipe and add a tap to your tank.

Simple Rainwater Harvesting

A few years ago we produced a documentary in Zimbabwe for a Swedish client. We were filming smallholder farmers and one of them showed me his simple, yet very effective rainwater harvesting system. He didn't have money for gutters or tanks. Instead, he had dug neat channels around his house, exactly where the rainwater ran off his roof. These channels all fed into one larger channel, leading the water down the slope past his citrus trees. Each of these had a large square dug around their trunks, about 15 cm deep, filled with a thick layer of compost. The main water channel had smaller channels leading off to each tree. These channels could be opened or closed with a piece of metal slotted into the opening. As soon as the first tree's square was full of water, it would be closed off and the water would run to the second, with the pattern repeated until all the trees were watered. The channel continued on to feed his vegetable beds in a similar manner. The channel ended in a dam at the bottom of his property, where any water that hadn't soaked into his garden was stored.

This system can be adapted to any garden that is on a slight slope. With some creativity it can be both functional and create an interesting feature in a garden. The channels can be turned into rock-lined streams, branching off into a network through the garden.

Another simple solution is to install rainwater barrels at the bottom of downpipes to collect the rainwater. A number of them can be joined together to create more storage space.

RAIN WATER HARVESTING TIPS

- Keep your roof clean during dry weather. This is when dust, leaves, animal excrement and dead insects accumulate on the roof.
- To avoid contamination of the runoff, rooftops used for water harvesting should be hosed down regularly, even if a first-flush diverter has been installed.
- Keep your gutters clean.
- A mesh screen can also be fitted into the gutter leading into the tank as an additional precaution to prevent debris from falling into the tank.
- Trees and plants hanging over the roof should be pruned back.

GREY WATER HARVESTING

Grey water is the relatively clean water that comes from showers, baths, sinks, washing machines and other kitchen appliances. Water that comes from the sewerage system is black water and should never be recycled. Nor should water from dishwashers be re-used. About 60 per cent of household water that leaves the home as wastewater is re-usable as grey water. It might look a little yucky but it is perfectly safe to use in our gardens (if the proper precautions are followed), wash cars and driveways, and flush toilets. By recycling our grey water we are reducing the load on increasingly stressed municipal systems. Plus it connects us urbanites to a natural water cycle.

Grey water storage is a bit more complicated than storing rainwater. If it sits for longer than 24 hours it becomes increasingly stinky and foul. This is because anaerobic bacteria move in and start feeding on all the yummy gunk in the water. If this happens, it should not be used. The simplest way to use grey water is to gravity-feed it to a section of your garden where a wetland is planted with water-loving plants. Or it can be gravity-fed to a drum, filtered and then drip irrigated every day into the flower garden.

I have followed my father's example by recycling our en suite bathroom's grey water – but instead of the water just flowing into the garden, we have a tank collecting the water. I knew I wouldn't be watering my garden every day,

All Natural

When recycling grey water, all products used in the areas where the water is generated must be biodegradable and environmentally friendly. This is becoming increasingly easy to do as these products are becoming more readily available commercially. Or you can choose to make your own, ensuring you know exactly what is going into them. Ingredients such as vinegar, lemon juice, baking powder and pure soap will take care of pretty much all your household cleaning needs.

plus I was planning to use this water for my vegetable garden. So I needed to make sure I wasn't going to make us all sick in the process! You have to be careful when using grey water on edibles, as harmful bacteria and other pathogens can be carried onto the leaves.

The first step is to place a filter on top of the tank to remove fluff, hair and debris. This must be cleaned weekly. We then installed an ozoneater inside the tank to clean the water. However, this required a small electric pump to circulate the ozone. It was a bit noisy and I was concerned that I was using extra electricity in the process of saving water. So we removed the ozoneater and its pump and tried beneficial bacteria instead. And this works perfectly.

A small submersible pump aerates the water (similar to a fish tank) and once a week we add a teaspoon of powdered beneficial organisms that clean the water so it is healthy and doesn't smell. To provide more surface area for the beneficial organisms to live and breed on, we cut up about 20 plastic two-litre bottles and put them in the tank. As an additional precaution, we installed an irrigation system in the vegetable beds using soaker hoses (see page 72). Using these, water soaks into the ground and doesn't splash on the leaves. Beneficial organisms in the soil and the roots of the plants provide a final filter.

The irrigation system operates off a pressure-activated pump. We had to trouble-shoot this because when we first installed the soaker hose, we were quite conservative about spacing and the lengths of hose we used. However, because the pump was pressure-operated, it needed more pressure and therefore more soaker hose to reach its optimum functioning. Otherwise the pump kept turning itself off. This is something to keep in my mind if you are installing one of these systems in a small garden. I would recommend using a specialist when installing a grey water system. JoJo Tanks has a list of preferred contractors on their website.

MAINTENANCE

I try to walk through my vegetable garden at least once a day. By doing a daily walk I can see very quickly if there are pests or diseases starting to bother my plants. The quicker these are spotted and dealt with, the less chance they have of becoming a major problem.

On my morning walkabout I take a notebook so I can jot down ideas and things that need doing. I also carry a harvesting basket, some twine or stretchy green ties for controlling and tying back plants, and secateurs for trimming. Summer tomatoes, cucumbers, squash and to a lesser extent beans, all have tender growing points and stems. If these are left to ramble too far in the wrong direction it is very easy to break them when you try to redirect them up a support. By doing it every day, it takes a short amount of time and it becomes a morning meditation. If left too long, it becomes far more of a mission.

In my vegetable garden I have a couple of logs and benches. These invite me to sit, observe and enjoy it. This is all part of the morning meditation. Because a vegetable garden is not only for feeding our bodies, it also feeds our souls.

WEEDING

Weeding is vastly reduced with no-dig gardening, mulching and by planting intensively. Filling beds cheek to jowl with vegetables simply crowds the weeds out. Weeds can be a problem when preparing new beds, when using compost that wasn't hot enough to kill seeds, or where nearby plants have sown their seeds. Even a tomato can become a weedy plant if it is growing where you don't want it to be.

MULCHING

Mulching (adding leaves, compost or other organic matter to the surface of the soil) is one of the simplest yet one of the most beneficial things we can do in our gardens.

A mulched surface creates a forest floor environment that plants love. It reduces weeds, retains moisture, reduces spread of disease, regulates temperature, strengthens roots and improves the quality and fertility of the soil. Some people say they don't mulch because it looks messy, but with all the benefits, how can you possibly choose not to mulch?

A variety of materials can be used as mulch. I prefer using organic mulches such as compost, straw, leaf mould, grass clippings, autumn leaves and clippings from shrubs – especially artemisia, sage and lavender, which constantly need trimming. Artemisia has the added benefit of repelling bugs, which hate its smell. (Don't mulch with hay, as it can still have seed heads attached that can become weeds. Rather use straw, which is made from stalks.)

Mulch should be applied when seedlings are about 3 to 5 cm high. Depending on the material, mulch can be anything from 5 to 15 cm thick. If using fresh grass clippings, mix them with leaves first, otherwise they become dense and slimy, preventing water and air from reaching the soil. Leave a mulch-free circle of about 3 to 5 cm around stems to prevent rot. For larger plants with woody stems, leave a mulch-free zone of about 10 to 15 cm to prevent the bark decaying. Always weed and water the beds well before applying mulch.

PLANNING AND RECORDKEEPING

Benjamin Franklin said, "By failing to prepare, you are preparing to fail," and when it comes to vegetable gardens, this is very true. To keep a garden productive throughout the year requires planning.

Plants such as broccoli and cauliflower form the largest heads in the coolest months. A plan for a winter garden should be drawn up in mid-summer, to ensure that these go into the ground at the right time. And a plan for a summer garden should be done in front of a winter fire, so you are ready to transplant spring seedlings as soon as the weather warms up.

Planning successive sowings of fast-growing, cool season crops in winter and quick-to-bolt crops in summer ensures continual harvests.

Keeping records of when and where you fertilised reduces wastage. Notes about which seeds were successful and which weren't will help you plan a more productive garden the following season. Keeping records of what you have planted where will help you work out rotations. Observations, notes and records all increase your knowledge of your garden.

The most common problems a beginner gardener experiences is either over-enthusiastic planting, resulting in crowded beds, or planting too much of one thing and being overwhelmed by the harvest. With good planning, this can be avoided. Jeremy Dore is a UK computer programmer who dug up his front lawn in 2004 to start growing organic vegetables. He realised quickly that he could put his computer skills to good use by creating a programme for gardeners to design and plan their vegetable gardens so they provide a balanced and steady harvest all year round. The result was the easy-to-use, yet powerful *Garden Planner*, now used by thousands of vegetable gardeners all over the world. When Jeremy approached me to adapt the planner for South Africa, I jumped at the opportunity.

Jane's Delicious Garden Planner makes it easy to draw out your garden plan and decide what to plant. It is an online programme with software that shows you exactly how much space each plant requires, how to group them, and when they should be rotated. Using your postal code, the planner provides location-specific information. It includes detailed planting and growing information on over 130 vegetables, herbs and fruit. It is versatile and adaptable, with space for you to add notes and customise varieties. Every two weeks, the planner sends out an email with reminders of what to plant and what to harvest, all based on your garden plan.

If going high tech is not for you and you prefer to plan with good old pen and paper, buy a large book as a dedicated garden diary.

PLANTING GUIDE FOR A KITCHEN GARDEN

Here is an approximate guide of how many plants you will need to grow per person. These numbers depend on your tastes and on whether the garden is providing all the food or if it supplements your needs.

Plants per person

Artichokes 1 – 3	Cauliflowers 3 – 5	Peppers 5 – 6
Asian greens 20 – 40	Cucumbers 4 – 6	Potatoes 10 – 30
Asparagus 10 – 12	Eggplant 2 – 5	Rhubarb 1 – 3
Beans (bush) 4 – 8	Garlic 12 – 16	Spinach 10 – 20
Beans (climbing) 4 – 8	Lettuce 10 – 15	Summer squash 2 – 4
Beetroot 15 – 25	Melons 2 – 5	Sweet potatoes 5
Broccoli 5 – 8	Mielies 15 – 20	Swiss chard 2 – 3
Cabbages 5 – 10	Onions 40 – 80	Tomatoes 3 – 5
Carrots 30 – 40	Peas 25 – 60	Winter squash 2 – 4

CONTAINER
AND RAISED BED
GARDENING

CONTAINER GARDENING

Having limited space doesn't mean you can't grow your own food. Even the smallest patio, window sill or garden patch can boast a crop of vegetables. The rewards are large, even if the space is small. Many vegetables and herbs are suited to container planting and they will grow in just about anything, from an old wheelbarrow to a fancy pot. Smaller herbs grow happily in recycled olive or tomato cans. Even milk and juice cartons can be recycled into nifty free containers.

More and more vegetable gardeners are choosing to construct raised beds. Differing from containers, raised beds consist of four sides, with an open bottom. They can range from beautifully crafted cedar boxes to recycled wooden fences. They are a popular option, especially in gardens where the soil is poor, or if you are growing on a non-soil surface, such as a rooftop. Both containers and raised beds create an almost instant vegetable garden. For more on raised beds, see page 90.

WHY CONTAINERS?

The advantages of growing in containers are many. Containers make good use of limited space and a surprising amount of harvest can be gained if they are fed and watered correctly. Soil disease is much easier to deal with in a container as the soil can simply be replaced. They are practical to feed and it is easier to protect them from pests. Containers can be moved to take advantage of the sun and to protect them from frost. The best beefsteak tomatoes I have ever grown were in boxes placed on the paving next to my swimming pool. The hot western sun warmed up the paving all afternoon, retaining this heat well into the evening – and tomatoes (along with eggplants and chillies) prefer warm night time temperatures. The tomatoes thrived far better than ones in the ground in the vegetable garden. Even if you have a fair-sized vegetable garden it is a good idea to keep a few containers outside the kitchen door filled with chives, mint, parsley, spring onions, basil and thyme. These are especially useful on a rainy night, when the last thing you want to do is go foraging in the garden. With a quick nip and snip out the back door, you can add a fresh touch to a meal.

When gardening in urban areas such as rooftops, or on cement or paving, containers are a practical choice. The soil in many urban public spaces might not be suitable for growing vegetables and using containers is a good solution. Containers create a planting area instantly and they can be moved to a new site if their current location becomes unavailable. They also make sense if you are gardening in a city area where you are not sure about the safety of the soil, such as a former industrial site.

WHAT CONTAINER?

Choosing a container depends on many things – style, budget, space and what you plan to grow. With large containers, an entire edible garden can be planted, giving you everything you need in one place. There are endless choices of containers – from pots to boxes, crates to barrels, and metal drums, buckets and tins. If you are gardening on a budget, you don't have to spend a fortune on pots. Wine barrels, paint cans, colourful plastic buckets and biscuit tins can all be used as planters. Ensure that the container has sufficient holes in the bottom for drainage. Many pots are sold with a single hole in the bottom, which won't let water drain properly. Plants' roots will rot and die if they sit in water.

Bag Containers

Large polypropylene bags make very practical and affordable growing bags. These are the bags in which building supplies such as sand are sold. They are strong and durable, and drain well. If you buy them from a building supply company, you will find sizes ranging from 50 kg up to 1 000 kg – big enough for a fruit tree. The bags come in different thicknesses and if you are planting trees, choose the thickest. For planting most vegetables, you don't have to fill them all the way to the top. Place some gravel in the bottom to keep it stable. Roll the sides down and start with a layer of container mix (see page 92) about 40 cm deep. Every season, simply add more container mix. Trailing plants, such as strawberries, cherry tomatoes and nasturtiums planted around the edges, will quickly hide the rather ugly white bag. For climbing plants, fill the bags nearly to the top and push poles right down to the base of the bag to create a sturdy tripod. For potatoes, start with the sides rolled down and as they grow, roll up the sides and earth them up.

Tyres

Recycled tyres are also a good choice as a no-cost container. There is debate (especially on the internet) about the safety of using tyres to grow edibles, with many sites warning of dire consequences of toxins leaching into the soil. Tyres do contain potentially harmful chemicals, but there are no credible studies that prove these are released from whole tyres used in the garden. Research has shown that if toxins (not only from tyres, but from any other source) do leach into the soil, they do not travel very far sideways (about 5 cm). Thereafter, they travel downwards. So, if you want to be on the safe side, position non-edible plants, such as marigolds, around the perimeter of the tyre and keep your vegetables in the middle. And don't disturb the soil. I have been growing potatoes in tyres for nearly 20 years and have suffered no ill effects. In hotter climates, tyres can heat up in the sun, killing plants inside them. Prevent this by painting them white or other light colours.

Recycled Pallets, Crates and Drums

Recycled crates make excellent containers, especially if you source ones that are made from strong wood. You can either scavenge your own or buy ready-made containers such as The Urban Box. These come in different colours, sizes and heights and can be flat-packed for easy storage. Wheels and handles can be added, making them easy to move when full of soil. Wooden barrels cut in half make a deep container. When creating containers from wood, paint the inside with a non-toxic, waterproof paint to prevent them from rotting too quickly. Half metal drums will need drainage holes drilled. Painted bright colours, they are ideal for a school or rooftop garden.

RAISED BEDS

The benefits of using raised beds are many. They warm up more quickly in spring and won't get as cold in winter. It is easier to protect raised beds from pests as the edges provide a barrier. The sides can also be used to attach supports for bird netting or frost cover. If you have a problem with disease, simply replace the soil. When beds are constructed to the approximate size of a door, they lend themselves to intensive gardening, providing a large harvest from a relatively small space. Raised beds can be constructed in bespoke shapes to fit into odd corners and angles. If you suffer from mobility or back problems, a high raised bed is the answer.

CREATING A RAISED BED GARDEN

When designing a raised bed garden, make the beds just big enough so you can reach the middle without having to stand on the soil, and leave sufficient room in between them for pathways. These can be gravel, paving, grass or simply earth covered with straw. If the planned vegetable garden area is grassed or weedy, see page 248 for a very quick way of creating an almost instant vegetable garden.

If you have trees nearby, their roots will sniff out the fertile soil in your raised beds and make a beeline for them, eventually finding their way into the beds. To prevent this, extend the weed cloth from the pathways under the raised beds (or recycle old carpeting). This also prevents unwanted weeds from popping up. To stop moles and other critters from tunnelling in under your beds, attach a layer of weld mesh to the bottom of the beds. This allows drainage and root growth but keeps unwanted eaters out.

The most common material used for raised beds is wood. The harder the wood, the longer it will last – but the harder the wood the more expensive it is. Cedar is a very good (but costly) option as it is long-lasting and insect-resistant. Gum is also insect-resistant and is a lot cheaper (or free, if you scavenge logs from tree fellers). Gum trees grow very tall and straight and these are ideal logs for creating a solid frame.

Raised beds constructed using bricks, either left bare or plastered, result in an elegant long-lasting vegetable garden. Don't forget to include drainage holes when you are building them. The hard edges of the raised beds can be softened by planting companion herbs around their bases.

There are many creative options for raised beds. I have used empty wine bottles turned upside down and stuck into the ground to create a solid yet interesting edge. Tyres (see page 88), straw bales (see page 151), cinderblocks, tree stumps, metal half drums, old baths, recycled packing crates and pallets, stones, woven sticks (fresh wattle, bamboo or bay sticks are good) and even broken crockery can all be used to create a raised bed.

GROWING AND MAINTAINING

When growing vegetables in containers and raised beds, almost all the information in the section on Urban Vegetable Gardening (see pages 12 to 83) is applicable. However, where things differ a little is with growing medium, watering and feeding. If you spend some time getting these three right, you will increase your chances of success.

GROWING MEDIUM

A good growing medium in both containers and raised beds is vital. Its functions are to provide water, nutrients and support for plants' roots. Using just compost or digging up some garden soil won't result in happy plants. An ideal mixture should be light, airy and long-lasting, without breaking down or becoming compacted. It should retain moisture but not become waterlogged and, most importantly, it must be nutritious.

Container Mix
A good recipe for both containers and raised beds includes a mixture of:

- 1 part pre-soaked coir peat (also known as coco peat, this waste by-product of the coconut industry is a renewable resource).
- 1 part pre-soaked vermiculite.
- 2 parts sieved nutrient-rich compost. If you make your own compost using manure and nutrient-rich herbs, the compost will provide nutrients as well as retain moisture. Vermicompost is an excellent addition.
- ½ part disease-free topsoil, to provide nutrients, density and natural organisms.
- If your compost doesn't contain manure, add a few scoops of well-rotted kraal or horse manure.
- A slow-release organic fertiliser, applied according to the packet instructions. If you are using a deep container, only add this to the top third of the container.

When mixing, use a shallow wheelbarrow or wide-mouthed tub (such as a plastic or galvanised metal drinks tub or dog bath). This makes it easier to blend everything together rather than using a bucket. Use a face mask when mixing – especially on a windy day. When filling a container or a raised bed, add the growing medium in batches, spreading and wetting each layer until it is thoroughly soaked before adding the next batch. Don't fill containers level to the brim – leave a gap of about 10 cm at the top to allow for watering. Once full, don't ever let it dry out completely.

REPLACING AND REVITALISING GROWING MEDIUM

This is an ongoing maintenance task for container gardeners. But how often should the growing medium be replaced? And can it just be topped up instead? The answers depend on a number of factors: the quality of container mix you began with; what you have been growing; and how often you have been adding organic matter and mulch.

The first step in deciding is to assess your containers. The first candidates are those that have had vegetables growing in them for one and a half to two years. All container mixes will eventually compact over time as the structure breaks down. Once this happens, the mixture can dry out more quickly, resulting in water running straight down the insides of the pots and not being absorbed by the growing medium. If you see the water coming out of the drainage holes almost immediately after adding water, it is time to change the medium. Or if your plants are weak or turning yellow, it is time to replace. Don't throw used container mix away – add it to your compost pile or to garden beds, unless you have had problems with disease. If the level of the container mix has dropped by quite a few centimetres, then it is time for a top-up.

A good reason for completely replacing the growing medium is disease. If you have experienced problems with diseased vegetables (especially tomato or potato diseases), then you need to replace the soil. Give the container a good scrub with soap and hot water before reusing it.

For perennials in small containers, a bit of care is needed when repotting them. The day after watering is a good time as the soil is moist enough to hold together but not too wet to handle. Loosen the sides using a spatula and slide the plant out of the pot. Look for any roots that are circling the sides and pull them to loosen. If they are very long and winding, cut them off. Replant in a container with fresh container mix.

Large containers with perennials won't need the mix replaced as often, as long as they are kept topped up, fertilised and well mulched. Large containers will replicate the natural process, where mulch and compost on the top layers break down, creating fertile, loose soil below. The plants will tell you if there is a problem with the soil and if it needs replacing: look for signs of yellowing or disease-prone plants.

Changing the soil in a large container with perennials is more of a transplanting process. To ease transplanting shock, the roots should be cut in stages, when the plant is dormant. Two weeks before repotting, use a sharp spade to slice down on two sides of the plant, 30 to 50 cm away from the stem (depending on the size of the plant), and deep enough to sever all the roots on that side. A week before transplanting cut the other two sides. On the day, prepare the new container mix and have it ready. Remove the plant from its container and place it in the shade. Empty the container, give it a scrub and fill with the new mixture, wetting

DRAINAGE

When you water, you want it to soak into the soil and not just run straight through. The growing medium needs to retain moisture, but also needs to drain so the roots don't sit in wet soil. The value of placing gravel or stones in the bottom of a pot to improve drainage is in fact a fallacy. Tests done at the University of Georgia in the USA proved that this method actually decreases drainage.

To ensure that your plants' roots remain moist but not waterlogged, start by using a good-quality container mix, with a combination of ingredients as listed on page 92. Before filling the pot, place a layer of sponges along the bottom of the pot – which will improve drainage. I recycle all my old kitchen and bathroom sponges into the bottom of my pots.

and firming the soil as you fill. Place the plant in the container facing the same way and at the same depth it originally was, back-filling and firming the soil. Water it in well afterwards. Keep it well watered for the next few weeks until it settles.

WATERING

Both raised beds (especially higher ones) and containers dry out more quickly than normal garden beds and need regular watering, sometimes as often as once a day in the middle of summer. The bigger and deeper a container, the less quickly it will dry out. Get into the habit of checking your plants every day or invest in a timer and a drip irrigation system (see page 72). Position the drip hose evenly across the surface and connect it with a hose attachment.

Self-watering Containers

More container plants are killed because of over or under watering than any other reason. Self-watering containers will prevent this. They are ideal for people who travel or those with long days at the office. Self-watering containers work on the principle of providing a reservoir of water that feeds into the soil of the container using osmosis, supplying a steady and natural flow to the plants' roots. This method ensures your water-hungry vegetables never dry out, reduces disease and conserves water. Self-watering containers can be made using many different methods – even recycled two-litre plastic bottles. There are many methods and plans available on the internet.

Watering Tips

- When checking, don't just look, use your fingers to feel. The surface can look dry even though it is still moist underneath. Push your fingers about 5 cm into the soil and if it is dry at your fingertips, then you need to water. Over watering can drown plants.
- When watering containers, water deeply until it runs out of the bottom. This encourages roots to fill the pot.
- Water the soil, not the leaves. This reduces risk of fungal disease.
- Get to know your plants. Some, like Mediterranean herbs, prefer to dry out between each watering. Others, such as Asian greens, lettuce and spinach, will suffer if this happens.

FEEDING

Raised beds and containers require extra feeding because nutrients are washed out more easily. Get your containers off to a good start by using a well-balanced soil mix (see page 92). This will gradually subside as it is

WISE WATERING

After I wrote my first book I met Sam, an avid gardener in Lenasia. Sam's entire garden is grown in containers, and he has worked out an innovative method of watering them.

When he fitted his small garden with an irrigation system, he added nozzles to all his pots. They did the job of watering the pots – but they also wasted water by spraying the surrounding paving. Sam soon solved this problem.

He cut the bottoms off plastic bottles and propped the top section over the pots on sticks. He positioned the nozzles inside these plastic 'caps'. As the spray from the nozzle hits the curved plastic, it showers downward, watering only the pot perfectly.

washed out through the drainage holes. Top it up in spring with a layer of topsoil mixed with rich compost. This will give your plants a boost at the beginning of the season.

When planting, add a handful of organic fertiliser or vermicompost to the planting holes. Add a dry organic fertiliser every three months and use a liquid organic fertiliser every month. If your containers are close to the house then choose a spray made from beet, such as Biogrow's Biotrissol, rather than a seaweed one that will make everything smell horribly fishy.

PLANTING GUIDE FOR CONTAINERS

PLANT	ABOUT	SOIL DEPTH	SUN/SHADE
Asian greens	Quick growing, provide a wide range of greens year round for salads and stir fries	30–40 cm	Full sun to part shade in summer
Beans	Runner beans will need a support, such as a tall trellis or tripod	30–60 cm	Full sun
Beetroot	Grow well in containers as long as they have regular water	30–45 cm	Full sun
Broccoli	Sprouting broccoli is a good container choice	30–45 cm	Full sun
Cabbage	Miniature cabbages are ideal for small containers	30–45 cm	Full sun
Carrots	Carrots are great in containers as they provide a clod- and stone-free soil, ideal for long juicy roots	45–60 cm	Full sun
Chillies	Wide variety to choose from and in frost areas they can be brought inside during winter	45–60 cm	Full sun
Chives	Chives grow easily in pots and are a good addition to the container garden as they chase pests away from other plants	30–45 cm	Full sun
Citrus trees	Choose a small variety. Use the space around the base to plant parsley, pansies and nasturtiums	80–120 cm	Full sun
Cucumbers	Will need a trellis or support to grow up	45–60 cm	Full sun
Edible flowers	Don't forget to include plants with edible flowers. Nasturtiums, pansies and violas are particularly easy and suitable	30–45 cm	Full sun to part shade

PLANT	ABOUT	SOIL DEPTH	SUN/SHADE
Eggplant	As eggplants only bear later in the season, combine them with shallower-rooted lettuces, greens and herbs. This allows you to harvest other things from the pot until the eggplants are ready	45–60 cm	Full sun
Garlic	Grows well in containers and moisture can be controlled, allowing them to ripen properly in areas with a very wet spring	30–45 cm	Full sun
Herbs	Almost all herbs do well in containers. Thyme makes a good groundcover	16–60 cm	Varies, but most prefer full sun
Kale	A good provider of healthy greens	45–60 cm	Full sun to part shade
Lettuces	A shallow container can be used if you use the 'cut and come again' method, where lettuces are sown thickly and leaves are cut from young plants every two weeks or so	25–45 cm	Full sun to part shade in summer
Onions	As with garlic, the moisture can be controlled in a container	30–45 cm	Full sun
Peppers	Crunchy, healthy and colourful addition to a container	45–60 cm	Full sun
Radishes	Quick-growing radishes can be popped into most containers	30–45 cm	Full sun to part shade
Rocket	Quick-growing filler	30–45 cm	Full sun to part shade in summer
Spinach	Spinach benefits from regular moisture and is a quick-growing, healthy green	30–45 cm	Full sun to part shade in summer
Spring onions	Love growing in containers and seed themselves	30–45 cm	Full sun
Squash (gem squash, patty pan, sweet dumpling and miniature pumpkins, zucchini)	These need a wide container and climbing varieties require support. All squash are hungry feeders and need regular fertiliser to keep them producing fruit	45–60 cm	Full sun
Swiss chard	Hardy and easy to grow, providing year round greens for salads and stir fries	30–45 cm	Full sun to part shade
Tomatoes (cherry)	Either let them trail over the edges of a large container, or provide a support	60–100 cm	Full sun

THEMED CONTAINERS AND BEDS

With so much choice of suitable plants, selecting a theme for each container or bed will help focus your planting, adding fun and interest to your vegetable garden. Colour, taste, scent and cuisine all influence the choice. The first thing to consider is what you and your family eat. It might be a great idea to plant a hot-flavoured Mexican garden but not if you're the only one who likes chillies. Also consider what plants like – don't mix and match plants with completely different watering or sunlight requirements. And remember – companion planting guidelines also apply to pots, so mix different plants together in containers. (For more on companions, see page 30.) Here are some ideas to get you started.

An Asian Oasis

Love Chinese food and Thai curries? Then an Asian-themed garden is for you. Grow in full sun and provide regular, deep watering.

What to grow

- Asian greens (bok choy, Chinese cabbage, mizuna, mustard and tat soi) grow well grouped together. They prefer cooler weather – during hotter months use the lemon grass and Asian lime for shade.
- Asian lime leaves add a distinct lemon flavour to coconut soups and curries. A small citrus tree, it does well in a container as long as it's fed regularly with slow-release organic 3:1:5 fertiliser.
- Chillies provide essential Asian heat. Plant near the front edge, where it is slightly hotter and drier.
- Coriander also goes to seed quickly in hot weather – but the seeds are delicious. For continual leaf supply, sow seeds every few weeks.
- Lemon grass grows quite tall, so plant it towards the back. It loves being cut regularly. It dies down in frost but will pop up again in spring.

Essential Italian Herbs

The flavours of Italy combined in one place makes for easy picking, whether you are cooking pizza, pasta or creating a robust salad. This container is filled with herbs that like full sun and don't need too much water. Use a well-drained growing medium.

What to grow

- Marjoram and oregano are undemanding plants. Marjoram is more sensitive to frost, whereas oregano is hardy.
- Perennial thyme bears pretty pink and white flowers in summer. Plant a selection (such as lemon, golden and variegated) to provide colour and flavour variation.
- Rosemary will grow tall so keep it towards the back. It benefits from being pruned regularly to prevent it from becoming woody. Cut it back in late spring.

A Gourmet Salad Box

A raised bed or container are both ideal for salad ingredients. If you choose a large box you can include a lime or lemon tree for a salad dressing. Position in full sun, or a spot with some afternoon shade.

What to grow

- Place a tall tripod securely in the centre and wind a cherry tomato up it.
- Sow a block of mixed loose-leaf lettuce on the southern side of the tripod to prevent them from getting too much sun.
- On the other sides of the tripod, plant basil and spring onions. Choose a selection of basils – from lemon-flavoured to mint. Leave some spring onions to flower and they will re-seed themselves.
- Around the edges, plant pansies and dianthus to add colour to salads.

Other Ideas to Try

- Cottage garden (mixed edibles, such as parsley, rocket, Swiss chard and spring onions, planted with flowers, such as calendula, California poppy and cornflowers)
- First Aid box (herbal healing plants such as *Aloe vera*, calendula and thyme)
- Fragrant garden (lavender, mint, pineapple sage and rose pelargonium)
- Mexican (chillies, coriander and tomatoes)
- Vegetable soup (carrots, celery, chard and onions)

CONTAINER AND RAISED BED TIPS

To maximise growing space, add a vertical tripod to the centre of larger pots or the end of a raised bed. Make it out of bamboo or wooden rods, burying the bases securely into the earth. A simple tomato or bean support can be created out of a tube of plastic chicken mesh, with a diameter the same as the pot or bed.

Keep the surface of the soil well mulched to prevent it from drying out.

Fill beds or containers with as many plants as they will hold, creating a living umbrella to protect the soil. If you have gaps in your planting, grow groundcovers, such as thyme.

Many soil-borne diseases are easier to prevent in pots as the soil can simply be sterilised or replaced. Fungal diseases can become a problem if containers are too close together or if there is not enough air circulation. This can happen on a closed-in veranda. Leave sufficient space between pots and place them on bricks or tree stumps to create varying heights and increase airflow.

Choose the right plants for the right container. For smaller boxes, choose shallow-rooted vegetables such as Asian greens and lettuces. In wall-mounted boxes, select rambling varieties of cherry tomatoes and nasturtiums to trail over the edges. For more robust vegetables, such as eggplant and squash, choose large, wide containers.

Drainage holes can become blocked if the container is placed flat on the ground. Raising the pots with small blocks of wood or bricks will prevent this.

THE URBAN ORCHARD

Our house was built in 1906. A gnarly old plum tree on the northern side of the house is the last remnant of what was probably once a large orchard. A few years after we moved in, an elderly woman rang our buzzer. She had lived in the house from the early 1930s, when she was a little girl, through to the 1970s as an adult after she inherited it. She was visiting Johannesburg and asked if she could come and see her old home. I loved walking around with her and listening to her take a journey down memory lane in my home. The pool was once a rose garden and the en suite bathroom, her sewing room. Then she asked, "Is the old plum tree still here?" As soon as she saw it she gave it a hug and told me it had been an old tree when she was a little girl. This meant that the tree, still providing abundant fruit every year, was probably planted when the house was built, making it over 100 years old. In those days, it was common practice to plant an orchard, especially as the stand sizes were large enough to accommodate them. Sadly, with the increase of easily available fruit at supermarkets and greengrocers, and the decrease of space, people have stopped planting fruit trees.

Then and there I decided I was going to make the most of the harvest that this elder of my garden produces so generously every year. I also decided to recreate an urban orchard. Over the years the plum tree has been joined by many others and my orchard now includes: a tea tree, a myrtle, a bay, a walnut, a pomegranate, two grapevines growing up over a pergola, a quince, an apricot, nine citrus, two apples, three figs, two peaches, an elderberry, two blueberries, strawberries, a granadilla, gooseberries and four types of rambling berries. Many of these are growing against walls or fences, some are in containers and others are pruned to fit into smaller beds.

PLANTING AND MAINTAINING AN URBAN ORCHARD

rban orchards are becoming increasingly popular as more people realise how delicious and rewarding it is to grow their own organic fruit. Nurseries are recognising this edible trend and are supplying a wider variety of fruit trees and bushes suitable for smaller urban spaces.

PLANNING

Do some research before just buying whatever is available at your local nursery. This includes: making sure the trees you like are suitable for your climate; checking to see what size a mature tree will be; and finding out whether it needs a pollinator or if it's self-pollinating. This is very important if you want your fruit tree to produce fruit!

When planning an orchard, it helps to know when plants produce their fruit. Avoid planting trees that will all fruit at the same time otherwise you will be overwhelmed by the harvest. Ideally you should aim for something to be fruiting each month, from early spring right through to late autumn. In warmer climates, your garden can provide fruit year round.

A useful resource is Stargrow's website (see page 251). They sell wholesale fruit trees to the nurseries and on their website is a list of fruit, along with photographs and descriptions, and useful information about when the trees flower and fruit, whether they need a pollinator and which varieties pollinate others.

PLANTING

With many fruit trees, bushes and vines, it is cheaper to buy bare-rooted stock in late autumn for planting in winter. Bare root plants are exactly that – they don't have any soil around their roots. Keep the roots moist and plant them within a few weeks of purchase. They must be planted while dormant, that is while they still have no buds or leaves on them. Plants in bags or containers can be planted at other times of the year, depending on the variety. With all deciduous fruit, it is preferable to plant them in winter while they are dormant. This gives them a chance to settle and develop their roots before putting their energy into spring growth.

Most fruit trees need full sun and space so they are not crowded, otherwise they will compete for nutrients and sunlight. Group similar trees and plants together, making it easier to water and feed them. Exceptions to the full sun rule are some of the berries, such as strawberries and cane berries, which don't mind dappled shade or afternoon shade. The soil should be fertile and well-drained. For

perennials that will be in the same place for many years, enrich the soil with compost, a slow-release fertiliser such as Vita-Grow 2:3:2 and well-rotted manure before planting. When transplanting, position the plant at the same level as it was in its container or previous site. Don't make the planting hole too small and cram the roots in – dig a big enough hole with plenty of room for the roots. Fill gently and firm the soil down as you go. Water well, providing regular, deep watering, especially during dry periods for the first year or two, until the roots are well-established.

Young fruit trees will need support until their trunks are strong. A firm stake in the ground when it is planted will do the trick. Tie it to the stem with figure of eight loops, ensuring they don't become too tight when the trunk grows. After a few years, when the trunk is sturdy enough, the support can be removed. Lateral branches might need support when bearing fruit, especially as a tree grows older. Wedge a bamboo or gum pole under the branch, leaning it at an angle, while the fruit is still small.

PRUNING

Pruning is done for a variety of reasons. Some trees are pruned to a specific shape and size to encourage fruit production. Others only fruit on new wood therefore pruning is essential to encourage new branches to grow. Pruning maintains a tree's health by removing dead or diseased wood, which in turn encourages healthy new growth. When trees become too dense or tangled, pruning opens them up, creating airflow and reducing disease. Pruning can also be done to encourage a tree to grow into a specific pattern (see espalier on page 125). If a tree produces excessive amounts of young fruit, thin these out selectively. The remaining fruit will be healthier and bigger. Thinning, or even removing fruit completely, during a fruit tree's first two to three years will encourage new growth and establish strong limbs.

Pruning Techniques

When a branch is cut off, the tree forms a protective layer – like scar tissue – to cover the cut, preventing disease and decay. Correct pruning will assist the tree in doing this efficiently. Cuts must be clean with no tears in the bark, which can lead to disease. One of the first principles of pruning is to have sharp, well-maintained tools. A blunt saw or secateurs will result in tears and the branch being crushed instead of cut.

When pruning, avoid creating snags – short pieces of branch sticking out from the stem or beyond a bud. These most often die back, leaving dead wood, which is an invitation for disease.

Cuts of smaller branches should be made tight against the stem or, if removing the end of a shoot, just above a bud. A bud cut should be made at an angle away from the bud, allowing water to drain away, reducing risk of rot (see left).

Cutting through a larger, heavy branch should be done using three cuts (see right). This prevents its weight causing it to fall before you have finished cutting, thus tearing the bark open along the branch and sometimes down the trunk. Make the first cut (1) about 60–90 cm away from the trunk, cutting in an upward direction, only cutting about a third of the way through. This will prevent the bark splitting to the trunk. Make the second cut (2) about 8 cm further out from the first cut and cut all the way through. The final cut (3) is the most important – especially when pruning a large branch. If you look at a branch, you will see a swollen ring or collar where the trunk bark transitions into a smooth branch (4). The final cut should be made following the angle of this collar, cutting the branch flush against the collar, but not cutting into it. The branch collar forms the scar tissue and if it is removed, the cut will not heal properly. Although sealing cuts with a pruning seal used to be common practice, these days most gardeners prefer to leave cuts open to the air to seal naturally.

Pruning should be done when the tree is young, from its first winter. Pruning stimulates new growth and by selecting which branches we want to grow, we can shape the tree into a strong frame that will support fruit. This should be repeated every year in June or July, until the shape is established, which will take about three years to achieve. In subsequent years, maintenance pruning should be done to keep the shape by selectively removing trunk and branch suckers. Remove any crossing branches or diseased limbs.

1.

2.

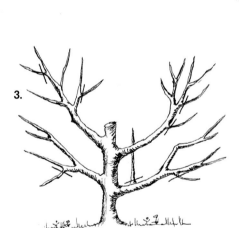

3.

AN OPEN VASE

This method of pruning shapes a tree to a short trunk with three or four main (scaffold) limbs, each with several lateral branches, radiating from the trunk at a similar level, like spokes of a wheel. A vase shape creates an open centre, allowing light and air to reach all the branches. It is ideal for smaller gardens, keeping the tree low for easy harvesting and care. It also encourages fruiting on lower and interior branches. It is suitable for most deciduous fruit and trees in containers. In larger gardens the open vase shape can be modified by allowing the tree to grow taller, with alternating scaffold branches radiating out at different levels, but still maintaining an open centre. The illustrations above show two layers, pruned in an open vase shape.

Year one: Choose three or four main branches that are evenly spaced around the trunk. Prune the central leader and any other side branches. **Years two and three:** Prune the end of each branch to an outward-facing bud. This encourages strong growth at the end and establishes the shape. Remove branches in the centre of the tree, keeping the central vase empty. Remove any crossing branches.

Grafting point

MAINTENANCE

When you have learned the basics of pruning, it is not difficult to keep on top of it. Once established, most fruit trees are relatively hassle-free, and don't need much other than regular watering and feeding when required.

One of the products that I use regularly on my fruit trees is Talborne's Vita Fruit & Flower. This organic fertiliser has been formulated to provide a balanced supply of nutrients to fruit trees. When feeding dry fertiliser, it should be applied to the ground under the drip line of the tree and watered in well. The drip line is the outer edge of the tree, where the furthermost branches are. A tree mirrors its upper growth in its roots, with the newest and most efficient roots being quite far away from the trunk. This is where you want the fertiliser to go. Liquid fertiliser can be sprayed onto the leaves as a foliar feed or used as a drench onto the soil. This is useful if a plant is struggling, or to give it a boost after fruiting.

Many fruit trees are grafted onto root stock of another variety. This is done for various reasons. Some cultivars do not grow true from seeds and can only be reproduced by grafting. Other reasons include: to produce dwarf varieties; to increase disease- and pest-resistance; to create a tree with two or more varieties on one trunk; or to increase hardiness, sturdiness and strength. One thing to watch out for on grafted trees is for growth coming from the root stock. Called water shoots, these unproductive stems need to be removed, as they will pull energy away from the fruiting sections and create unwanted growth. There are two ways in which you can identify a water shoot. Firstly it will be coming from below the grafting point – a bumpy section, low on the stem. Secondly, it will look different to the upper section, with dissimilar leaves or larger thorns, for example.

PESTS AND DISEASES

Some fruit trees are pest- and disease-free, while others battle an attack of one or the other constantly. Here follow some of the more common pests and diseases you might encounter, with non-toxic solutions to deal with them. When using organic pest control, don't forget that a small population of pests is welcome, as these attract predators such as ladybirds. However, this does mean that some of the fruit might not be perfect. I would rather have a slightly imperfect fruit than one covered in toxic pesticides.

Underplant your orchard with a variety of flowers and herbs, such as basil, borage, chives, comfrey, daffodils, feverfew, garlic, marigolds, nasturtium and tansy. Creating diversity encourages a balance of insects and helps prevent disease.

For more detail on the sprays and solutions recommended below, see page 56. For making traps, see page 110.

1.

Aphids and whitefly (1)

Plant basil, chives, garlic, nasturtiums and tansy under trees. Use a garlic, chilli and oil spray (see page 60) or an insecticidal oil such as Biogrow's Neudosan or Vegol to control heavy infestations.

Birds

Deter birds by placing twirling reflective items in the trees. The best protection is to use nets to cover fruit as it ripens. Individual fruit bags can also be used, but this is more labour intensive than putting up netting.

Black spot (2)

This is a fungal infection that makes round black marks on leaves and citrus fruit. It causes leaves to fall and reduces yield. Use a milk spray (see page 60) or spray with Biogrow's Copper Soap as a preventative to protect fruit trees during wet and humid weather.

Citrus psylla (3)

Citrus psylla is a tiny scale pest that sucks juice from the underside of

2.

leaves, causing bumpy curled leaves. Spray leaves and tree trunk, as well as drenching the soil around the tree, with Biogrow Pyrol to kill off these pests and to control the ants that spread them. (For more on ants see page 56.) Feed trees regularly to prevent stress (which makes them vulnerable to pest attack).

Codling moth

A light grey moth with black-headed, yellow larvae. The female lays eggs on fruit or leaves and the larvae attack the fruit as soon as they hatch. After chomping for about three weeks, the fat larvae head down the trunk to pupate for the following spring. To break the cycle, place collars of corrugated cardboard around the trunk as soon as the fruit is ripe. The larvae will head down the trunk and hide inside the cardboard furrows. Check the cardboard regularly and squish them. Spraying young fruit and the soil around the tree with Bioneem will also help break the cycle. To trap moths before they lay, make a molasses fruit trap (see page 110).

3.

BELOW: Underplant fruit trees with companions such as comfrey, chives or basil to confuse pests and prevent disease.

Fruit beetles

Chafer beetles, which turn leaves into lacy tatters, and the large smelly black and yellow beetles that make a beeline for ripe fruit, can both be repelled and controlled effectively using Bioneem. You can also trap them (see page 110).

Fruit fly

Fruit fly is responsible for more cursing gardeners than most other pests. Fruit fly females lay eggs under the skin of ripening fruit. Larvae burrow into the fruit and munch their way to maturity, destroying the fruit in the process. Prevent fruit fly by encouraging vigorous growth with good feeding, pruning, regular watering and mulching. Practise good sanitation by removing any fallen fruit regularly. If left, ripe fruit attracts fruit flies and makes it easy for larvae to tunnel into the ground to pupate. Companion planting of basil, chives, garlic, nasturtiums and tansy under trees will help confuse them. Use traps to attract and kill them (see page 110). Eco Fruitfly Bait GF-120 can also be applied to the tree fortnightly. (Use a brush to flick large droplets over the tree.) For more on fruit fly control, see opposite.

A fruit fly infestation can lead to significant loss of fruit. This can be devastating for a commercial grower. But more problematic is the loss of access to export markets, where requirements are so strict that a single fruit fly can lead to suspension of the export. Commercial orchards are adopting a 'sterile insect technique' (SIT) whereby sterile male fruit flies are released, ultimately reducing the population. However, one of the main sources of fruit fly is private gardens and neglected orchards, where they continue to breed unchecked and reduce the efficacy of the SIT programmes in nearby commercial orchards. Even if you don't plan to harvest your fruit, the responsible thing to do is to control the fruit fly in your garden.

Leaf curl

This fungal disease causes reddish blisters on leaves, distorting and thickening them, eventually reducing both leaf and fruit production. The spores live in protected areas over winter and then regenerate in spring. Prevent by using a seaweed foliar spray or Biogrow's Biotrissol to toughen the leaves. If you had leaf curl the previous year, prevent it attacking again by spraying with Biogrow Copper Soap in winter as soon as the leaf buds begin to swell, and repeat seven to ten days later.

Mildew

Prevent with a milk spray (see page 60) or Biogrow Copper soap.

Pumpkin flies

These are similar to fruit flies. The flies lay eggs in the fruit, which in turn develop into maggots that munch their way to maturity, destroying young fruit. Once they leave the fruit, they fall to the ground. They have a very distinctive habit of 'springing' themselves along the ground to move to another area where they burrow under the soil to pupate.

Good sanitation is the first step of control. Remove all fallen fruit and remove any early unpollinated fruit. These develop as normal at first, but then turn yellow, shrivel up, and eventually die off. Use a fruit fly trap (see page 111) and spray young fruit with Bioneem.

The incidence of stings can be severe towards December and January if the pumpkin fly populations are not controlled early. Start a regular spray programme with Bioneem every seven days when the plant starts flowering. If a serious problem develops, combine Pyrol and

Jenny Slabber from Talborne Organics recommends the following approach. Every winter after pruning, spray the trunks of trees and branches with Lime Sulphur or Biogrow Pyrol to flush out eggs and insects over wintering in the bark. Spray a preventative spray of Biogrow Pyrol just after petal drop, as newly formed fruits appear, to knock back early populations that may be around from the previous season's crops. For example, an infestation from winter citrus could invade your early spring peaches.

Neglected loquat trees in the neighbourhood are perfect breeding grounds for fruit fly as loquats are often left rotting on trees at the time that other summer fruits start to ripen. As soon as fruits start to 'swell and smell' (which often coincides with the heat and first spring rains in summer rainfall areas), a regular programme for prevention must be started and stuck to. Spray alternately with Pyrol and Bioneem every 14 days initially and closer to harvest, every seven days. For best control spray during the late afternoon, when the beneficial insects and bright sun are both on their way to bed.

Bioneem at 5 ml each per litre of water and spray during the late afternoon when the pollinators are resting.

Scale
These tiny parasitic insects stick to the trunk and live off the tree's sap. Spray with an organic insecticidal oil, such as Vegol, and in heavy attack use Pyrol. Scale is usually planted by ants on distressed plants that are under-watered and underfed.

Slugs and snails (see page 53)

Stem borer
The female stem borer beetle lays eggs under the bark. The larvae then drill holes in the bark and into the trunk. If left, they will tunnel deep into the tree and can destroy it. They are particularly prevalent in the Western Cape. Prevent the female from laying eggs by protecting the stem with shade cloth (leave a gap between the stem and the cloth). If borer holes are spotted, clear them as much as you can by poking wire into the holes and then squirt Pyrol into them.

Wasps
Although they prey on many unwanted insects such as worms and grubs, wasps love munching on ripe sweet fruit, particularly peaches. Use a trap (see page 111) or bags to protect the fruit.

TRAPS AND BAIT

With a little effort and ingenuity, you can protect your harvest from insect damage. The following are very effective solutions.

Fruit Bags
Bagging individual fruit, although a little labour intensive, will protect against insect and bird damage. The cheapest way to do this is to purchase dozens of little polyester draw-string gift bags, available from bulk gift stores for about R2 each. Tie them on as soon as the fruit begins forming. They can be reused season after season.

Fruit Beetle Trap
Yellow-and-black fruit beetles are attracted to the smell of ripe fruit and can do considerable damage. You can make an effective trap using a plastic milk container. Cut a couple of rectangular holes into the sides (about 4 cm x 2 cm). Place some scraps of fruit (especially banana) in the bottom of the container and hang it in the tree. The beetles climb in but can't get out again. Empty the bugs out regularly and refill with fruit.

Homemade trap

1. Cut the top cone section off a two-litre plastic bottle (remove the lid first). Place the bait in the bottom of the bottle. Turn the cone upside down and place it inside the base of the bottle, and use metal clips to secure it. (The tops of these can be used to hang it in place.)

2. Place strips of masking tape up the sides of the bottle. (This gives insects a 'ladder' to grip onto when climbing up the sides.) For larger insects, leave as is. For smaller insects, cover the top with plastic and secure it with an elastic band.

3. Make holes in the plastic that allow tiny insects in. Hang them in the fruit trees. Check every second week. If you don't like the look of plastic bottles hanging in your fruit trees, decorate them with twine and beads.

1.

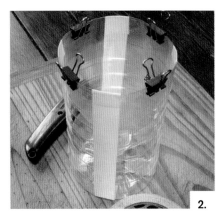

2.

3.

So now that you have caught all these insects in your traps, what are you going to do with them? If you have hens, they love the treat of a trap full of bugs being emptied into their run. Otherwise, the most humane way to kill them is to put them in the freezer. Once frozen, put them in the compost.

Bait for Traps

Soak a sponge in any of the following bait mixtures and place it in the trap. Replace every week while the fruit is ripening.

For pumpkin and fruit flies use apple cider vinegar and over-ripe pieces of banana or apple. Eco Fruitfly Bait GF-120 is an organically certified bait that attracts and kills fruit flies. It contains spinosad, an insecticide derived from soil bacteria. It also contains protein and sugar, both of which attract the flies.

For wasps mix a cup of apple juice, 1 teaspoon of sugar, and a few pieces of wet cat food.

For codling moth mix molasses and water using a 1:10 ratio.

Solar Light Trap

Many insects, such as chafer beetles, are active at night. You will notice this if you go out with a head torch to harvest dinner after dark. Bugs, attracted to the light, will buzz around your face. You can make use of this behaviour by placing a solar-powered LED light inside a trap.

Follow the instructions opposite for making a trap. Cut a small hole in the base and insert the spike of a garden solar light through it. Attach the top of the solar light to the spike so the light is inside the trap with the spike sticking out the bottom. Cover the clear plastic at the bottom of the trap with dark tape, but not so high that it blocks the solar panel's sun. Position it in the sun near where the pests are active.

DECIDUOUS TREES

Many trees can be grown in smaller urban gardens. Here follows a selection of popular fruit. Not included are trees that are on the alien invasive plant list, such as loquat and mulberry. Although these produce delicious fruit, they can rapidly become invasive weeds, as their fruit is spread by birds.

Apple

Apples are hardy trees that grow up to ten metres high. They can be grown in medium-sized gardens, but are only suitable for small gardens if pruned or trained as an espalier (see page 125). They have a long lifespan and bear fruit ranging from green to yellow and red, with flavours and textures from crispy and tart, to sweet and juicy.

Although there are some self-pollinating varieties, most apple trees need a pollinator otherwise they won't bear fruit. To ensure good pollination, plant at least three varieties. Apples prefer fertile, loamy soil but will grow in poorer soils. They do not like being waterlogged nor damp frosty corners. Apples need cold winters and mild summers and won't do well in warmer climates.

Growing and maintenance Apples need to be pruned for their first three years to create an open vase shape that allows light in (see page 105). Fruit is borne on spurs (short side shoots) and two-year-old laterals (horizontal stems). Every winter, while the tree is dormant, the tree should be lightly pruned, maintaining the vase shape but making sure not to cut off the fruit-bearing spurs. Fertilise in spring.

Encourage vigorous growth by foliar spraying with a liquid organic fertiliser once a month until the fruit has been harvested. In late spring, remove any damaged or diseased apples to allow the remaining ones to flourish. Good companions to plant under apples are chives, nasturtiums, stinging nettles and tansy.

Diseases and pests Codling moth, fruit fly and powdery mildew

Harvesting and eating Fruit is ready to be picked when they can be twisted off the stem easily. Apples are delicious baked whole, or made into crumble or apple pie.

Apricot

Apricots are suited to medium-sized gardens as they are self-fertile and grow up to six metres tall. Hardy and deciduous, they produce soft sweet-flavoured fruit that bruises easily when ripe. Store-bought apricots, picked when unripe so they can travel, seldom match the sublime flavour of a sun-ripened freshly picked apricot.

They like well-drained, fertile soil. They need a cold winter but produce flowers early, so won't do well in areas with late frosts.

Growing and maintenance Shape them in their first winter. After that the only pruning required is to remove any dead or diseased wood. They bear fruit on spurs and the branches can become brittle and break with the weight of fruit. Either thin the fruit out, or prop up vulnerable-looking limbs.

They need regular deep watering, especially during dry weather, and benefit from a thick layer of mulch. Good companions are all members of the onion family.

Diseases and pests Codling moth, fruit fly, powdery mildew and scale

Harvesting and eating They are best picked when soft and ripe – but check them every day as they can go over very quickly. They make delicious jam and can also be preserved in brandy.

Cherry

Cherries need a cold winter and won't do well in warmer areas. Some varieties are self-fertile, others are not. A good choice for urban gardens is the self-fertile Stella, which has sweet, dark fruit.

Growing and maintenance Cherries will grow up to ten metres unless trained as an espalier (see page 125). Cherries, more than any other stone fruit, do not like soggy feet and need well-drained, fertile soil. They grow on spurs on two-year-old wood. Cherries like having the ground around them covered with grass, alfalfa or clover.

Diseases and pests Birds

Harvesting and eating Cherries don't ripen much after being picked so are best harvested when fully ripe. They are delicious preserved in sugar syrup.

Fig

This is one of my favourite fruits. Easily bruised, the best way to savour the flavour of a fully ripe fig is to grow it yourself. They are self-fertile with many different varieties, ranging from the dark, almost black Turkish figs to the light pink White Genoa. If you have space, plant a few, providing figs at different times of the year.

Growing and maintenance Left to themselves, they can become large and sprawling trees. However, if espaliered, pruned or planted in a container, they grow happily in smaller gardens. Fruit grows on older, stronger branches.

When the tree is young select four or five of these branches to grow. In late winter prune all long, soft shoots that are not part of these main branches. Prune any shoots off the main branches that are growing at less than a 45 degree angle, preventing branches growing too close to one another.

Finally, prune the main branches back by a third or a quarter.

Diseases and pests Birds and stem borer

Harvesting and eating Harvest when the fruit is fully ripe and soft – they will not continue to ripen when picked.

Peach and Nectarine

Peaches and nectarines are compact, self-fertile trees, suitable for smaller gardens. Nectarines are very similar to peaches, but don't have the peach's distinguishing downy fuzz on their skin.

There are many different varieties of peaches, ranging from white to yellow or orange. These are divided into two groups: clingstone, where the flesh is tight around the pip; and freestone, with a looser flesh and easily removable pip.

Growing and maintenance Prune when young to create a good shape. They fruit on young shoots, and in late winter the top ends of higher branches should be cut back to encourage new growth from the lower branches. They do well as espaliers and can be trained to grow against a wall, up an archway or over a pergola. Peaches benefit from fruit being thinned, which reduces disease and keeps the trees strong and healthy.

Good companion plants include alfalfa, chives, clover, garlic and nettles.

Diseases and pests Birds, fruit fly and leaf curl

Harvesting and eating Picked when the fruit is soft and fully ripe, a peach straight off the tree is sublime. They will ripen a little if picked when underripe but will lose their flavour. Rather use these for jam or chutney.

Pear

Pear trees look similar to apples and like apples they enjoy cold winters and mild summers. They flower early in the season and need protection in areas with late frosts. There are a few self-fertile varieties, but most of the tastier ones will need a pollinator.

Growing and maintenance They respond very well to pruning and can be trained into a variety of shapes (see pages 125 to 128). They will also do well in a large container, but will need to be pruned.

Good companions are alfalfa, clover and grass – although lawn should preferably be grown only once the tree is established.

Diseases and pests Codling moth, fruit fly and scale

Harvesting and eating Pick pears before they ripen fully, as they tend to go floury if left on the tree. Similar to apples, they love being baked.

Plum

The stately plum tree contributes to the garden year round, with snowy blossoms in spring, fruit and shade in summer, and architectural interest in winter. Most

TIME-SAVING TIP

For years I spent ages cutting up plums and taking out the pips. In the process I would lose fruit and have cuts all over my fingers from the sharp plum stones. There had to be another way. After experimenting I came up with a much quicker method. This recipe is the base for all my plum jams, jellies and cordials. It can be adapted to many types of fruit, especially those with large pips.

Method

Collect a large colander of fruit and dump them into a basin of water. Wash well, rubbing or cutting off any bits that have been bitten by birds or gone bad. Put the washed fruit in a large pot and add water so it is about a quarter of the depth of the fruit. Bring to the boil and simmer, partially covered, for 6 to 8 minutes. For fruit with firmer flesh, such as peaches, increase the cooking time. Turn the heat off, cover and leave until cool.

At this point you have a choice. If you are making jelly or cordial, mash the fruit thoroughly with a potato masher. Pour the mush into a bowl lined with mutton cloth. Gather the edges and secure them with a strong rubber band. Tie the resulting 'bag' above the bowl and leave to drip overnight. Don't squeeze or disturb the bag as this will result in a cloudy liquid.

If you are making jam or chutney, pour the cooked fruit into a colander and, using a potato masher or wooden spoon, push the pulp through the holes, until just the pips and some of the skins are left behind.

The strained liquid or the pulp can be frozen in zip lock bags for later use. This takes the pressure off having to cook the entire harvest as it ripens.

varieties require a pollinator but some of the tastiest, such as the Santa Rosa and Methley, are self-fertile.

Growing and maintenance Plum trees require full sun and well-drained, fertile soil. Prune when young to shape into a good frame, and thereafter only cut back dead wood. The weight of the fruit can cause horizontal branches to break unless fruit is thinned or the branches are supported. Good companions are chives and garlic.

Diseases and pests Birds and fruit fly

Harvesting and eating Pick when soft and completely ripe – fruit will continue to ripen off the tree if picked unripe, but the flavour is not as good. Plums make excellent jelly and jam, and can also be made into cordial or preserved in brandy.

Pomegranate

A sprawling tree with antioxidant-packed fruit, the pomegranate is suitable for medium gardens. It grows up to five metres tall with stiff spiky branches and leathery leaves. It is ideally suited to Mediterranean climates with warm dry summers and cool wet winters. However, it can grow in a variety of climates. It is self-pollinating.

Growing and maintenance

Pomegranates need full sun and well-drained soil. They benefit from plenty of well-rotted manure and compost being added to the planting hole. They are drought resistant but need regular water to prevent the fruit from cracking. Prune in the first winter to develop a strong framework of three to five branches. Flowers appear in August and fruit ripens in late summer and early autumn. Remove all flowers for the first two years, and limit to 50 to 60 fruits in the third year.

Diseases and pests Codling moth

Harvesting and eating Fruit is harvested from year three onwards. The fruit is ready when it changes colour to deep red and the calyx closes and becomes indented. Cut the fruit off rather than pulling. If there are no cracks, the fruit can store for five to seven months and the juice becomes sweeter the longer it is stored.

Quince

A quince is a good tree for a small garden as it is self-fertile, small and bushy. The older they grow, the more knotted and gnarly their branches become, creating trees with great character. They prefer moist soil and need plenty of water throughout the summer. They will grow in most areas, except in warm sub-tropical gardens.

Growing and maintenance Prune when they are young to create a good shape, and thereafter only to remove dead wood or crossing branches.

Diseases and pests Birds, black spot, codling moth, fruit fly and stem borer

Harvesting and eating Harvest when the fruit is yellow and smooth, and has lost its fuzz. Quinces will continue to ripen after being picked. They have a tart flavour when raw, and are best eaten cooked or made into delicious jelly.

EXTRACTING POMEGRANATE JEWELS

The most efficient way of removing juicy pomegranate seeds is to first roll the whole fruit to loosen them. Then cut it in half around the middle. Hold one half cut-side down in the palm of your hand over a bowl. Using a wooden spoon, tap the skin firmly to release the seeds, squeezing a little if necessary. The seeds can be frozen.

EVERGREEN FRUIT

Bananas

Bananas, with their large glossy green leaves and beautiful flowers, create a luscious corner. They are best suited to sub-tropical gardens, but can be grown in areas with mild frosts if they are planted in a sheltered sunny spot. They like rich soil with plenty of organic matter. Protect from wind and grow grouped together.

Growing and maintenance

A banana is similar to ginger, growing from an underground rhizome that spreads by sprouting new suckers. New plants can be propagated using these. Bananas are shallow rooted and heavy feeders. They like fertile, well-drained soil and need regular watering and feeding to ensure good fruit. Mulch well to keep the soil moist.

After it flowers, the purple petals peel back and reveal a 'hand' of baby bananas. These quickly turn upwards towards the light. Over the next few months the bunch becomes heavier as the bananas ripen and could do with some support to prevent the tree from breaking.

Diseases and pests Monkeys

Harvesting and eating They are ready to be picked when they are well rounded, even if they are still green. They will continue to ripen after being picked. If you pick the whole bunch they will ripen at once so be ready! The leaves are edible and make lovely serving platters. Young leaves can be used to wrap food for steaming.

Citrus

Hardy, evergreen and essential for G&Ts, a lemon tree is a must-have in the urban orchard. But many other citrus trees, with their glossy green leaves and deliciously healthy fruit, are also ideal for city gardens. They are self-fertile but if you have space, plant a few different varieties.

Citrus is best suited for sub-tropical gardens, but some varieties will survive mild frosts if protected when young. In colder areas, don't worry too much if citrus leaves go yellowish in winter – it is just a sign of them not enjoying the cold. In gardens where the temperatures drop below −5 °C there is the option of growing them in containers that can be moved into a warm, sheltered area during winter.

For small gardens, all citrus trees do

well in containers as long as they are fed and watered regularly. Or follow the Italian example of training lemons to grow over a courtyard as a roof.

Growing and maintenance Citrus trees need fertile, well-drained soil, full sun and regular water. A good general rule is to water more in spring and summer and cut back in autumn and winter. Remember to water lemons regularly throughout the winter in summer rainfall areas as they need water to produce their juicy fruits, but don't overdo it. A sign of too much water is yellowing leaves dropping. Container-grown citrus should be watered three times a week in summer and twice a week in winter to prevent the blossoms from dropping.

To keep your citrus flowering and fruiting, feed with Talborne Organics Vita-Grow 2:3:2 once a year for root conditioning, followed by Vita Fruit & Flower 3:1:5 every four months thereafter. Keep the ground under the trees well mulched to suppress weeds and retain moisture. Leave a mulch-free space around the trunk to prevent rotting.

Feverfew, lemon balm, tansy and yarrow are all good companions to plant under and around citrus trees.

Citrus trees need little pruning other than to remove weak, broken or dead branches and spindly growth. Prune after they have finished bearing. Aim for a well-balanced framework of larger branches. The centre needs to be open to allow good air circulation and light penetration. Cut out smaller branches rather than removing larger ones.

Diseases and pests Aphids, black spot, citrus psylla and scale

Harvesting and using Fruit can take six to eight months to ripen. They are ripe when they have reached full size and colour. The fruit does not all ripen at once, providing a harvest that can stretch over many weeks. Undamaged fruit will store for several weeks in the fridge.

All parts of citrus fruits are edible, creating a wide variety of options from marmalade, preserves or juicing, to candied peels and zest. Lemon juice rubbed on fruit or vegetables before drying will prevent them turning brown and help preserve them.

Citrus pips, particularly lemon, are full of pectin, which makes jam and jellies jell. When using fruit low in pectin, gather citrus pips in a muslin bag and immerse it in the jam or jelly while cooking to help it set. And of course, a gin and tonic is not ready to drink unless it has a slice of lemon in it.

Mango

Mango trees are an indelible part of my childhood endless-summer memories. The poolside mango trees provided delicious fruit but they had to be eaten on the top step of the pool because they were so stringy and messy. I tried to grow mangoes in my Johannesburg garden but they succumbed quickly to the frost as they are only suited to hot climates. They are attractive trees, growing up to seven metres high, with spreading branches and dark green narrow leaves. They are great for tree houses.

Growing and maintenance Although they can be grown from pips (which sprout in the compost quite often) this can result in a tree that produces horrible-tasting mangoes. Rather buy a sapling of a non-stringy variety.

They prefer well-drained, fertile soil and plenty of moisture throughout summer.

Diseases and pests Monkeys and scale

Harvesting and eating Mangoes soften and the skin changes from green to yellow or red as they ripen. They do continue to ripen if picked slightly underripe. They are best fresh but also make delicious chutney.

Pawpaw

This is another fruit from my childhood as Mom always had a few pawpaw trees outside the kitchen door. They grow best in sub-tropical gardens, but will grow in areas with mild frost if protected.

They can be propagated from seed easily. Select an overripe pawpaw and wash the seeds. Sow in fertile soil and keep watered until they germinate.

They are ornamental plants, suited for small gardens. They require male and female plants for successful pollination and fruit, but only one male plant is needed for more than 20 females.

Growing and maintenance Pawpaw trees like rich, well-drained soil and need support when young or bearing lots of fruit. Their life span is about five to eight years, after which they should be replaced.

Diseases and pests Monkeys

Harvesting and eating The challenge of harvesting pawpaws from a tall tree that won't support the weight of a ladder has resulted in many innovations. My Dad rigged up a system with a blade attached to a swimming pool net to catch the pawpaws. It worked about 50 per cent of the time and we often had broken (but still tasty) pawpaws in our fridge.

They are best harvested when the skin has ripened to a rich yellow, but can be picked earlier and will ripen at room temperature. Although they are delicious when fully ripe, this is one of the few fruits that can be eaten when unripe, especially in spicy Thai salads. Hens adore the pips.

Pineapple

Pineapples are surprisingly easy to grow from an existing fruit. They don't take up too much room and are as pretty as a bromeliad (a close relative). They are tropical plants and won't grow in frosty gardens. However, they do grow happily in containers and can be moved to a warm, protected spot in winter.

Growing and maintenance Slice the leafy top off a ripe pineapple, removing any of the yellow flesh. Let it sit for a day or two to dry out and then plant it, about 5 cm deep, in a sunny spot. (They don't mind a bit of dappled shade.) Pineapples can also be grown from suckers taken from an existing plant, which start forming when it is about 18 months old. These will begin to bear more quickly than ones grown from pineapple tops.

They are drought resistant and don't need particularly fertile soil. They have a very small root system and will benefit from a foliar spray as they absorb many of their nutrients through their leaves. They

grow about a metre wide and a metre high and have spiky leaves, so position them away from a pathway.

Diseases and pests None

Harvesting and eating It will take about two years for pineapples grown from the tops to begin bearing fruit. A flower appears first and the fruit takes about six months to develop. It is ready to be picked when it starts turning yellow.

Tree Tomato

This evergreen, shrubby tree is a member of the tomato family – although its tart fruit tastes nothing like a tomato. It is a pretty tree, particularly when the fruit is ripe. In warm climates it will continue to fruit for most of the year, making it a good choice for small gardens. It prefers warm climates but will survive mild frosts.

Growing and maintenance Tree tomatoes can be grown from seed or slips from an existing tree. They will begin fruiting at two years old. They like fertile, well-drained soil in full sun. Good companions are marigolds and tansy.

Diseases and pests Whitefly

Harvesting and eating They are ready for harvest when the fruit has ripened to a deep red, almost purple, colour. They can be eaten raw, but are very sour. They make excellent jelly and jam.

BERRIES, BUSHES, CLIMBERS AND CREEPERS

Blueberries

Blueberries will grow only in areas with cold winters, as they need a long period of cold during dormancy. If the weather is too warm, they will not develop fruit. However, newer varieties are being developed that don't require such a long cold dormancy period.

Blueberries need full sun, acid soil (pH 4 to 5) and benefit from plenty of organic matter in the soil.

Although most varieties are self-fertile, they will produce bigger fruit if they are cross-pollinated by another bush.

With a shallow root system, they don't like moisture fluctuation. Keeping the surface well mulched will help maintain consistent moisture. They can grow in containers, in which it is easier to ensure that the soil is the correct pH. Use a large container to prevent moisture fluctuations.

Growing and maintenance Fruit is produced on side shoots of year-old canes during December and January. Older canes will stop bearing after about four years. Every year (either after harvest or during winter, depending on the variety) cut out older, non-productive canes, pruning the whole bush back by about one third. This will encourage productivity and prevent the centre from becoming congested and blocking air circulation.

Diseases and pests Aphids and birds

Harvesting and eating Blueberries are very high in antioxidants, making them one of the healthiest fresh fruits to eat. To retain these nutrients, they are best eaten raw or lightly cooked in a tart or crumble. They are excellent as toppings for various desserts such as pancakes and cheesecake.

Bramble Berries
(blackberries, raspberries, tayberries)

Packed with nutrients, easy to grow and quick to bear fruit, berries are becoming an increasingly popular addition to urban gardens.

Home-grown blackberries and raspberries are much sweeter than store-bought ones as we can harvest them when they are fully sun ripened without worrying about damaging them on the way to market.

There are various hybrid crosses of the blackberry and raspberry, such as the loganberry and the tayberry. The tayberry is a particularly good hybrid, producing large sweet fruit. It is not a commercially grown crop as it is difficult to harvest.

Most of these are rambling fruit and, if left, will quickly grow into a wild and thorny tangle. However, with the right support and by keeping them under control, you can create a delicious berry corner, even in a small garden.

Bramble berries prefer full sun or dappled shade. They like well-drained soil and don't do well with cold wet feet. They prefer slightly acidic soil (pH 5.6 to 6.2).

SPOT THE DIFFERENCE

Blackberries are black and raspberries are red right? Well, no. Blackberries are red before they ripen, and then there are black varieties of raspberry. However, there are distinct differences between the two types of berry – the main one being the rasp. When a raspberry is picked, its centre, or rasp, is left behind and the fruit is hollow. A blackberry breaks off cleanly at the stem and isn't hollow.

Growing and maintenance Bramble berries will ramble over a vast area if left unchecked. They spread vigorously as the canes root themselves whenever they touch the ground. They can be contained by providing a frame – or as I call mine, a Berry Alley.

To control their rampant growth, place poles along either side of a narrow bed and use wire or string to create two parallel fences running alongside the bed. The poles can be at an angle to create a V shape or vertical to create a rectangle. Plant the canes 30 cm apart (roughly 15 canes per square metre). As they begin to grow, wind any growth that heads out of the fenced area back inside. Once the designated growing area is full, remove any new growth that emerges outside this area. Keep the new growth thinned out to about 15 canes per square metre. In late winter or early spring, cut the canes back to encourage new growth in spring.

The fruit will begin to form in early summer. The berries are ready to be harvested when they can be pulled easily from the bush. Be careful when working with these plants as the canes are covered in little prickles that hook you unmercifully. On some varieties, the first year of growth will produce berries. On others, the first year of growth produces leafy canes up to 5 m long. In the second year, fruit-bearing side branches develop. After fruiting, these canes will turn brown and die back – this is when they are ready to be removed.

Diseases and pests Birds

Harvesting and eating Raspberries and blackberries can be eaten raw or made into jellies, syrups and jams. They are an excellent fruit to bake in a tart or to flavour vinegar. The leaves are high in vitamin C and can be made into a delicious midsummer iced tea.

Fruit Salad Bush

This sprawling bushy plant is a member of the tomato family. A tender perennial, it produces white egg-shaped fruit that ripen to a creamy colour with purple stripes. It can be grown in containers and should be protected against frost in cold areas.

Growing and maintenance It likes full sun, fertile soil and plenty of regular water. Every two to three years, prune it back after it has finished fruiting. Feed it twice a year with an organic fertiliser.

Diseases and pests None

Harvesting and eating The ripe yellow fruit has a mild melon flavour and can be added to salad or eaten as a dessert. It pairs well with spicy flavours and makes a good salad to go with hot curry.

Gooseberries

I used to think this plant got its name because it came from the Cape. I then discovered it was named after the cape-like husk that grows over the fruit. It is a member of the nightshade family of plants, along with tomatoes and potatoes.

This is a rewarding and easy plant to grow. It does well in poor soil and too much fertiliser will result in more leaves than fruit. It is a water-wise plant, surviving periods of drought.

Growing and maintenance Sow from seed or transplant seedlings throughout spring into early summer. It is happiest in full sun but doesn't mind semi shade. It prefers well-drained soil and won't do well with muddy, wet feet.

Although it is a perennial, it is grown as an annual in colder parts of the country as it dies back in a hard frost. In milder frost areas the leaves will die back in winter but the roots survive.

Cut back all the dead branches in early spring and it will pop up again. This is a rambling plant, which benefits from having space to spread or something to climb up. I have found it does well in amongst shrubby plants, where it climbs up and through them for support and in return the shrubs protect the gooseberry from frost.

Birds are fond of the fruit and they can spread seed (and gooseberry plants) all over the garden. Learn to recognise the seedlings and pull them out when young otherwise you will have gooseberries everywhere.

One dedicated bed with four or five gooseberry plants will provide you with sufficient harvest that you can freeze and use for a year.

Diseases and pests Birds

Harvesting and eating Fresh gooseberries have a unique tart yet sweet flavour, making them the perfect match for meringues or a good addition to fruit salads. Their tartness mellows with cooking and they are delicious baked in a crumble or tart. They have a high pectin content and set quickly when used for preserves or jam. They can be dried or frozen whole.

Granadilla

The vining passion fruit is an exotic addition to the orchard with one of the most extraordinary flowers of any edible plant. The fruit is deliciously sweet.

Granadillas need a protected sunny area, rich well-drained soil, and regular water. They won't survive a hard frost. Yellow varieties are more susceptible to frost than purple ones.

Growing and maintenance They are vigorous climbers and need a pergola, fence or other vertical structure to climb up. After flowering in spring they produce a summer crop and then flower again in autumn for a smaller winter crop. They have a deep root system and benefit from well-mulched soil, but not close to the stem.

Prune in spring every two years, thinning out if necessary and removing branches below 60 cm to encourage air circulation.

Feed with a slow-release organic fertiliser, compost and well-rotted manure twice a year after fruiting.

Granadillas are perfect to cover an existing fence or to train up a trellis against a wall.

Diseases and pests Monkeys

Harvesting and eating Granadillas are ready to eat when their skins have ripened to their full colour and have started to wrinkle (about 80 days after flowering).

Grapes

Use deciduous grapes to cover an archway or to create an edible pergola, providing shade in summer and sun in winter. They are self-fertile so you only need to plant one.

Growing and maintenance Grapes prefer a hot sunny position with well-drained, gravelly soil. Most do better in winter rainfall regions but some cultivars are bred for summer rainfall areas – check your nursery.

For the first few years, prune the vines to grow up a trellis or pergola. After that, prune every year in winter to cut back the

previous year's fruiting stems. Fruit is produced on spurs from one-year-old stems, so it needs to produce new stems every year. Vines will grow rampantly if left to their own devices and will produce less and less fruit if not pruned.

In spring, feed with organic slow-release fertiliser, compost and well-rotted manure. Fruit ripens in late summer to early autumn. Good companions are mustard and sage.

Diseases and pests Beetles, downy and powdery mildew

Harvesting and eating Harvest when the grapes have ripened to their full colour and sweetness. They will not continue to ripen off the vine. Grapes are best eaten fresh, but if you have excess they can be frozen whole. These can be popped into drinks as fun edible ice cubes or eaten whole as a cooling snack.

Kiwifruit

My aunt has a rambunctious kiwi forest in her garden, with two or three kiwifruit rambling over pergolas. She often provides me with baskets of this delicious exotic fruit. It is a deciduous climber that prefers a temperate climate. It will survive mild frosts but won't do well in hot summers. As with the pawpaw, a male plant is needed for pollinating the female plants. One male will pollinate up to nine females.

Growing and maintenance Kiwifruit likes fertile soil and plenty of water. It will need a strong support as it is a vigorous plant. Early shaping and pruning is required to encourage the plant to grow where it is wanted. It can become very unruly if not kept in shape. Fruit is produced on side shoots, so don't hard prune these back otherwise you won't get any fruit.

Diseases and pests Birds

Harvesting and eating Fruit will continue to ripen after being picked and this is the best way to prevent birds eating your harvest. They are delicious when ripe and are the best ingredient (along with strawberries) for a classic pavlova. They make a tasty and unusual-looking jelly.

Rhubarb

This bushy perennial plant with its long, edible red stems is a popular fruit plant in many gardens. It is an attractive plant and can be grown just as easily in a flowerbed as in the vegetable garden. It likes cool winters and is fairly hardy. In colder climates its leaves will die back over winter.

Mulch well and new leaves will unfurl in spring. If it is grown in semi shade, it sends out longer stems. The leaves contain high levels of oxalic acid, which makes them poisonous to humans but helps prevent disease in other plants (see page 59).

Growing and maintenance Rhubarb needs about one square metre per plant. It can be grown from seed, but it is much quicker to buy small plants. If looked after, it will continue providing for many years. It likes rich, fertile soil and regular water throughout summer. Enrich the soil with compost and plant crowns 10 cm deep in early spring. For the first year after planting, leave it to become well established.

Similar to asparagus, a rhubarb's root system is called a crown. The more robust this is, the stronger and more prolific the plant will be. If it starts sending up flower stalks, remove them before the plant's energy is put towards flowering. After about four years, rhubarb tends to become straggly and needs to be divided. Dig up the crown and divide it into sections using a sharp knife. Make sure each section has a strong bud.

Diseases and pests Rhubarb can be infected with a fungal disease called crown rot, often caused by poor drainage. This causes the whole plant to wither and the roots to die. The only remedy is to pull the entire thing out and throw it away.

Harvesting and eating The edible part of rhubarb is the red stem. Start harvesting in the second year by twisting at the base of the stem and pulling outwards. Cut the leaves off immediately to prevent the stems wilting.

Sufficient leaves need to remain on the plant for it to continue feeding its crown underground. Be careful when harvesting not to damage any tender new growth.

Rhubarb is rich in vitamin C and has a unique tart sweet flavour, ideal for baking. Try mixing it with strawberries for an extra zing.

Strawberries

I love strawberries and a recent addition to my garden is a vertical strawberry 'patch' that covers a rainwater tank (see pages 142 to 144). By selecting a number of varieties, this supplies us with strawberries at different times of the year. Strawberries are a useful addition to the vegetable garden, with their low growth and spreading habit making them an ideal groundcover.

Growing and maintenance

Strawberries are grown more easily from seedlings than from seeds. They like very fertile soil and a sunny spot, but don't mind some afternoon shade.

They spread by sending out runners, which root themselves to form new plants. Once you have a few plants, spread them to other areas of your garden (after they have finished fruiting) by cutting a runner and digging up the new plant.

They are low-growing and ideal for edging pathways. They are also good container plants, growing happily in small spaces as long as they are well fed and watered. They like being planted together with Asian greens, beetroot, borage, French beans, lettuces, spinach and spring onions.

Keep strawberries well watered, as they don't like dry soil, but be careful not to waterlog them. Using an anti-bug mulch of artemisia, lavender and sage helps keep pests away.

After about four years, a plant will become unproductive. If you create new plants regularly using runners from existing plants, you will have a constant supply with which to replace the tired ones.

Diseases and pests Birds, slugs and snails

Harvesting and eating Pick strawberries when the sun has been shining on them for a few hours as the heat brings out their sweetness. They also are best when picked fully ripe. Strawberries pair well with mint and chocolate. If you have a bumper harvest, they make a delicious jam.

ANNUALS

Melons and Watermelons

Melons are vining plants that ramble across large areas of ground. However, by choosing smaller varieties and space-saving tripods and trellises (see page 139) these delicious summer fruits can be grown in smaller spaces.

Growing and maintenance
All melons like very fertile soil and do well in a humid environment. Enrich soil with well-rotted manure before sowing seeds. They need plenty of water and sunshine. To encourage earlier fruiting, pinch out the growing tips of the vine. If growing them up a tripod you will need to support the fruit. Create a 'hammock' by tying an old T-shirt or stocking under the fruit.

Diseases and pests Mildew and pumpkin flies

Harvesting and eating Melons should be fully ripe when picked as they don't continue to ripen afterwards. With watermelons, look for the small tendril where the stem is attached to the fruit. When this dries out it indicates ripeness. It will also sound hollow when tapped. With melons ripeness is indicated when the blossom end softens, their scent increases and the skin changes colour.

NUTS

I am lucky enough to have a large walnut tree in my garden and there are many of a similar age in the surrounding neighbourhoods. There must a have been a fad for walnut trees about forty years ago – or else a very good walnut tree salesperson in the area. Generally suitable for medium to large gardens, almonds, pecans and walnuts are good for cooler areas. Cashews and macadamias are suited to more tropical, warmer parts of the country. Once established, nut trees are low maintenance, providing a bountiful harvest in autumn.

Diseases and pests Stem borer, husk fly

Harvesting and eating Nuts are ready when the outer green husk has dried to brown and peeled back to reveal the nut inside. Shaking branches gently will make them fall. Leave them to dry for two to three weeks and then shell them. If you don't plan to eat them within a few weeks, seal in airtight containers and freeze to prevent them from going rancid.

DOGS AND NUTS

Most dogs love nuts. We know it is walnut harvest time when Tilu and Tosca begin snuffling for fallen nuts. They bring them inside, crack them open, and delicately pry delicious pieces of nut out with their teeth. In the process they leave sharp bits of shell everywhere for unsuspecting bare feet.

ESPALIER AND OTHER FRUIT TREE SHAPES

Many fruit trees can be trained to grow flat against a wall or a frame, by pruning the branches and tying them to a support. The French term *espalier*, which means shoulder support, is a decorative and space-saving method of growing fruit. The term originates from the Italian word *spalliera*, meaning 'something to rest the shoulder against'. I love the idea of a tree resting its fruit-laden shoulders against my wall.

In my garden I have a number of espalier fruit trees in progress, including two figs, an apple and a peach. In Europe this horizontal method of growing fruit is often used along passageways or in smaller gardens where space is limited. As so many people are now growing their own fresh produce here in South Africa, it has caught on locally too.

A painting of an espaliered fig tree on the wall of an Egyptian tomb shows that this fruitful and ornamental technique has been around for thousands of years. It was used extensively in European walled monastery gardens and in castle courtyards from the Middle Ages onwards. In a modern-day urban garden, creating an espalier might take some time and patience, but the resulting edible sculpture is well worth the effort. Training an espalier might be a long process, but once established, fruit trees grown this way are attractive and striking, whether blossoming, fruiting or bare in winter. It is also a very productive method of growing fruit.

BENEFITS OF ESPALIER

Apart from being space-saving and attractive, espalier trees have other advantages.

- Fruit on an espalier tree will receive more sun, improving the flavour by creating more natural sugar.
- Espalier fruit trees do best on a sunny wall. This creates a warm microclimate, enabling gardeners in colder areas to choose from a wider range of varieties.
- It is easier to protect an espalier from both birds and frost than a free-standing full-sized tree.
- An espalier can be trained to grow up an existing archway, flat against a wall or on a free-standing frame to create a living fence.

OTHER FRUIT TREE SHAPES

The term 'espalier' refers to a specific pattern of a central trunk with evenly spaced horizontal branches. However, fruit trees can be trained into a variety of decorative shapes, from a simple cordon or fan to a complicated candelabra, spiral or whimsical heart. For some ideas, see the illustrations below and on pages 127 and 128. Whichever style you choose, it will require regular pruning, especially in the first few years, to keep the tree flat and two-dimensional.

SUITABLE TREES

The best fruit trees for espalier are those that continue bearing fruit for many years and have supple new growth that can be trained easily. Preferably buy a one-year-old tree with a strong central stem.

Stepover

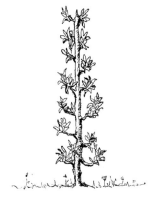

Single cordon

Oblique cordon

- Apples and pears are the most commonly espaliered and can be trained into many different shapes.
- Grapes are also easy to espalier into a variety of shapes.
- Figs are a good choice for a small space. As their branches aren't very pliable, start training them when they're quite young.
- Apricots, cherries, peaches, plums, pomegranates, quince and nectarines can all be espaliered into fan shapes, but they require more careful pruning.
- Citrus trees can be trained to grow onto a pergola, creating a shady citrus roof. This is a common practice in Italian courtyards.

CREATING A SUPPORT SYSTEM

A strong support system is essential as it needs to carry the weight of the branches and fruit for many years. To create a support against a wall, rawlbolts inserted into the wall with strong cables or wire stretched between them are recommended. The first line should be about 50 cm off the ground and each subsequent line 50 cm above the one below it. An average wall will accommodate three to four lines.

When inserting rawlbolts into the wall, leave a gap of 15 cm between the wall and the wires to give the plant some breathing space and allow air to circulate. When creating a free-standing structure, sink poles into the ground and connect the wires between them. You can also use an existing fence or an archway, if it is sufficiently sturdy.

TRAINING, PRUNING AND MAINTENANCE

Trees should be spaced about 3 m apart. (See page 103 for more information on how to plant.) The aim of an espalier is to train the tree's branches to grow into a pattern of easily accessible low branches.

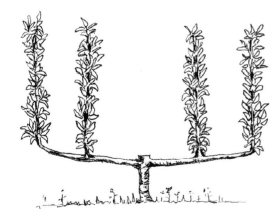

Multiple cordon

Fan

To create a classic espalier shape (see drawing below right) cut the central shoot so it is level with the first wire. Allow the top three buds to grow. Leave the central shoot to grow vertically to reach the second wire. While they are still young and whippy, gently bend the outside two shoots 90 degrees so they are parallel to the first wire. Attach them to the wire using cable ties or strong twine tied in a figure of eight. The ties should be firm but not tight, otherwise the bark will be damaged. The following year, cut the central vertical shoot just below the second wire and again allow three buds to develop. Let the central one grow vertically and train the other two horizontally. Repeat each season until you have reached the top wire and then remove the central shoot.

To speed up the process, remove the blossoms or young fruit for the first two to three years. This will focus the tree's growth and energy into root, branch and leaf production until it is completely established.

Unlike most free-standing fruit trees, which require pruning once a year, an espalier will require regular trimming throughout summer. As the tree begins to grow, develop the basic structure by pruning unwanted branches as often as necessary throughout the growing season. Remove any vigorous shoots that don't fit into your design, especially those growing off the main central stem. There should be a solid arm on each line of wire with spurs growing off it, from which the fruit will develop. Remove the whips – the thin long stems that come off the horizontal branches – as these will not produce fruit. In midwinter, trim back all the lateral shoots on the main arms so three buds remain above the basal cluster.

Trees should be watered regularly during hot weather. North- and west-facing walls are hot and trees planted against them can dry out quickly. Drip irrigation with a timer will ensure that they are watered adequately.

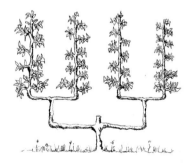

Double U

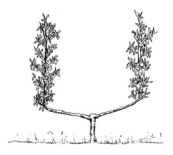

Double cordon

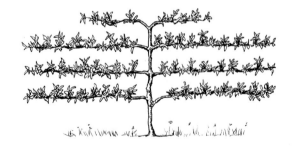

Classic espalier

MAXIMISING
URBAN
SPACES

When we choose our homes, there are many factors that influence the decision, but growing food is usually not high on the list. You might love a house with a great sea view but vegetables won't enjoy the wind and salt. A petite apartment that suits your budget will only have a small – or no – space for a garden. And you might have a decent-sized garden, but it's shady, because you love trees. Growing food in the city can be challenging but there are many ways around these obstacles.

GROWING UNDER COVER

Vegetables are grown under cover for various reasons. In Cape Town, when the South-Easter blows, a greenhouse or tunnel protects vegetables from the blasting wind. On the Highveld, they will shield vegetables from a vicious summer hail storm. In colder parts of the country, where the winter temperatures drop below −5°C, greenhouses provide a sheltered and warm area, extending the growing season by many months. And then there are dogs, birds, monkeys, squirrels, baboons and other vegetable-damaging creatures. A cage or a greenhouse will keep them out. A greenhouse is not just for the plants, it creates a sanctuary for gardeners too, protecting us from sunburn and rain, and providing an inviting and luscious haven.

GREENHOUSES

It was the Romans who first created greenhouses, developing simply heated, walled-in structures where frost-tender vegetables could be grown year round. Technology has improved since 30AD but the concept remains much the same – to create a protected and environmentally controlled area for growing plants. Greenhouses range from home-made structures using recycled windows, or even an enclosed veranda, to specifically constructed units with purpose-built shelving, breathing vents and drip irrigation.

The first step towards successful greenhouse construction is to use the right material. I once tried growing my seedlings in a greenhouse but I made every mistake in the book. I bought an inexpensive DIY unit, with no instructions and a jigsaw puzzle of poles. Once we figured it out and connected all the pieces successfully, I placed it in a sunny spot and filled the shelves with trays of seeds. It was late winter and the greenhouse was pleasantly warm inside. But the very first hot day of spring turned it into a sauna. With no ventilation, the temperature went over 50°C and cooked my seeds to oblivion. Even after I moved it to a more suitable spot (and sowed all the seeds again) it only lasted one season before the plastic shredded.

Our South African conditions are harsh and, as I learned, our intense UV radiation will destroy cheap plastic quickly. Likewise, if you use clear plastic, the radiation will burn your plants. Plastic sheeting that is specifically designed for greenhouses will cost more, but it has many advantages. Urban Freedom, a family-run manufacturer specialising in innovative greenhouse designs, uses a special film that suits South African conditions. It is 200 microns thick and is UV-stabilised, extending its life span. It has built-in light-diffusion agents that soften the radiation and distribute it evenly onto the plants, encouraging uniformity and increasing yield.

> **"The only way to guarantee truly organic eating is to grow your own food. If you want to do it easily – the greenhouse can do it for you. Then you can have herbs and vegetables all year round."**
>
> *Luana Pasanisi, Urban Freedom*

Another problem encountered in greenhouses is condensation. Droplets forming on the inside surface reflect the light away. This reduces light, and moisture falling from the roof onto plants increases the risk of fungal and bacterial disease. Sheeting that has a built-in anti-drip agent prevents this. It should also contain UV blockers, which reduce the transmittance of harmful UV rays to plants.

To prevent your seeds from being cooked like mine, placement is important, with the ideal position receiving six to eight hours of mostly morning sun. Sunlight can be reduced by adding shade cloth, and ventilation controlled by opening windows and doors. Micro-jet irrigation can also take the edge off the heat, with a little spritz of water here and there during the day.

And then there are the pests, many of which love nothing more than the increased humidity and warmth inside a greenhouse. Once they get in, they will be quite happy to stay. Urban Freedom recommends vigilance and catching pests early before they settle in. Diatomaceous earth (see page 56) and colloidal silver work wonders for fungal infestations, and a rooibos mulch makes surfaces very uncomfortable for slugs to move around on. Recognising insects is important and treating plants immediately is the key to successful organic control. Ideally, working daily in your garden and greenhouse and being present as often as possible is the best deterrent: removing the odd slug by hand; clipping off a leaf with a fungal disease.

Space can be maximised inside a greenhouse with layers of shelving. When purchasing a greenhouse, check that it is strong enough to hold multiple layers. This literally doubles the growing space of the greenhouse.

If you prefer not to purchase a prefabricated greenhouse, you can convert an existing area quite easily. My creative friend Allison Forgèt-Deyes turned a corner of her garden into a magical greenhouse, where she propagates her seedlings.

It was once a cottage veranda and much of the basic support structure was already there – it just needed to be enclosed. She bought new greenhouse-rated Perspex for the roof, but for the rest she used recycled material. For the front enclosure, second-hand metal windows were sanded, painted and glazed, letting in maximum light. The entrance is a salvaged wooden door, sanded and varnished. Simple shelving was created by placing wooden sleepers on top of stacked bricks. Attached to one wall, a nifty fold-down table provides a work surface and there are hooks for essentials: tools, gloves and a hat. Against another wall, a hose with a soft spray attachment is looped neatly. It is connected permanently to a tap outside, which makes it easy to water everything as often as needed.

Allison's converted greenhouse is a haven for both plants and their gardener, where young seedlings thrive in a variety of recycled containers, such as old biscuit tins and enamel mugs.

TUNNELS

A tunnel is a version of a greenhouse, where vegetable beds are covered with plastic or frost-proof material. Also called hoop gardens, these range from temporary bamboo poles bent over a bed and covered with shade or frost cloth when required, to more sophisticated permanent tunnels, created from PVC piping and strong UV tunnel plastic. These tunnel gardens have all the benefits of a greenhouse.

I have used low temporary tunnels in my garden, but they pale by comparison to the one constructed by Bev and Gary Brice. It is an excellent example of this efficient way of growing a successful harvest. When Bev's vegetables were destroyed by a severe Highveld storm one November, she and her husband decided to build raised beds covered with a protective tunnel. Using clay stock bricks that wouldn't require plastering and painting, they built the beds 700mm high so that she didn't have to bend down to weed the garden. They left sufficient space down the middle to pass through comfortably with a wheelbarrow. PVC pipes were used to make hoops above the beds, which were covered with strong UV-resistant plastic. Finishing touches include irrigation pipes that are watered from two rainwater tanks. (See next page for step-by-step instructions.) Bev has had tremendous success with growing a wide range of vegetables. She also finds it very convenient that she can take her time picking vegetables for dinner, whatever the weather.

MAKING A TUNNEL

Bev's tunnel functions more like a greenhouse, as it is a permanently enclosed walk-in space. A low hoop tunnel to protect beds from frost or pests can similarly be created using flexible PVC pipe. These can be placed over a raised bed or a normal garden bed as a temporary or permanent structure.

1. Cut flexible 40 mm PVC pipe into equal lengths, depending on the width and height of the finished tunnel.

2. Hammer short lengths of rebar or wood into the ground, 50 to 70 cm apart, along either side of the bed's lengths. (With raised beds, secure planks of wood along the outside of the beds. Drill holes into the timber to fit the PVC pipes.)

3. With two people standing at opposite sides, bend the PVC pipe and push each end firmly over the rebar (or push each end into the holes in the wood) to create a hoop. Repeat to cover the bed. (Secure the PVC pipes in the holes with screws through the timber into the PVC pipe from the outside.)

4. PVC pipe can also be attached to the outside of a raised bed using cable ties.

5. For stability, securely attach a piece of pipe lengthways across the top of the hoops.

6. Cover with shade cloth, frost cloth or UV tunnel plastic.

Freshly-cut bamboo poles can also be used to make hoops. However, a thick cane won't be flexible enough to bend into a narrow hoop. Instead, bundle together three or four skinnier, flexible canes, about 1.5 m long, tying them together at 30 cm intervals. Dig holes where the hoops will be and bury the bases of two bundles firmly opposite each other. Bend each bundle towards the centre of the bed, twist the tops together and tie them securely. Repeat until you have done all the hoops and then secure them with a length of bamboo along the top.

A CAGED GARDEN

One way to ensure that your vegetable garden will not be demolished completely by monkeys or birds is to enclose it with a cage. Kathryn Kure, a keen gardener in KwaZulu-Natal, lives very close to a nature reserve. This means regular monkey visitors and she soon realised that if she wanted to grow edibles, they would have to be protected from the vervets. The answer was to construct a monkey-proof cage over the entire garden.

Luckily, her husband Fem is a handyman. Construction began using bitumen-coated poles, chosen for their water- and termite-resistant properties. The poles were buried in holes about 600 to 900mm deep and no other foundation was used apart from hard earth, as the clay content in the soil was sufficient to hold them tight. The design included a roof with an apex, which mimics the neighbouring roofs aesthetically and ensures that the leaves falling from surrounding trees slide off it. For the covering, strong weld mesh was used, chosen on the premise that it would be sturdy enough to handle a troop of monkeys jumping around on it. Shade netting would not have been a good choice in their forest environment as it would have resulted in the underlying area becoming too moist and humid.

On the first day the cage was fully enclosed, after about 200 hours of labour by Fem, he came home to find the entire troop of about 40 monkeys sitting on top of the cage, looking mightily disgruntled. The monkeys soon discovered that they could stick their arms through the weld mesh, so the side walls were given an additional covering of smaller mesh chicken wire. "They could reach in to an arm's length all around the cage, which meant we were losing quite a substantial amount of space. The chicken wire has stopped that."

Kathryn makes great use of all the space, planting a variety of herbs and companion plants in the nooks and crannies, and particularly in the holes of the bricks Fem used to make the terraced beds. Many plants, herbs in particular as well as ferns, are used to clinging amongst bare rock and in tight, constricted spaces. Rocket, mint and strawberries thrive in these small holes, in some instances out-growing their nearest, non-restricted counterparts planted out at the same time.

Most importantly, the cage has proved to be worth all the hard work as it has kept the monkeys out. "As an organic gardener, you have to shift your mind-set from complete annihilation to thinking about how best to thwart your opposition. Or rather, how best to live in peaceful co-existence," says Kathryn. It also prevents birds from eating the crops, while the weld mesh allows beneficial insects to access the garden.

HAIL AND SUN

Many gardens in South Africa receive too much sun for vegetables. And in some areas, the harvest can be devastated by a few minutes of severe hail. An effective solution is to erect a shade cloth roof. Keep the sides open to allow air to flow through and insects in. Make the roof pitched, so the hail will slide off easily. If it is flat, the stones will quickly collect and their weight will break the supports or tear the shade cloth.

VERTICAL GARDENING

No matter what the size of our gardens, we run out of space eventually. The vegetable garden is no exception. Lured by the pictures on the seed packets, we plant until our gardens burst. A simple solution is to grow upwards – I call it 3D gardening. Adding tripods and other vertical structures to our vegetable gardens maximises space. Vegetables, such as butternut and gem squash, which normally ramble across metres of ground, can be trained to grow up a tripod. Tomatoes, instead of sprawling across a bed, smothering everything else, can be tied to a trellis or grown inside a cage.

Vertical gardening has many other advantages:

- Vegetables are lifted off the ground, limiting attacks from bugs and assisting all-round ripening.
- Airflow is increased, reducing disease.
- Plants with differing needs, which are beneficial to one another, can be combined.
- Instead of squeezing a sun-loving plant into a small space on the ground, a vertical support will let it reach for the sun.
- The ground around the base of the vertical support can be utilised for non-climbing plants.
- The shadier side of a large trellis or arch provides a perfect spot to place a bench for a hot gardener to rest. This is also a good position for plants that appreciate some shade in summer, such as coriander and lettuce. This will prevent them from going to seed as quickly in hot weather.
- Many plants, such as eggplants and peppers, become top heavy when they are bearing fruit. If they lean or fall over, their stems and roots are compromised, affecting the health of the entire plant. Attaching them to a simple vertical structure prevents this and keeps them healthy.

CREATING VERTICAL SUPPORTS

Adding tripods, arbours, archways and trellises to our gardens creates visual appeal and interest – even when there is nothing growing on them. Attach a trellis or a grid of gum poles to a wall (as long as it is not south-facing, as this won't receive any sun during winter) for tomatoes and beans. A trellised archway can be added over pathways to grow beans, cucumbers and other climbers. Create an arch at the entrance to your vegetable garden and combine flowers and vegetables on it. Beans will climb up happily through wisteria or roses. Tall, sturdy tripods allow gardeners with limited space to experiment with melons and squashes. Wire mesh, used to reinforce concrete, can be used to create custom-sized cylindrical supports for tomatoes, runner beans and cucumbers. Use your imagination to create structures that reflect your style and suit the plant's needs.

I love creating new designs and I am always experimenting with different vertical supports. My two most recent tripod creations are polar opposites. One is completely organic, created from bamboo and vine, while the other is industrial looking, with metal poles sunk into solid concrete blocks, wrapped with blue washing line. I once created a copper tripod by soldering plumbing pipes together. It looked beautiful but was disastrous as a plant support. Copper is an excellent heat conductor and burnt everything that grew up it. However, there is wide range of suitable material for tripods; gum poles, thatching laths and bamboo are all ideal. Metal is fine – just don't use copper! (The copper tripod didn't go to waste – it is now a birdcage for my colourful collection of wire benders' beaded parrots.)

I use many recycled objects, from abandoned burglar bars to leftover plumbing pipes. Although a recycled fence converted into an arbour does not look nearly as beautiful as a cedar wood gazebo, it costs next to nothing, and once it is covered in plants you can't see it anyway. Many of my supports are made from natural materials, which disintegrate slowly over a few seasons. Bamboo wigwams with long, whippy bay tree trimmings wound around them create a bean-loving support. Wisteria and jasmine stems, especially those trimmed in late spring after a growth spurt, are flexible and can be woven into wonderful patterns around a sturdy gum pole tripod.

USING EXISTING VERTICAL SPACES

Often, when visiting someone's garden to give them advice on growing vegetables, I hear them bemoan their lack of space. Looking around their garden, I invariably spot an unused vertical space that could be utilised for growing vegetables – a north-facing wall, a fence or a warm courtyard wall. Many existing structures can be used to support fruit and vegetables. A swimming pool fence is an ideal place to grow a granadilla. A strong archway can be used to espalier a fruit tree or for a grape vine. (See page 125 for more on espalier.)

EDIBLE WALLS

Edible walls have become an increasingly popular option for gardeners looking to maximise their space or to add edible greenery to an otherwise bare wall. From slick corporate headquarters to shacks in a low-income housing area, edible walls are a viable option for increasing food as well as greening our environment. A green wall creates cleaner air by acting as a natural filter, and the foliage reduces noise pollution by absorbing and reflecting sound.

Creating an edible wall can range from using a sophisticated modular system, designed specifically to create a self-watering edible wall, to a homemade system using recycled pallets or other items. Even recycled gutters attached to a wall will provide a shallow growing area for salad ingredients.

Many edible walls are created using a pocket system. This looks similar to a hanging shoe bag, with panels of pockets that are filled with growing medium and plants. You can purchase custom-made pockets from landscaping companies or you can make you own. I have seen wonderfully quirky edible walls created from canvas shopping bags, cloth shoe bags or even old jeans cut off and sewn along the bottom. None of these will last very long, but they make creative use of something that would have been thrown away. Whatever you choose, bear in mind that both the wall and the material used have to be strong enough to support the weight of wet soil and the plants. Because of the increased moisture, it is a good idea to cover the wall with a sheet of strong plastic before starting. This will prevent damp seeping into the wall.

Watering is an essential component of an edible wall. Because of the limited amount of growing medium, it will dry out very quickly. To prevent this, an irrigation system is recommended. A drip system is best, with each pocket having its own dripper. The components are easy to

WATERING AND FEEDING

- Before planting multiple vegetables in and around one tripod, enrich the soil with a mixture of well-rotted manure and compost.
- Underneath the centre of the tripod, create a mound, using the same mixture.
- Dig a hole in the middle of the mound and bury a plastic nursery pot, leaving its rim sticking out a few centimetres above the mound. The earth should be mounded up around the pot, with its rim at the top of the slope.
- Sow your seeds in the mound (not the pot). As the plants grow, their roots spread around the bottom of the pot. When you fill the pot with water, it drains slowly out of the holes at the bottom, watering the roots directly and gently.
- Once the plants start bearing, use the central pot to feed your plants with organic liquid fertiliser. This delivers the food directly to the roots without any wastage.
- Watering into the pot avoids wetting the leaves and lessens the chance of disease.

install and a simple timer will ensure that your plants stay moist. Ideally, the water that drips down through the edible wall should be collected and directed somewhere useful. If you don't install an irrigation system, water your wall daily.

Because the pockets or modules contain a relatively small amount of growing medium, nutrients will drain out quickly and the plants will require far more regular feeding than those in the ground. Sprinkle a slow-release organic fertiliser into the pockets every month and spray with a foliar feed every three to four weeks. The growing medium should be replaced every year. A good mixture consists of coco peat, vermicompost, organic slow-release fertiliser, compost and vermiculite.

Plants most suitable for vertical walls depend on position. On a hot north-facing wall, cherry tomatoes, Mediterranean herbs and chillies will do well. On a shadier wall choose lettuces, leafy herbs and Asian greens. Strawberries do well on a wall with morning sun. Don't forget to include some companion plants, such as trailing nasturtiums and pansies.

A GARDEN ON A WATER TANK

Many people would like to install a water tank but they don't want to waste limited garden space. But by wrapping a tank with a vertical garden you can actually create more garden space.

Our grey water tank is in a hot position on the north-facing side of the house. I decided to cover it with hardy succulents as they would need very little water (see page 144 for how to do it). On the tank in the driveway, which receives morning sunshine, I planted a mixture of strawberries and herbs. I chose a number of different varieties, with some producing in early spring and others producing well into autumn. The final step was to install irrigation on the strawberry tank wrap, which is part of a series of rainwater harvesting tanks connected to a pressure-activated pump. We installed a drip irrigation system with each pocket having an individual dripper. This is attached to a timer that turns the pump on at the same time every day for about ten minutes. Now the vertical strawberry and herb garden is being watered by its own rainwater. The succulents didn't need a watering system as they don't mind a drier environment. During dry periods I water them whenever I water my nearby containers.

So far I haven't seen any birds on my strawberries or any bird damage as the tank is too close to the house. I did discover a couple of fat snails hiding behind the planting bags. I removed them and placed a barrier of rolled pot scourers (see page 53) around the bottom to prevent the blighters from climbing up again.

I am now eyeing my remaining rainwater tanks and planning what to plant on the next vertical garden.

VERTICAL COMPANIONS

Be creative and combine climbers. The following are good companions:

- Cherry tomatoes and a granadilla – the strong granadilla stems support the tomato's vines easily.
- Beans up an apple tree – especially an espaliered one.
- Sunflower and mielie stalks (after they have been harvested) make good supports for cherry tomatoes, beans and cucumbers.
- Tall asparagus ferns (mature, strong plants only) can be joined together to form a tripod for cherry tomatoes to scramble over.
- Sturdy amaranth can provide a support for beans or cherry tomatoes, especially if three of them are leaned towards each other to make a tripod.

How to Do It

- Measure your tanks and, using strong landscaping material (such as bidim® or strong shade cloth), create panels that will cover the area you want to plant. My tanks are against a wall, so we only covered the front-facing half. If you plan to cover the entire tank, I'd recommend that you create two or three separate panels.
- Turn the top over and stitch a 2 cm-deep channel for the support cable to thread through. For all sewing, use an industrial sewing machine and very strong thread – the panel needs to hold the weight of the planting material and the plants.
- Cut out pockets big enough to each hold one plant comfortably and sew them onto the panel.
- Position the panels and make holes where necessary to accommodate the tank's pipes and taps.
- Thread stainless steel cable through the turnover on the top of the panels.
- Connect this cable to form a circle and tighten it around the top of the tank so the panels hang securely off it.
- Position a second cable about midway down the tank, over the top of the wrap, positioned so it doesn't block any pockets. This provides additional support as the panels are heavy once they are full of plants and soil. Leave this slack until the bags are filled and planted.
- Half fill the bags with growing medium and transplant the seedlings. Fill the bags and water well.
- Tighten the middle cable fully.

VERTICAL GARDENING TIPS

- Always install supports before planting. If you decide to put a stake next to a tomato plant once it is already flourishing, you will disturb its roots.
- When constructing vertical supports, check that they won't block the sun.
- To prevent impacting the soil while you are building a support, use a few wide planks to stand on.
- Start training the plants up their supports as soon as possible. Natural climbers like pole beans won't need much assistance to wind their way quickly toward the top. But others will benefit from a little help, especially in the beginning. Tomato and squash stems, for example, are very fragile and if you try to corral them once they have started to sprawl, the chances of damaging them are high.
- Every few days check your plants to see if they need to be twisted around a pole, tucked into netting or woven back into a tripod.
- The growing tip is the most flexible part of the plant, and can be manipulated quite easily, but be gentle and don't bend it too far or it will break.

GROWING MICROGREENS

Microgreens are an easy-to-grow choice for city dwellers with very little space, as they can be grown on a kitchen counter or even a windowsill. They are quick-growing and add a healthy dash of home-grown taste to a meal. Although suited to mini spaces, they can just as easily be grown outdoors in a larger vegetable garden. Bigger than sprouts and smaller than baby salad leaves, microgreens are picked once they have developed two 'true' leaves. These are ones that are produced from a stem, not the seed. This means the plant has already developed roots and therefore contains more nutrients and flavour than a sprout. Unlike sprouts, which need only water, microgreens are rooted in a thin layer of fertile growing medium. Although they require a bit more care than sprouts, microgreens provide a much wider range of textures, shapes and colours.

When growing microgreens, start with untreated seed as you don't want them contaminated with pesticides and fungicides. Often we have many more seeds than we can use in our vegetable gardens and, as seeds have limited viability, growing microgreens is a great way to use these up. All of the following and more are suitable: alfalfa, amaranth, Asian greens, beetroot, broccoli, buckwheat, cabbage, cauliflower, celery, chickpeas, chives, clover, flax, kale, lentils, lettuce, mielies, mustard, onions, peas, quinoa, radish, rocket, sesame, spinach, sunflowers, Swiss chard, turnip, watercress and many herbs.

Recycled plastic takeaway containers are ideal for growing microgreens, with the lid creating a moist microclimate, which germinating seeds love, as well as allowing light in. (Don't forget to punch some drainage holes in the bottom, otherwise you will waterlog the seeds.) Shallow bonsai containers are also a good choice.

Different seeds will germinate at different rates, so don't mix varieties together unless you know they will grow at the same speed. If you want mixed microgreens, rather grow each type of seed in a separate container. (Larger seeds, such as peas, mielies and chickpeas, benefit from being soaked for 24 hours before sowing.) Add a 4 to 6 cm-deep layer of fertile growing medium (see page 92) to the container. (If growing in an outside bed, the soil should be raked as smooth as possible before sowing.) Moisten the soil and firm it down gently. Sprinkle the seeds evenly over the entire surface. Sow the seed quite thickly – you will be harvesting them quite small, so they don't need the same space as an adult plant.

For small seeds, cover them with a layer of finely sieved compost, and press down again gently. Larger seeds don't need this. An alternative to covering with compost is to cover the seeds with thin cloth or paper towel and spray with a mister until completely damp. This creates a moisture-retaining blanket for the seeds and works well for larger varieties. (Once the seeds germinate they will start pushing the paper towel or cloth up and it needs to be removed.) Covering the containers with a lid will speed up germination. Either use the takeaway plastic lids, or thin clear plastic shower caps. Place the containers on a warm light windowsill or shelf.

They need to be watered every day so position them where you will see them. Check that they don't get too humid and hot under the lids, otherwise mould can form or the heat can even 'cook' the seeds. A germinating seed must stay moist and if the growing medium is allowed to dry out, the seed will die. Water the seeds every day, and in hotter climates twice a day. Once the seeds have all germinated, remove the lids.

Depending on the microgreen, they can be harvested within 7 to 14 days by snipping them off at the surface with scissors. They do not keep well, so it is best to harvest them just before eating.

SQUARE FOOT GARDENING

First developed in the USA by Mel Bartholomew in the 1970s as a more efficient way to garden, Square Foot Gardening (SFG) is ideally suited to small urban gardens. As SFG was developed in the United States, it uses feet and inches as a system of measurement. Although we are a metric country, it is easier to stick to the imperial system as the support information you will find on most websites uses these measurements.

SFG is ideal for anyone with a small urban garden, or for those who live in a rental property and are reluctant to invest too much time or money in a garden that is not their own. This method of gardening utilises intensively-planted raised beds that produce a surprisingly large amount of produce from a small space, with the added advantage that they are not permanent fixtures and can be moved easily.

The raised beds are small enough for the gardener to reach the middle without stepping on and compacting the soil. Each bed is divided into clearly marked 1 foot by 1 foot squares, hence the name. Different vegetables are planted in each square. The number of plants per square depends on the size of the vegetable. For example, 16 or so smaller plants, such as carrots, radishes or onions, can fit in one square, but larger plants such as broccoli, peppers and tomatoes have only one plant per square, or might even use up a few squares for each plant.

Mark and Kathy Roach are enthusiastic Square Foot Gardeners. A few years ago they decided to try their hand at growing their own vegetables. However, as they rent their townhouse in Pretoria, they needed approval from the owners and had to undertake to return the garden to its original state when they moved out. After researching possible alternatives online, they decided that Square Foot Gardening was the answer.

They set about measuring and building frames for the beds, working out the ideal soil mix, buying and planting seeds and learning, from the ground up, how to grow vegetables. One year later, they had grown a wide range of vegetables successfully and had turned their new passion into a flourishing business, now teaching and sharing what they have learned – and continue to learn – through workshops and demonstrations. In addition to an informative website, they also run an online shop, selling organic and heirloom seeds, as well as the accessories required to get a square foot garden started.

Their vegetable garden has now spread throughout the entire townhouse complex. "I have been living here for nine years," says Mark, "and before I started this project I knew only two neighbours. Now I know all of them." What began with a few beds has now grown to include six other gardens in the complex, feeding 13 households with fresh produce. People either pay to receive a harvest basket or they donate time to working in the gardens, or even donate space in their own gardens to the project.

Growing methods have also been adapted to suit the space. In some gardens the walls have been used for hanging vegetable gardens, while in others they have planted up large 5 litre and 20 litre containers with vegetables. These methods are especially suitable for small gardens. "Crop rotation is often difficult in small spaces. If only one wall in a garden receives enough sun for tomatoes, you can't rotate them. So instead we just rotate the soil," explains Mark.

There has been enormous enthusiasm among the residents for the project. One of their neighbours, for example, is in the roofing business, and he supplies off-cuts with which they create planting boxes. An unexpected benefit has been that the vegetables themselves have helped people to come together. Neighbours, who were once strangers to one another, are now sharing recipes for cooking unfamiliar produce.

"Instead of us all being isolated, the garden has created a village type of community here."
Mark Roach

Square Foot Gardening Tips

As a rough guide of how many boxes you would need, Mark advises that one 4 foot by 4 foot (1.2 m by 1.2 m) box will produce sufficient ingredients to make a salad for one adult every day. An additional box of the same size will provide supper vegetables. For each child, add a smaller 3 foot by 3 foot (90 cm by 90 cm) box. When calculating the space, make a 1 m wide pathway between the boxes. The depth of the boxes should be 20 cm, and be sure to fill them with a good-quality growing medium (see page 92).

Although SFG is best suited to raised beds, the concept can be adapted to existing non-raised beds. Most SFG growers, however, use raised beds, with all the benefits that come with them (see page 90). The squares can be delineated using lines of string, bamboo poles or even strips of recycled advertising boards. The idea is simply to demarcate the squares so you can see them when sowing seeds or transplanting.

Once plants have been harvested, add a layer of fresh growing medium and transplant new seedlings or sow new seeds in the squares, keeping the principles of crop rotation in mind (see page 39).

Because spacing is an important component of a successful SFG garden, it is recommended that seeds (of plants that don't mind being transplanted) are sown in seed trays first and then transplanted into the squares. Once a year replace the growing medium.

How to Plant

Depending on the mature size of the plant, grow either 1, 4, 9 or 16 plants per square, fitting the maximum amount of vegetables into the space.

To work out how many plants fit into one square, use the seed packet spacing as a guide, and follow this planting suggestion:

- One plant per square for 12 inch (30 cm) spacing, for example broccoli and cabbage
- Four plants per square for 6 inch (15 cm) spacing, for example celery, lettuce and parsley and thyme
- Nine plants per square for 4 inch (10 cm) spacing, for example bush beans, leeks and spinach
- Sixteen plants per square for 3 inch (7 cm) spacing, for example carrots, beetroot and radishes.

A STRAW BALE GARDEN

Using straw bales to create a vegetable garden requires no digging, no weeding and can be set up in any sunny space. Ideal for a one-season garden, the bales slowly decompose creating compost. Straw bales are ideal for rooftop gardens as they are so light. They are also a good option if you want to create a low-impact garden.

How to Plant a Straw Bale Garden

- Position the straw bales to create the shape you want. They can be used to make rows, a square with a hole in the middle, or simply placed in a line against a wall.
- Place the straw stalks horizontal to the ground. If they are vertical, water will run through too quickly. And don't cut the bailing twine that holds them together, otherwise you will have straw everywhere.
- Sprinkle with a slow-release high-nitrogen organic fertiliser, such as Talborne's Vita-Green. Cover the tops of the bales with a 5 to 7 cm layer of compost. If you created a hole in the middle, fill it with a mixture of coco peat, well-rotted manure and compost.
- Soak the bales with a mixture of water and liquid organic fertiliser (such as Biogrow's Biotrissol) every day for ten days. This will kick-start the composting process, breaking the bales down, ready for your plants.
- Use a trowel to pry holes and transplant seedlings. Direct sow root crops or plant potatoes into the central area. Or install a vertical support for a gem squash or cherry tomatoes.
- Install a soaker hose and in dry periods water every day or two so the bales don't dry out. (See page 72 for more on watering.)
- By the end of the season the bales will have broken down. These can be used to start the next straw bale garden or they can be added to the compost pile.
- If you are in a windy area, straw bales can be placed as a wind break around a bed. Dig a hole in the centre of each bale, fill with growing medium and plant your seedlings.

SHADY GARDEN SOLUTIONS

One thing we always hear about growing vegetables is that they need sun, sun and more sun. But what if you don't have a sunny garden? Many urban gardens have large trees that provide welcome shade and people are understandably reluctant to remove them. Or a neighbour's trees or surrounding buildings block the sun. Living in a city we don't have the luxury of being able to choose a sun-soaked section of farm for our vegetables. But before you abandon your dream of growing an edible garden, there are solutions for shady areas. Although you won't be able to grow tomatoes or mielies, there are other vegetables that grow happily in less than optimal sunlight. It helps to understand a bit about shade and how plants utilise sunlight.

Plants need sunlight to manufacture food. They capture the sun's energy and, using green chlorophyll in their leaves, transform it through photosynthesis into energy they can store and use. The better the plant is at this, the less sun it actually needs. Vegetables and herbs with large, flat, green leaves growing at various angles are ideal solar accumulators. Think Asian greens, lettuces, rocket and Swiss chard. And the more leaves they have, the more shade they can handle. Plants that grow large sweet fruit (such as eggplants, melons and tomatoes) won't do well in shade at all.

Shade is shade is shade – right? Wrong. There are different types of shade and before you start growing vegetables, first assess your garden and the quality of shade. Track the sun's progress by observing where the sun moves and making rough sketches to work out the number of hours of sunlight different sections of your garden receive. Vegetables will yield more in an area with bright dappled shade all day than in an area that receives only a few hours of full sun per day.

Shady areas can be altered to increase the amount of sunlight.

- Open up the area to more light by cutting off low-hanging branches. The higher the branches are, the 'brighter' the shade and the more energy the plants can tap into.
- Paint surrounding walls, particularly north-facing ones, white or a light colour to reflect the sun's energy into the garden.
- Use reflective white stones or light-coloured gravel on pathways.
- Use reflective mulch to bounce sunlight up onto your vegetables. Metallised reflective mulch sheeting is available overseas (and online via Amazon) but we can make do with sheets of reflective white paper or recycled inners from box wine.

GROWING IN THE SHADE

Dappled shade is light speckled shade, caused by high branches or feathery trees. The higher the branches, the brighter the shade.

Semi shade is shade for part of the day, with full sun for a few hours of the day. Afternoon sun is stronger than morning sun.

Seasonal shade moves as the angle of the sun changes through the season or as a tree loses its leaves. For example, a north-facing bed under a deciduous tree will receive plenty of sun for most of winter but will be in full shade for most of summer. The angle of the sun also makes a difference: one hour of winter sunlight in Cape Town has far less energy than one hour of summer sunlight in Pretoria.

Full shade is solid shade caused by dense trees, low-hanging branches, a building or a wall. Solid shade caused by a wall or house, is generally drier than under a tree.

Tips for Planting in Shade

Moveable containers
Make good use of seasonal sunny areas by simply moving containers to where the sun is. (See page 86 for more on growing in containers.)

Soil
Growing vegetables in less than optimal conditions requires fertile soil. Add plenty of compost and manure to your beds before planting and keep the soil enriched throughout the growing season with balanced organic fertilisers.

Roots
Growing vegetables in a tree's dappled shade means there are roots to contend with. These pull water and nutrients away from the soil and the roots will be drawn towards the vegetables' fertile soil. To get around this, build raised beds and line the bottom of the beds with old carpeting to keep unwanted roots away. Install an irrigation system to keep vegetables well watered.

Pests and diseases
More vigilance is required in a shady garden where diseases and pest infestations can be aggravated. Slugs and snails love moist, shady conditions.

Seeds
Shady areas are cooler and this affects germination of seeds, particularly early in spring. Start seeds in seed trays and transplant them. If sowing seeds directly, sow them more thickly than usual.

Choose the Right Vegetables

VEGETABLE	HOURS OF SUNLIGHT	GROWING
Asian greens	3–4 preferably midday, or 6–8 bright dappled shade	Do well in bright dappled shade
Beans	4–5 preferably midday and afternoon	Bush varieties crop better in less sun than climbing ones
Beetroot	4–5 preferably midday	Will take longer to reach harvest size
Cabbages	4–5 preferably midday and afternoon	Chinese and baby cabbages do better than large ones
Carrots	4–5 midday or afternoon	Will take longer to reach harvest size
Edible flowers: calendula, nasturtium, pansies	4–5 any time of day	All do well in semi or bright dappled shade
Herbs: borage, chives, comfrey, coriander, fennel, golden marjoram, lemon balm, lovage, mint, oregano, parsley, pelargonium, pineapple sage, sorrel	3–4 any time of day	All do well in semi or bright dappled shade
Horseradish	5–6 dappled shade, midday	Won't spread as quickly
Kale	3–4 any time of day	Leaves will be smaller
Lettuce	3–4 morning to midday	Choose leafy lettuces rather than heading ones
Mustard	3–4 any time of day	Leaves will be smaller
Peas	4–5 any time of day	Sugar snap and petit pois do better than larger varieties
Potatoes	4–5 preferably midday	Will take longer to reach harvest size
Radishes	4–5 morning to midday	Will take longer to reach harvest size
Rocket	3–4 any time of day	Does well in bright dappled shade
Spinach	3–4 any time of day	Does well in bright dappled shade
Swiss chard	3–4 any time of day	Leaves will be smaller

ROOFTOP GARDENING

Using rooftops to grow vegetables is an option for many city dwellers with limited choices. Edible urban rooftops take previously sterile and unused areas and convert them into productive and healthy living spaces that reduce the eco-footprint of your home or office. If you look out of your window right now you will probably see a roof you could use on a shed, a garage or a cottage. If you live in an apartment block, most of them have a flat top or a level section over the parking. City office blocks often have flat, easily accessible roofs.

In South Africa, edible rooftop gardens are becoming increasingly popular and there are several that provide inspiration for small-space gardeners. The Saxon hotel has created an edible wonderland above a parking garage, which provides one of their restaurants with daily fresh produce (for more, see page 196). In Johannesburg's city centre, The Star newspaper has made clever use of The Urban Boxes on their flat rooftop to create an edible garden that was installed in a couple of days. In Durban, two particularly well-designed rooftop gardens are flourishing in the city centre.

INSPIRING ROOFTOP GARDENS

When the Priority Zone Project (PZP) was initiated by the eThekwini Municipality to improve conditions in the Durban inner city, one of their first projects was to create a rooftop garden above the PZP offices. The one-storey building's large roof has been transformed from a flat expanse of hot concrete to a luscious and thriving rooftop garden, with inviting recreational spaces. Wide pathways, made from wooden pallets covered with recycled Astroturf, meander between beds packed with an abundance of organic vegetables. Half drums and recycled tyres are filled with brinjals, chillies, madumbi, Swiss chard, tomatoes and herbs. Colourful marigolds pop up in the gaps. Low tunnels covered with greenhouse sheeting and shade cloth provide a sheltered area for seedling propagation and for vegetables and herbs needing protection from Durban's hot sun.

The rooftop was designed and installed by Marc Nel of Eva Group. There were several factors that he needed to consider when designing the garden. It covers a large area and the design had to take into account not only the water flow, but foot traffic too. As the garden is used as an educational tool and a venue for functions, it had to have easy entry and exit points, plus areas for people to congregate.

Marc's design includes benches and tables, inviting office workers in the area to come and enjoy their lunches in the garden or to have a meeting. A giant chess board adds attraction. Sharing the rooftop with the food garden is a low-maintenance succulent garden, planted with indigenous plants. The wide variety of vegetation attracts not only bees but also butterflies and birds to a previously barren area. The reaction from users of the garden has been overwhelmingly positive, and it continues to draw local and foreign visitors, who come to spend time enjoying the rooftop.

One of the visitors to the garden was Yanni Vosloo, Merchandise Director of Mr Price Home. He had been challenged by his CEO to come up with a creative concept to beautify a bare thoroughfare on the roof of Mr Price Group's head office that connected the different divisions to the canteen. After seeing the PZP garden, the idea sprouted to build a rooftop garden on the unutilised concrete space. And to assist him in creating his vision, Yanni called in Marc.

The Mr Price rooftop proved to be a challenging area, with the loading restrictions resulting in an extremely shallow planting depth. The shallow soil coupled with direct sunlight and strong winds made for very difficult growing conditions. But despite this, with the correct plant choice and careful attention, the rooftop garden has flourished into a beautiful and functional space.

Both roofs' productive organic vegetable gardens are planted with seasonal crops that are rotated, as well as companion plants. In the PZP garden, jobs have been created through the maintenance and sale of

"**People are blown away by what is possible in a high traffic area; it's fantastic to see people sitting in the garden having a meeting or a cup of coffee.**"
Marc Nel, Eva Group

the produce grown, while a large portion is also donated to charities in the area. At Mr Price, the rooftop garden supplements the canteen with fresh produce. The canteen staff harvest from the vegetable beds, but as the strawberries and granadillas are a popular lunchtime treat for staff members, they rarely make it to the kitchen.

Marc loves creating these oases and he is now working on greening more urban rooftops. "A rooftop garden need not be big or expensive. It just needs to cover a bare area that is a waste of space. Plant herbs or a small succulent garden. And use an old bath or cut a drum in half. Once you see how satisfying and easy it actually is, you'll be searching for more wasted space."

INSTALLING A ROOFTOP GARDEN

Before you start piling soil or placing boxes on your roof, there are a number of practical factors to take into consideration. Apart from the usual elements that go into any well-planned vegetable garden, a rooftop garden needs to allow for weight, safety, water flow, usage, drainage, wind and access.

Weight Bearing and Safety

Whether you are creating a small garden on top of your garage or a large one on an apartment rooftop, before you begin consult a structural engineer to assess the type of roof and whether it is suitable for a rooftop garden. You might find certain areas can carry higher loads than others, or you might have to create a reinforcing framework. Once the loading capacity has been measured, a kilogram per square metre rate is given. These vary greatly from building to building and it is advisable to keep well within the loading specs. Remember to calculate your garden in a 'wet' state as water is heavy. Choosing light materials, such as straw bales (see page 151) also helps keep the weight down.

Working on a rooftop to install a garden brings other challenges, such as safety. A balustrade is generally the cheapest method to ensure that there are no accidents. This needs to be installed before work can commence.

Drainage, Water Flow and Waterproofing

Water drainage should be assessed before construction begins. The surface intended for your rooftop garden needs to be able to drain water off quickly as stationary water not only increases the risk of damp, but also adds to the loading weight.

Understanding water flow is also extremely important when planning a rooftop garden. Although flat roofs look flat, they are designed for water to flow off them. A structural engineer will give you the percentage fall and anything greater than one per cent is good. Ascertain where the lowest point of the roof is and aim all the water in that direction. Ideally, install pathways in the natural path of the water flow, to assist the

water in exiting the garden. In both the PZP and Mr Price gardens, Marc made use of recycled plastic decking for pathways as it is hard wearing and requires zero maintenance. The pathways have a dual function of providing access to the beds and creating water channels, with the water flowing freely under the plastic decking towards the drains.

A rooftop garden also needs to have a waterproofing system applied before construction can begin. Marc recommends the torch-on method; a heat-fused UV-stable membrane that provides complete waterproof protection. If the roof already has one, ensure that there are no cracks that might compromise the waterproofing.

Access

Safe access to the rooftop is essential. For garden sheds and garage roofs a sturdy ladder will do, but for larger rooftops on taller buildings, if there is no ready access, stairs will have to be installed. For city centre rooftops, planning is crucial to streamline the installation process. "A bill of quantities needs to be established and the materials need to arrive like clockwork. Where possible use a rope-and-pulley system, especially for the growing medium," says Marc.

Watering

Rooftops tend to dry out more quickly than a normal garden and a reliable water supply is important. If possible, harvest water from gutters or neighbouring buildings (see page 75), but remember to take into account the loading weight if you want to keep tanks on the rooftop itself. Mulch is also essential for retaining moisture. For a large garden, a drip irrigation system is ideal (see page 72).

Wind and Sun

On a rooftop – especially in a coastal city – wind can blow a garden to smithereens. To prevent this Marc ensures they don't use excessively tall plants. "Vegetables like tomatoes are staked to prevent them from being blown over and having their roots exposed. Again, mulch is key to combatting the plants drying out quickly from the wind."

The tunnels on the PZP rooftop have been limited intentionally to 1m in height, to avoid wind interference. When creating permanent structures for seating or pergolas for shade or support, design them to be wind permeable, otherwise they can create wind tunnels or be blown over.

Bare concrete rooftops can be very hot zones, but by simply planting a garden this is mitigated and a cooler environment is created. Water-wise methods such as mulching, intensive planting and grouping will all help a garden to survive the hot sun. "The beauty of rooftop gardens is what happens below them," says Marc. "At one of our gardens the ambient temperature inside the building below it has dropped by an average of 3 °C." This has reduced their air conditioner use by 40 per cent during the summer.

Other Elements to Include

- An electrical point is useful, especially during construction. If the rooftop is a large one, a permanent electrical point will enable you to install lighting to access and use the garden in the evening.
- Provide a space for a storage shed where tools, implements and fertiliser can be kept.
- Provide shady seating nooks for visitors.
- Think of setting up a worm farm. Both rooftop gardens have worm farms, with Mr Price recently adding a second 1.5 m by 1.5 m unit to assist in composting more of the canteen's organic waste. This is fed to the wormery where it is converted into a natural fertiliser for the garden.
- Recycle whatever you can. In keeping with the ethos of improving the inner city environment, both gardens make creative use of recycled products. Marc tries to utilise as much as possible: old tyres, recycled plastic benches, recycled plastic walkways, reject drums, water tanks made from recycled plastic, and reject pallets. Even the waterproofing used as a layer on top of the torch-on is made from recycled plastic.
- Consider keeping bees. The PZP garden also has two honey-providing bee hives. "We consulted with a bee expert who advised us on ideal plants for bees," says Marc, "and the bees are always extremely busy collecting pollen. And no! Even though the garden gets hundreds of visitors a week, no one has been stung." (See page 215 for more on urban beekeeping.)

GARDENING IN PUBLIC SPACES

Growing your own food creates plenty of benefits and pleasure. It provides you and your family with healthy nutritious food right from your own doorstep, it cuts down on the monthly grocery bill and it gives you the satisfaction of looking at your edible garden and saying, "I did that!" But perhaps most fulfilling of all is the empowering knowledge that is gained through the very process of gardening – to know that if push came to shove and the supermarket couldn't provide you with enough food, you could dig up your lawn and plant tomatoes, potatoes, onions and more. But what if you don't have that lawn? What if you live in an apartment, with no balcony and nowhere to grow vegetables other than perhaps a windowsill for herbs?

There are many public spaces just begging to be rejuvenated into an edible garden. All it takes is a motivated person or organisation to make it happen. Urban public spaces are not the easiest places to grow a food garden. The soil is often not ideal, water can be a problem and security a concern. But many people have taken up the challenge and have transformed urban public spaces into edible havens.

GUERRILLA GARDENING

Guerrilla gardening first began in New York in the 1970s, when a group of green activists transformed an abandoned lot into a community garden. Part social activism, part political protest and mostly about enriching or beautifying unused or abandoned ground, there are now Guerrilla Gardeners worldwide. At one of Johannesburg's busy intersections in Parktown there is a perfect example of a Guerrilla Garden. A local resident and keen gardener has spent many years creating a beautiful space for public enjoyment where before there was just a weedy island. There are many other spaces that can be utilised.

An Alleyway Garden

A few years ago I received a phone call from a friend of mine Brian Green, who was starting a vegetable garden from scratch and needed some help. Below his property in Forest Town is a public service alley and he was planning to start a guerrilla vegetable garden there. Brian has always been a bit of a maverick, so it was not surprising that his approach to vegetable gardening was a little unorthodox. He had never grown vegetables before but wanted to supply a local restaurant with fresh organic produce. And the best way to do so was to grow his own.

When I first visited, the service alley was heaped with piles of rubble and covered with weeds flowing from the walls. First the alleyway had to be cleared, which took a few days of concentrated sweat and labour. Then he could see the space he had to play with – and it turned out to be much

"You put seed in the ground, give it water, give it nice soil and voom, up it comes!"
Brian Green

GUERRILLA GARDENING TIPS

- Look for vacant untended land near you and start planting. It helps if you rope in a couple of neighbours who also want to be involved, as you might have to carry water to your plants during dry spells.
- Spend as little money as possible by using recycled material.
- Start small and add to your project as you go.
- Choose vegetables that are quick to grow, easy to maintain and will seed themselves. Beans, cherry tomatoes, gem squash, lettuce, mustard, rocket and Swiss chard are all good choices.
- Include companion plants such as California poppies, cornflowers, marigolds and nasturtiums. These will fill the spaces in between vegetables and reduce weeds.
- Add a selection of perennial herbs.
- Involve the people the garden is aimed at.
- Another version of guerrilla gardening is seed bombing. A selection of easy-to-sow seeds is mixed into a ball of clay and fertiliser, which is then tossed into vacant land. As the rain breaks the clay apart, the seeds spread and germinate, creating a patch of edible garden.

bigger than expected. After deciding to go with raised beds filled with enriched soil, he also set himself the challenge of spending as little money as possible on his new venture. Brian proved to be a master scavenger and collected boxes, crates, metal sheets and boards off the side of the road to create a mixture of containers without spending a cent. His gravel pathways were created using leftover stones from work done on his house. The soil and compost to fill the beds came from his own garden, and the fertiliser from a wormery he had started a while back.

The resulting garden is a medley of pleasing shapes and colours enhanced by the fact that this is a food garden situated in a reclaimed alleyway where graffiti still adorns the walls. There is a vital grittiness to this garden. Real work goes on here, and the beds are bursting with beetroot, carrots, eggplants, herbs, spinach, tomatoes and more. "It's fabulous! The taste of organic vegetables picked an hour ago, now on your plate. I feed the house and the restaurant gets dollops, kilos a week." As part of his intention to create a self-sustaining cycle, all the organic leftovers from the restaurant are recycled back to the large worm farm and compost pile.

Brian plants his vegetables from seed, using heirloom varieties as he has been impressed by their yield. His approach is entirely organic. "One of the most beautiful things about this organic vegetable garden is using companion plants to keep the nasties out. What I've found is that if you plant marigolds you don't see a single bug. Another example is onions planted with lettuce – pests don't like a strong oniony smell. So I'm not going out and buying loads of things to kill the bugs. Everything is here. It is all about finding a balance."

It has not all been smooth sailing, but he has learned from his mistakes and his enthusiasm is refreshing. "For me it's not about becoming a garden scientist. It's about experimenting, getting my fingers dirty and having fun. I am hooked."

AMbush Gardening Collective

An active South African guerrilla gardening gang is the AMbush Gardening Collective. Armed with gumboots and gloves, Liliana Transplanter and WayWord Sun (not their real names!) are changing their environment for the better, one edible garden at a time. Liliana is an ethno botanist and while doing research in the Western Cape she "became very aware of the unused, vacant, wasted spaces, what we call 'forgotten spaces' throughout the cityscape. AMbush emerged as a collective, aiming to transform space, and the perception of space, and the perception of waste, and to bring people into the conversation about how this space can be used. We aim to transform these 'forgotten spaces' into productive, multifunctional, beautiful and meaningful spaces, which reflect local realities and interests," says Liliana. Inspired by this desire to make urban landscapes more productive and beautiful, they work with communities, rather than just bombing in and planting. They try to uncover the local knowledge and

> **"By finding ways to celebrate our ecological and cultural heritage we can co-create more sustainable, resilient cities and societies."**
> *AMbush*

engage with communities about what they would like to have planted, thereby creating meaningful greener spaces.

One of their main challenges is the sustainability of the gardens they create, partly due to the lack of adequate financial resources. But despite this they continue to try to get people to celebrate themselves and the diversity around them. They hope that their gardens will create positive change within their lives and in their communities.

Gardening or cultivating in public areas can be tricky. Problems encountered by the AMbush collective include: people walking on newly-planted seedlings; rats invading the gardens; people stealing the crops; and their gardens being used as dustbins or toilets (which is often what the space was used for before they began planting).

Despite this, Liliana has yet to encounter someone who hasn't liked or appreciated the fact that they are cleaning and greening an area. And, as Liliana has discovered, the cleaning and greening does not just benefit the recipients. "Our guerrilla gardening acts as a participatory performance, where we share information, and learn more about each other and the world that surrounds us. For us it's very beneficial to work with local people, as that is where we get the most out of this, creating community."

PAVEMENT GARDENING

Most of us plant vegetables in our gardens with the intention of growing food for ourselves and our family. However, Denise O'Callaghan's vegetable garden is on her pavement. And she grows her vegetables for the dozens of people who walk past her home in Parktown North, Johannesburg, on their way to catch a bus or taxi. "When I first started planting vegetables on the pavement in 2009, I was quite surprised to find that the people the vegetables were meant for walked past the ripe tomatoes and did not touch them. One day, I asked an elderly gentleman, who had stopped to look at my vegetables, why he did not help himself. He replied he could not because they weren't his." So Denise made a sign, encouraging the public to help themselves but to leave enough for others. Only then did people start picking. She was worried at first that the entire harvest would be picked all at once, but she found that passers-by picked only one or two vegetables for themselves and always left enough for the next person.

Denise believes that apart from providing nutrition for people who need it, her pavement vegetable garden is a way of connecting with the larger community. "When I am working in the garden, people always stop to chat to me and I get to know the regulars." She has inspired many others to grow pavement vegetable gardens too, and recommends planting easy-to-grow vegetables, such as beans, cherry tomatoes, marog and Swiss chard. "Sow them from seed in seed trays and then transplant them out when they are a decent size."

"The pavements belong to everybody. If each household planted spinach amongst their roses, or brinjals next to their flowers, Joburg would become known as a generous city."

Denise O'Callaghan

Pavement Garden Tips

- Include some easy-to-grow perennials such as oregano, rosemary, sage and thyme.
- Add some edible flowers such as California poppies, nasturtiums and sunflowers.
- Other suitable vegetables are Asian greens, beetroot, chives, kale, potatoes, rocket, spring onions and sweet potatoes.
- Put up a sign encouraging people to pick the harvest.
- Put up information signs about the various vegetables and when and how to harvest them.

SUCCESSFUL
URBAN
GARDENS

COMMUNITY, NON-PROFIT
AND EDUCATIONAL GARDENS

One thing I am increasingly asked is to assist in setting up community or non-profit vegetable gardens, which are springing up in many urban spaces, from neglected bowling greens in middle-class neighbourhoods to unused pieces of land in informal settlements. These gardens are a good choice for gardeners who don't have the space to grow vegetables, or don't have the time to maintain their own garden but would like to contribute to a nearby communal garden in exchange for organic vegetables. They are also ideal for schools, churches and charity organisations to provide healthy food for those who are not getting the nutrition they need.

Many community gardens begin with plenty of enthusiasm but then run out of steam after one short season. Likewise, many organic food gardens set up in underprivileged communities by charity organisations – with the best of intentions – are destined to fail. The reasons are varied: the initial enthusiasm fades; the community changes; the expectations are unrealistic; or leadership is lacking. However, there are many functioning and fruitful community non-profit and educational food gardens that have managed to find the right ingredients for success.

ABALIMI AND HARVEST OF HOPE

One of South Africa's most successful food garden projects is Abalimi, a non-profit association operating on the Cape Flats. *Abalimi* means 'the planters' in Xhosa, an appropriate name for an organisation that has educated and empowered thousands of people, teaching them how to set up and maintain organic food gardens. But it has not been easy. As Rob Small, founder and energetic motivator, says, "There is a mind-set in these communities, particularly among the younger generation, that does not believe micro-farming is worthwhile. This is compounded by a skills deficit, a shortage of start-up capital and lack of long-term training and support services to emerging micro-farmers. Many community gardens fail because they are based on an assumption of what people will do. These are human beings who have been disenfranchised, disempowered and have no sense of who they are – especially compared to the middle class. You can't go into these areas and give them a vegetable garden and walk away. It's good to give, but don't stop giving until you have empowered the community."

Abalimi runs hands-on training courses, providing students with the skills to either start their own food garden or become involved in a community garden. Farmers are taught the deep trench composting

system, where food waste is buried in a trench, creating a deep compost layer. Crops are planted above the trench and by the time the roots penetrate down, the compost layer has rotted, providing nutrients and retaining moisture. This is an effective method of composting for people without access to running water and where soil is sandy and nutritionally poor.

Abalimi's involvement doesn't end with education. As the farmers become increasingly skilled, they start producing more than enough to feed their families and begin to sell the excess. However, outside their immediate neighbours, there is little or no access to markets. And so Abalimi founded Harvest of Hope, a Community Supported Agriculture (CSA) scheme that provides a much needed outlet for these farmers.

Members of Harvest for Hope sign up to have a box of seasonal organic vegetables delivered to them every week. Harvest of Hope contracts with the farmers in advance, guaranteeing that their produce will be purchased, thus giving them income security. This has enabled people to move from growing subsistence food, to producing extra food and being able to earn a living from the excess. Not only has Abalimi succeeded in creating gardeners and farmers who are now eating and selling healthy organic food, it has also been a catalyst for social change and restored a sense of community.

"The focus of a CSA scheme is to re-establish our relationship with the food we eat and where it comes from; knowing how it's grown and who grows it. It connects and supports people and communities in a direct and friendly way."
Rob Small, Abalimi

ORANJEZICHT CITY FARM

This vibrant urban farm, at the base of Table Mountain, is the brainchild
of Sheryl Ozinsky who is passionate about greening urban spaces.
Exploring the rows and rows of abundant vegetables, it is hard to believe
that this farm was once a neglected bowling green and a refuge for
vagrants and drug dealers.

The site of the Oranjezicht City Farm (OZCF) comprises part of the original Oranjezicht Farmstead, once the largest farm in the Upper Table Valley. Seven generations of the Van Breda family farmed here from 1709 until 1901, and it has now gone full circle. A group of local residents has formed a non-profit organisation to celebrate local food, culture and community through urban farming. In keeping with its historic origins, the OZCF design is based on elements of Cape formal gardens from the Seventeenth century. The result is practical and aesthetically very pleasing, with wide pathways intersecting smaller ones, creating a geometric maze inviting visitors to interact with the garden.

The project is striving to be sustainable – solar pumps feed the pond and drip irrigation is gravity fed. An earthworm farm digests hundreds of kilograms of household waste per week, all supplied by local residents. The farm is headed up by two full-time gardeners, with help from many volunteers, both local and international. Their energy and skills are maximised by dividing the support required into categories, such as farming and operations, education, communication and administration.

Start-up funding and pro bono services were provided by various donors to cover the set-up costs. But, as a community-based non-profit organisation, OZCF is working hard to support itself, by selling T-shirts, vegetables, seedlings and more. Every Wednesday evening the farm is open from 4pm to 6.30pm for a guided harvest. Visitors arrive with empty baskets and are shown what and how to harvest. A buzzing weekly Saturday Market Day provides an outlet for artisanal food producers and local farmers, with the emphasis on local, fresh and seasonal. The innovative market organisers have also introduced a Kid's Market Day, where young entrepreneurs learn the skills of producing and marketing their own wares. A percentage of proceeds from these events goes to OZCF.

The farm is an important educational resource and school outings are encouraged. "Learning to appreciate the wonder and power of nature is at the core of the educational programme," says Sheryl. Pupils are taught about sustainability, water conservation, healthy eating and organic food production with practical, hands-on experience and a guided tour of the farm. With the farm's rich past, it is also an opportunity to learn about history and heritage.

A definite contributing factor to OZCF's success is the well-organised steering committee. With passion, dedication and clearly defined roles, it is the engine driving this flourishing farm. With the success of the OZCF, Sheryl is now looking at other unused or under-utilised public green spaces. "We are hoping OZCF will serve as a model, providing mentoring, support and resources to inspire and strengthen other groups keen to do something similar."

"There are hundreds of spaces that have the potential to serve our communities as places that beautify, educate, feed and strengthen residents."
Sheryl Ozinsky, OZCF

REEA VEGETABLE GARDENS

Tucked away in the Johannesburg suburb of Craighall, on the banks of the Braamfontein Spruit, the prolific and verdant food garden of the Rand Epileptic Employment Association (REEA) is an unexpected surprise. Gravel pathways frame geometric beds brimming with vegetables, herbs and edible flowers. Colourful and creative scarecrows, made by supportive residents from the surrounding neighbourhood, keep a watchful eye on the garden. Pansies and chives spill out of recycled tyres creating a living bank. At the entrance is a gazebo, its shelves piled high with seedlings, fresh vegetables and free-range eggs for sale.

This is one of the oldest existing urban farms in South Africa, having started well over seventy years ago. When REEA began in 1935, the vegetable gardens were established soon after, with beautiful greenhouses and glasshouses being built from 1946 onwards. Unfortunately, due to financial constraints and other factors, the gardens fell into disrepair and many of the glasshouses and greenhouses were demolished. Over the past four years the remaining gardens and heritage greenhouse have been undergoing refurbishments by volunteer community members led by local resident Daniella Alexander, who took it upon herself to create something meaningful for both REEA and the broader community.

Daniella is one of those people who makes magic happen – even when there isn't any money. With calm determination, passion and an incredible amount of hard work, the vegetable gardens have been rejuvenated into a thriving and abundant farm. Daniella has motivated many community members to become involved, both in the gardens and financially. The garden's running expenses are currently part-sponsored by a generous community member. But Daniella sees this as an interim measure. Her vision is to have the garden become completely self-sustainable and to generate a portion of REEA's 24/7 high-care medical and residential costs. Vegetable and herb sales, contract plant sales and an orchid rejuvenation project in its infancy stages are current revenue streams, with a future museum and education centre planned to make it a commercially viable operation.

The garden is a perfect example of a well-balanced and fertile vegetable garden. By using intercropping they produce the maximum amount of vegetables from a limited space. A 'no-dig' or 'dig as little as possible' policy is maintained to protect the bacterial and fungal populations within the soil and keep them in their correct places: aerobic organisms within the top 10 cm of soil, and anaerobic populations below this. To one side of the garden is a large chicken coop. The straw bedding, chicken manure and all the waste generated by the garden are composted. The food waste from the nearby Delta Café is added to a bokashi fermentation system (see page 69). When planting out seeds or seedlings, compost is added to the planting hole or drill. Struggling plants are watered with diluted bokashi 'tea'

"Dedicated committed volunteers from the community are like gold, and it is a struggle to find them. For those who do spend their time in our garden, it is a fulfilling exercise allowing them to reconnect with the earth, breathe fresh air, listen to the birds, insects and river, and be still and at peace in our busy, hurried, modern lives."
Daniella Alexander, REEA

to enrich the soil with organisms, increasing breakdown of organic matter and improving water retention.

No insecticidal sprays are used as these destroy beneficial insects, which are the food source of the predators. A healthy balance exists between 'good' and 'bad' with very little damage occurring to the vegetable crops. Snails, cutworms and slugs are eaten by the resident birds, frogs and 'Parktown prawns' or, when found, are fed to the chickens. Fungal diseases are controlled with a 50:50 milk and water spray, and sometimes a weak solution of bokashi 'tea' (a 1:200 dilution).

Daniella shares her considerable knowledge by running organic food gardening workshops. REEA also hosts children's workshops and school groups, introducing them to recycling, nature and life cycles. Every year a well-attended Home-grown Vegetable Exhibition and Scarecrow Festival is held, where local vegetable growers compete with their produce. For the last couple of years I have been invited to judge the Best Scarecrow and the Best Vegetables on show. This isn't an easy job, as the tables are packed with glossy, healthy vegetables – proof that Daniella's green fingers are spreading into the community.

URBAN HARVEST EDIBLE GARDENS

1.

2.

Ben Getz began growing herbs in his early teens, when he developed a passion for creativity, both in the kitchen and in the garden. Ten years later, in 2003, he established his first fully fledged food garden as his contribution to a Summer Camp in Michigan, USA. By the time he had completed his studies back home in South Africa, it was clear that there was a growing demand and need for food gardens.

In 2006 he established Urban Harvest Edible Gardens, a social enterprise specialising in the installation and maintenance of beautiful and highly productive edible gardens in homes, schools and businesses. In eight years Ben and his team have installed over 260 unique organic food gardens in Cape Town and he has found a way to live ethically, doing what he loves best. "I have always wanted to live a meaningful life and make a positive impact in the world, to improve people's lives. Urban Harvest provides people with an experience that is deeply nourishing and brings a unique and improved quality to home-time, family-time and food-time."

Ben believes people need 'time out' from their busy work lives and the constant buzz of technology. He has seen how people are nourished when slow-time is spent with nature, growing their own food. When it comes to school gardens, finding enthusiastic and involved leaders who are truly proactive and motivated is the most important element for success. He ensures that every garden is well positioned and well designed, resulting in beautiful, user-friendly, highly productive and inspiring gardens. Each new garden is pampered with plenty of good-quality compost and a variety of organic soil conditioners. Ben recommends using a mix of chicken manure, molasses, gypsum, seaweed and bone meal. Mulching both pathways and beds is fundamental. Establishing earthworm farms, composting units and liquid fertiliser barrels all ensure ongoing soil fertility.

The school gardens are funded by corporate social investments and part of these funds go towards training people to maintain them. An essential element in the sustainability of the school gardens is identifying a dedicated Garden Champion who is ultimately responsible for the day-to-day running of each garden. Resources are topped up until each garden is able to develop these on site. Wherever possible, upcycled materials are used, such as Ben's favourite reclaimed roof tiles. Wine bottles are another inexpensive and useful edging material he uses. Urban Harvest provides an 'Edu-maintenance' service, working with the Garden Champions on a monthly basis and training them through the seasons to become expert food gardeners. They gain skills, an income and an increased sense of worth as they help to feed hundreds of learners every day.

1. A sandy site before planting
2. Raised beds made using empty wine bottles, and tyres filled with fertile growing medium
3. A flourishing vegetable garden, protected by a shade cloth roof and plenty of mulch

> **"These are fully organic 'micro-farms'. The produce that we grow is used to educate the class in nutrition and food preparation."**
> *Brian Joffin*

SIYAZAKHA PRIMARY SCHOOL GARDENS

Brian Joffin has been growing organic vegetables and teaching people how to do so too for more than thirty years, both in South Africa and at thriving community gardens in England. He is currently involved in a number of community and educational gardens in the Western Cape and Gauteng. "Many food gardening projects do not last long, for various reasons. My main concern is to try to establish food gardens that flourish and thrive for years. These are, after all, really little farms. And farms go on for years, even hundreds of years."

One of his more recent projects is at the Siyazakha Primary School in Philippi, outside Cape Town. There, he is teaching a group of about 25 children, aged 11 to 14, how to grow a variety of crops. Brian feels that the project is successful largely due to the enthusiastic participation of the teaching staff, in conjunction with the SAEP (South African Education and Environment Project). The head teacher is fully committed and she has sourced funding from government to employ an excellent full-time gardener. One of the other teachers, together with an SAEP representative, works with the children in the classroom and in this way the lessons learned in the field are reinforced.

Brian designed the garden and plans the rotations and planting, setting the standards for this productive 'micro-farm' and ensuring that they are achieved. He also works continuously at improving the food garden's sustainability, by demonstrating how it can produce its own seeds, plants and compost.

Brian's aim is for the teacher and an SAEP representative to take over the full management of the garden in time. "I would then step back into an 'extension officer' role, monitoring, mentoring and being available to help solve difficult issues. Even old productive farms need this kind of support." The successful school garden is inspiring and other schools in the area are now using it as an example to start up food gardens in a similar way. Brian's hope is that there will eventually be a thriving urban food gardening culture in schools and communities in the Western Cape.

TYISA NABANYE

Situated on the slopes of Signal Hill in Cape Town is a flourishing and beautiful community garden. *Tyisa Nabanye* means 'feed the others' in Xhosa, and this garden is living up to its name. Within a year of being established it had grown enough food to feed its core members and their families, with sufficient surplus to donate to those in need and to sell at a bi-weekly market. The success of this garden lies in the commitment, dedication and knowledge of its core members. It was founded as a collaboration between passionate food security activists and community members. They all bring different skills to the garden, resulting in a balanced and effective team.

Both Mzu Zele, the head gardener, and his friend and co-founder Lumko Ningi, learned about growing vegetables from their grandparents when they were young. When an advertising colleague showed Lumko an available piece of unused land on military ground in Tamboerskloof, he and Mzu knew they had found a perfect place to start a community urban farm. With a third friend, Unathi Dyantyi, they started planting and Tyisa Nabanye was born. Within a few months Lizza Littlewort, who had been involved in the Oranjezicht City Farm from its inception, heard about the flourishing project and offered to share insights from her experiences. Catherine Nicks, an Urban Planning Masters student, joined soon after. They brought organisational and marketing skills. Volunteers began helping at the farm and a market was started where young entrepreneurs are invited to sell their products, ranging from pancakes to fresh vegetables. They have also started a nursery to propagate most of their own seedlings.

On their first birthday, fruit trees and hundreds of seeds were planted by volunteers, who also helped clear beds to make way for more vegetables. The organisation aims to become a model of sustainable living, by composting and recycling their waste, making use of whatever materials they can find and by eating the food that they grow.

The Tyisa Nabanye team is passionate about inspiring others to do the same. The group is using its influence to show youngsters that "gardening can be a cool thing". Two of the members come from a performing arts background and their lively shows in the barn help educate the community. And it is working – other residents who live in the area have been inspired to start growing their own gardens. Their advice to anyone starting a community garden is to consider the sustainability of those gardens. Proper training and ensuring that there are people in place to maintain the gardens will help them to succeed.

"The best part about what I do is imparting the knowledge I have to other people."
Mzu Zele, Tyisa Nabanye

Tips for Starting a Community Garden

- **Do some research** and speak to others who have experience. Almost all gardeners I know are willing to share information.
- **Define the roles and goals of the garden.** What motivates the project? Is it a social and community-based garden? Will there be educational aspects? Is it for food security or economic gain? Before you begin, all the members must lay out their project goals clearly to ensure that everyone has similar expectations.
- **Define the scope and size of the project.** Is it a short-term, one-season project or much longer term? Include in this assessment the physical aspects of the site, such as its size, soil, access to water, slope and climate, as well as the surrounding neighbourhood and its influence and involvement in the project.
- **Specify the type of garden and what it will contain.** Will it be purely a food garden for a feeding scheme, or will it be a commercial garden supplying herbs, vegetables and microgreens to select retailers? Include in this section an outline of what the design will entail (raised beds, pathways, containers, greenhouse, recycled elements). Include a list of plants you plan to grow, including long-term plants such as fruit trees.
- **Organise the people.** A committed group of core volunteers is essential, as a garden requires daily work. Make a list of everyone participating and include their level of gardening expertise and other areas of useful knowledge and contacts. Elect a project manager and a steering committee. Specify the roles of all members.
- **Draw up a project plan.** Take an inventory of the material, financial and human resources you have. Create a calendar, listing the planned phases and what resources each stage will require.
- **Contact all stakeholders and potential sponsors and funders.** Inform anyone who needs to know about the garden and if necessary get any permission required. You might be pitching the idea to people who are resistant, so put together a well-prepared presentation that shows all the benefits and plans of the project.
- **Use social media** to organise, communicate and promote your garden. Allocate this task to one or two members of the team. Photograph, document and share all stages of progress. The higher your visibility, the more volunteers and support you will attract.
- **Recycle and reuse** everything that comes your way.

Other Community Gardening Ideas

- Find a neighbour or relative who is willing to give you a corner of their garden in exchange for some of the harvest. Look for someone close by. If you have to travel miles to tend your garden, it won't happen.
- We often have far more seed than we can use. Set up a monthly community seed swap or a central seed swap location. A library is often a good place. Encourage everyone to divide their seed into small labelled envelopes, easy for swapping.

- Seedlings are usually a better price when bought in larger quantities, but we don't necessarily have space for them all. Gather a seedling-buying group in your area and share seedlings. This is great for gardeners with small spaces.
- If you have excess harvest, swap with a neighbour who has something different. This can be planned in advance, increasing the selection you all have available. Neighbours can also help with processing the harvest. One person can gather all the basil to make pesto, another makes the plum jam and the produce is shared.
- If you have always wanted an organic vegetable garden but simply don't have the time, pool resources with some neighbours to train and employ a dedicated vegetable gardener to rotate amongst all your gardens.

CORPORATE FOOD GARDENS

Much of a city dweller's time is spent at work, and for many of us that means in office buildings. Whether you work in a multi-storey high rise, an office block or a converted house, there is sure to be a space somewhere to grow vegetables. (If a rooftop is the only option, have a look at page 156 for more.) If your reason for not having your own vegetable garden is because you are too busy at work, perhaps you will be inspired by these corporate-sponsored gardens to initiate one at your workplace. As you will see from the following gardens, a corporate vegetable garden is far more than just about growing organic food.

DIS-CHEM'S VEGETABLE GARDEN

It is hard to believe that the flourishing vegetable garden adjoining Dis-Chem's head office in Midrand was once an open site that all the builders in the area used as a dumping ground. Penny Stein, who heads up the Dis-Chem Foundation, is the energetic founder and project manager of this garden, which began in 2013. After only a year, the concrete and rubbish had been replaced by rows of beans, chard and onions.

The Foundation is the beneficiary of Dis-Chem's loyalty programme. Every time a membership card is swiped, a percentage of the purchase goes to the Foundation's beneficial causes. It was through her work with the Foundation, where she was exposed to so many people in great need, that Penny was motivated to start a food garden. Inspired by a friend who had begun growing vegetables on her pavement, Penny decided to do the same – but on a bigger scale. "I looked at this piece of land and thought, why don't we create a food garden?" There was some resistance but Penny is the kind of person who brings solutions to the table, not problems. And very soon work on converting the site began.

Everything that was needed to create the garden came from the site or surrounding area. When preparing the beds, unearthed stones were used to form the pathways. Larger stones were stacked to create a rockery, now filled with herbs and companion plants attracting bees, butterflies and other beneficial insects. Topsoil was brought in from a building site nearby, and neighbouring stables supply plenty of manure. Penny sought advice both from farmers and the organisations the garden now supplies with fresh organic vegetables. "We have 25 feeding schemes that come every week to collect food. They are rotated, so everybody gets a share." In one year 35 different types of vegetables have been grown and more than 5 000 people have been fed regularly with healthy organic produce. The garden also supplies the canteen at the Dis-Chem head office, right next door.

Contributing to the garden's success is Jeanette Spence, the on-site manager of the garden, overseeing everything from the planting, harvesting and rotation plans, to managing the 15 full-time staff who work in the garden. "These were previously unemployed people from the surrounding area who we have trained. I have worked in many departments at Dis-Chem, from reception to HR. Now I manage the garden full time and I love it," says Jeanette. Although she had no previous farming experience, her enthusiasm combined with her good management skills led to her becoming the respected leader of this hard-working team.

On the day I visited, Swiss chard, onions, leeks and beetroots were being harvested. As they were washed and bagged, Penny told me about the future plans. "We still have plenty more space and we are dividing

that into allotments. Members of neighbouring communities, including the densely populated townships of Diepsloot and Ivory Park, will be given training, tools and seedlings to grow vegetables." These allotment gardeners will be encouraged to do more than just grow food for their families. They will be given advice on marketing their wares and skills, and the Foundation will provide information on preparing the produce to ensure maximum nutritional benefits.

"If you can use your skills to help others and to teach others, it is most probably the best gift you can have in your life."
Penny Stein, Dis-Chem Foundation

ROGZ FARM

"Your average director would jump for joy when a big deal goes through; I am more excited about the granadillas creeping into my office window. I believe that if people are content and happy in their work environment, they will produce excellent results."

Paul Fuller, Rogz Farm

Omuramba Business Park in Montague Gardens, Cape Town is an unlikely spot to find a pile of pumpkins or baskets of freshly harvested spinach. But at the Rogz factory, fitted between the palisade and aluminium siding, are rows and rows of carrots, Swiss chard, cabbages, tomatoes, onions and beetroot. Pumpkins trail out of their allocated spaces and spill into the parking lot, and the face brick wall of the Rogz head office is covered with trellises, which are rapidly being overgrown by granadillas. Apple and lemon trees line the edges of the parking lot, and boxes of potatoes are being harvested. This thriving urban farm in the middle of an industrial area is the brainchild of Paul Fuller, co-founder and director of Rogz, a company that makes gear for pets.

"Food, and growing food, has always been my passion," says Paul. "I studied farming at Stellenbosch and I love growing healthy organic things for my family and I always rushed home to enjoy my vegetable garden. It was a dream to provide most of my family's vegetables, fruit and herbs from my home garden. This proved to be a challenge space-wise, so I decided to start gardening in the industrial space around our business and incorporate my home lifestyle at work."

Paul's plan of using under-utilised space to extend his home garden quickly grew into something much bigger and Rogz Farm began. It now involves all the staff in one way or another. "Each member receives a compost bin that they fill at home and empty into our compost heaps. This assists us with our organic strategy, keeping the ground fertile and nutrient-rich."

The farm is 100 per cent organic and is tended by a small team of full-time gardeners, headed up by Farmer Williams. His mantra is something I relate to, "Soil, soil and soil … and make sure you prep your soil properly!" He maintains soil fertility through composting and mulching and is planning to add a large-scale worm farm soon. He prevents pests and diseases with companion planting, and keeps the crops strong as pests target weaker ones. His daily routine includes an early morning walk through the garden. "Eyes and hands are essential gardening tools. Early morning observation and critter removal is a great method of pest prevention. And occasionally some vinegar and a little soap. As the farm is in a built-up factory area, rats and mice can become a problem, but owl boxes are the solution – an owl can eat 1000 mice per year."

The garden produces a range of produce that is harvested weekly. "We have a market day every Friday," says Paul. "Working with 200 employees, various cultures and eating habits determine what we plant. It's important to cater to all their needs, and to grow what they like and can use. We also want to encourage them to adapt to an organic healthy way of living. The real heroes are the members of our kitchen team, who prepare food from the garden for 200 staff on Fridays."

The running costs of the farm are still partially funded by Rogz, but the aim is to make the project self-sustainable. "There is a growing demand for good-quality organic produce at a reasonable price," says Paul. "Products are harvested to order and purchased by both internal and external parties. Some of our customers include feeding schemes, schools and organic shops."

The reaction to the garden has been phenomenal. "People stop outside all the time and ask questions about what we are doing," says Paul. "They are amazed and very interested. Most people connect very strongly with food growing."

The farm's ethos is spreading to the neighbouring communities. "We are currently working with eight under-privileged schools to create urban organic vegetable gardens where the gardens support the food kitchen." And it is not just local communities who are benefiting. "We export Rogz products to 65 countries," says Paul, "and I believe we can get some of our partners to follow suit. Rogz Australia has already taken up the challenge and has developed its garden."

Paul's Tips for Setting Up a Corporate Vegetable Garden

- Keep it simple, fun and innovative.
- Have a key person, who is passionate about food and growing, driving the project. If you intend developing a large garden, you will have to employ or assign dedicated farmers.
- Start small with one square metre at a time; that way it's not daunting.
- Prepare the soil properly and start with hardy, easy-to-grow plants such as cabbage, spinach and tomatoes.
- Buy a few trays of seedlings from your local nursery to get started. This is expensive, so eventually find a local commercial seedling grower and buy in bulk.
- Start with seedlings, and then move to sowing seeds.
- Ensure you have access to water.
- Keep the integrity of your current garden, farming in between key structures and hero plants. This way no one is offended, the place always looks well maintained, and you don't get wind erosion.
- Involve all your team members on different levels – farmers, chefs, market staff, compost collectors, consumers and marketers. This way they all participate in the spirit of the project.
- Brand your produce.
- Keep it organic and promote the benefits associated with living healthily.

CATERING GARDENS

A recent surge in garden-to-table dining, with restaurants establishing productive vegetable gardens to supply their kitchens, means unique and interesting flavours are finding their way onto restaurant tables across South Africa. Apart from the obvious benefits of cost, convenience and sustainability, a restaurant garden provides the opportunity for creative collaboration between chef and gardener, resulting in diners being introduced to unusual new vegetables, freshly-picked microgreens and exotic flavours.

EATING ETHICALLY

Many people think that because I have written a best-selling book on growing vegetables, I must be a vegetarian. I am not. Although I do eat meat, it is seldom centre stage on the plate. That space is reserved for vegetables, with the meat providing the chorus.

However, I am a conscious carnivore. If I am going to eat meat, I want to know that the animals lived a contented healthy life, so I source my meat from ethical, organic growers.

Luckily there has been an increase in the last few years of farmers and suppliers who specialise in free range chickens, grass fed cattle, and pigs that spend their lives snuffling happily for acorns or wallowing in mud. If it is a little more expensive, well we just eat less of it.

If we choose to be carnivores, then we need to wake up and make informed decisions about the type of meat we are buying and eating.

BABYLONSTOREN

Situated in the heart of the Cape winelands, Babylonstoren is leading the revolution of garden-to-table dining. The eight-acre garden provides more than 300 varieties of edible plants and vegetables for Babylonstoren's two restaurants, Babel and the Greenhouse. Although this garden's name harkens back to the mythical gardens of Babylon, one of the seven wonders of the Ancient World, it feels more like the Garden of Eden. Inspired by the original 1652 Company's Garden in Cape Town, it was designed by architect Patrice Taravella of the well-known garden Prieuré d'Orsan in France. Liesl van der Walt, head gardener at Babylonstoren since 2010, recalls how "the beauty evolved from the ground up. Long before the plants that now steal the show, the structure for the creation was in place, with every line drawn with sense and purpose."

Walking through the garden, Liesl points out some more unusual varieties, such as the Braeburn apples, colourful prickly pears, stripy tiger figs and Turk's turban pumpkins. All these and more stimulate Maranda Engelbrecht's creativity. She is the author of the sumptuous *Babel* cookbook and a leading force behind the restaurant. "Every pick is unique and not a single item is wasted. The combination is always unpredictable with the journey of discovering something different every day. The health and well-being of the plants rubs off on me and I have to pinch myself to be reminded of the privilege of creating fresh from the garden."

Babylonstoren has established itself as a must-see destination and provides inspiration for those who grow and others who just enjoy the tranquillity, magic and being close to nature's bounty. During their daily garden tour the gardeners share stories of the farm and their growing experiences. And after the walk visitors enter Babel to experience a meal that has journeyed from seed to harvest in this extraordinary garden. Babel's trademark red, green and yellow salads are a symphony of flavours and textures, grouped according to colour. Maranda's simple and unique interpretation of dishes makes the most of their fresh ingredients and opens diners' eyes to seasonal, organic and local eating.

Liesl keeps the garden organic by "being hands-on and loving the garden daily. Seeing when plants are stressed and responding quickly. Also not expecting the garden to be perfect, but balance it with enough to harvest while the chickens and tortoises also have a bite." For me, one of the highlights of this garden is the endless array of espaliered fruit. From angled fig tree trellises to apple tree fences, every effort has been made to utilise all the spaces to grow edible plants.

An ongoing challenge for the gardening team is to ensure a constant supply of fresh produce for the kitchens. "We are firstly a garden that brings joy to visitors who walk through it touching, smelling, picking and tasting different varieties," says Liesl. "We harvest fresh every day for our restaurants, which luckily can adapt to what is available, but also buy in from local suppliers to supplement seasonally as necessary." She and her

"My inspiration is simply my love for cooking from the garden. The sense of smell, touch and taste. The perfection of harvesting and collecting. The imperfection of shape and size, free to grow the way nature intends."
Maranda Engelbrecht, Babel

team liaise regularly with the kitchens to determine their requirements, but they also have plenty of freedom to select seasonal vegetables for cultivation. "We always grow as many varieties as we can find and the new unknowns are often a surprise challenge for experimenting chefs."

Liesl's advice for any restaurant wanting to begin a garden is "to put energy into the ground with good soil preparation, compost and drainage. Plenty of sun is essential and chefs who love to harvest are a bonus!"

THE SAXON

In Johannesburg, David Higgs, executive chef of the Saxon Boutique Hotel's 'five hundred' restaurant, is making use of an extremely productive rooftop garden to bring fresh flavours to diners' tables. It all began when he was hunting for good-quality fresh produce. "As a chef, I am very specific about the ingredients I use in my kitchens and I only source ingredients from local farms and speciality purveyors to ensure that our guests can enjoy the best products we can offer." While on this quest he met Linda Galvad of Sought After Seedlings (see page 46). When David discovered a disused vegetable garden on the roof of the hotel's parking garage, he knew it was what his kitchen needed and immediately commissioned Linda to rejuvenate the abandoned garden.

"We were shown the existing rooftop area, which was largely barren except for the gum poles delineating the beds," says Linda. "We set about creating a beautiful, eye-catching garden that would be both practical and aesthetically appealing. A special place where you could lose yourself and enjoy the wonder of a garden." A few years later and the garden is all that and more. They use organic principles such as crop rotation, companion planting, soil health and excellent seeds, resulting in a garden filled with herbs, vegetables and flowers, pulsating with life and colour. In line with the organic philosophy of recycle and reuse, the garden includes a worm farm and compost heap, so the organic waste from the kitchen nourishes the garden.

It is obvious from the menu that this abundance inspires David and his team. "Almost the entire menu is harvested from our organic garden, save for protein items. For my team and me, the highlight is creating a menu that reflects their emotions, passions and inspired ideas, all with an effortless simplicity. When in the past we would have sat around the table and created a dish based on the protein source available at the time, now we walk through the garden to find vegetables that we can centre an entire dish around. For me, this is truly exciting. There is something inspiring about finding unique ingredients that are in season and creating a menu around those ingredients. Just this week we found the most delicious ripe green tomatoes, and created a delectable green tomato soup with garden beans and tarragon, and decorated the dish with the flowers from the beans." David emphasises that he wants his food to be approachable, "I want it to be the best quality, taste and texture without being pretentious. My philosophy is simple – use ingredients that people understand, use the best techniques and remain focused on the smallest details."

Linda's selection of vegetables in the garden includes many unusual varieties, typically not available from vegetable suppliers. These include leaves such as black kale and ten different types of tomatoes. As people become more aware of the need to reduce their carbon footprint and return to seasonal, organic eating, they are looking for restaurants

"Creating these dishes is the ideal way to showcase the ethos of the kitchen and our pride in the produce we harvest on the roof. When food is grown with respect, picked at its peak, served close to its source, and prepared with care, the finished plate is a culinary experience that nourishes and satisfies on many levels."
David Higgs, The Saxon

that serve locally grown produce. And it doesn't get any better than a restaurant that offers vegetables grown from their own garden. Says David, "There is no denying that once you have tasted the difference between organic and non-organic vegetables, you won't look back. It is evident that people are starting to become more aware of what they are eating and where it originates."

THE COMPANY'S VOC VEGETABLE GARDEN

"Heavy drizzle in the morning and a strong north-westerly wind blowing in from the sea. Today the first two ripe Dutch apples were picked in the Company's nursery garden." So said Jan van Riebeeck in April 1662, tasked with establishing a permanent supply station at the Cape of Good Hope on behalf of the Dutch East India Company. The result is the oldest garden in South Africa, with its first seeds having been planted in 1652 by Dutch master gardener Hendrik Boom.

And now, three centuries after vegetables were initially grown in the gardens on the fertile slopes beneath Table Mountain, they are back. The City of Cape Town has restored part of the Company's Garden to its original purpose by establishing a large vegetable and herb garden.

Roy Phelan, the Company's Garden manager, is passionate about the project, with aims to develop it into a significant historical garden and tourist destination. From the ground up, its history has been woven into this garden. "The design is based on the quadrilateral design of the original Company's Garden," says Roy. "This era of landscape design in Holland was known as the 'Dutch Baroque' period and emphasised classical lines of axis but also served practical functions in the context of producing fruit and vegetables." These included a *lei-water* system of flood irrigation via channels using run-off water from Table Mountain, and planted screens to protect crops from wind and animals. "Historical drawings and archive material indicated what the garden used to look like in this era (1652 to 1700s) and these were used as informants for the modern design and interpretation, right down to the finer details, such as the edges of the beds, where Table Mountain sandstone cobbles have been used for the borders."

The rejuvenation of the garden has seen an accompanying reinvention of the tea garden. The creative Madame Zingara team, renowned for their innovative eateries, has created a nature-inspired oasis in the middle of Cape Town's buzzing urban metropolis. And with the abundant VOC Vegetable Garden providing them with daily vegetables and herbs, the food is as fresh as it gets. As chef Jody Carolus says, "The excitement of fresh fruit and vegetables gets my imagination going at 100 miles an hour. It gives me the ability to see what fruit and vegetables can be, as opposed to what they are. Like a basic carrot could be a luscious, velvety purée with a hint of cinnamon." Keeping up a constant supply for the restaurant's popular salad bar means Roy plants on a rotation basis so that half the garden is ready to harvest while the other half is growing on. He liaises with Jody and crops such as green beans, interesting lettuce varieties, root vegetables and onions are planted with the salad bar in mind. The planting changes seasonally, with more root vegetables in winter and salad greens in summer. Jody loves the fact that he is able to see an ingredient grow from seed to plate and then to be served to a happy guest.

The fresh bounty is a reminder that the seed of Cape Town itself began in this vegetable garden. It also awakens people to seasonal eating. "Eating seasonally connects us to the earth and its seasonal changes. We are part of the cycles, but that is easy to forget if we eat only packaged and processed food. Eating organic, seasonal foods makes the changing cycle of the year more tangible and keeps one in touch with the natural world," says Roy.

Roy, a horticulturist with 34 years of experience, is committed to the garden being 100 per cent organic. He grows companion plants to encourage pollinators and inhibit pests, and uses organic pelletised chicken manure for fertiliser. He does not use pesticides but depends on manual control of pests and a daily maintenance programme.

This well-designed and functional vegetable garden is also being utilised as a resource to exhibit and teach urban farming skills. "Food is the most basic of needs and in these hard economic times most people can benefit from taking a look back at how things were done before the advent of supermarkets, and to experience the rewards of harvesting one's own produce," says Roy. "The Company's Garden aims to showcase this, by turning back the clock to simpler times." Schools and community groups are taught about herbs and their medicinal properties and how they can be used for entrepreneurial enterprises, such as candles, oils and soaps. Excess garden harvest is sold at the Oranjezicht City Farm market and at the VOC Farmer's Market, which provides an outlet for other community gardens and market gardeners to sell their produce, pickles and preserves.

Roy believes that no matter how big or small a restaurant is, there is always an opportunity to either grow herbs in containers for culinary use, or install larger containers to at least grow fresh garnish greens such as basil, marjoram, mint, spring onions, rocket, Swiss chard, thyme and the like. "Growing fresh vegetables can only improve the fresh and seasonal produce a restaurant can offer."

ALL CREATURES
GREAT
AND SMALL

What would an urban farm be without some livestock? As much as I love the idea of a sheep replacing my lawnmower, it is not a practical choice. But there are other options for urban dwellers. Aquaponic systems, which combine fish tanks and growing vegetables, are becoming increasingly poplular. And many urbanites are discovering the joy of keeping a few chickens or having their own honey on tap. These are all low maintenance and add tremendously to the quality of life in the city.

URBAN AQUAPONICS

Aquaponics is the combination of fish farming and hydroponics (growing vegetables in water). On their own they have their downsides, but combined they fit together like a jigsaw puzzle. In a hydroponic system, expensive nutrients are added to the water to feed the vegetables. And in aquaculture, the system has to be flushed regularly to keep it clean and maintain the correct pH balance, resulting in a wasteful loss of water. By combining hydroponics and aquaculture, the highly nutritious fish waste provides a rich food source for the vegetables, and the vegetable roots in turn provide natural filtration for the water.

Aquaponic systems are rapidly becoming a practical and water-wise choice for urbanites. This efficient way of growing vegetables uses 95 per cent less water than conventionally grown vegetables, and the systems are easily adapted to different environments. A small unit can fit on a balcony or a much larger operation can supply a restaurant with both protein and fresh vegetables.

SETTING UP AN AQUAPONIC SYSTEM

The two aquaponic systems used most commonly are the raft-based and media-based systems.

The Raft-based System

Plants are grown in polystyrene rafts that float on long channels of water about 40 cm deep. The fish are housed in separate tanks. The nutrient-rich effluent water flows continuously from the fish tanks via a biological filtration system, through the raft channels, and back into the fish tanks. Seedlings are placed in perforated pots that are sunk into holes in the polystyrene rafts and, as they grow, their roots dangle freely in the fertile water below. Air bubblers in the channels oxygenate the water for the plants. This is a stable and productive method of aquaponics, used in most commercial set-ups.

The Media-based System

For home gardeners, this is a common choice. Water is pumped from a fish tank into an equal-sized container above it called the grow bed. This is filled with an inert medium. The water trickles down through the medium, which acts as a bio-filter, past the roots of the plants and back into the fish tank. The most commonly used medium is expanded clay or shale pebbles, which are organic and sustainable. They are fired at an extremely high temperature, resulting in a medium that is pH neutral, with a good balance of both air and water, keeping the roots oxygenated. The clay provides an ideal surface for both roots and beneficial bacteria that live in the growing medium.

Other Components

Bacteria are essential in aquaponics. Fish give off ammonia in their urine and their gills. If this builds up in the water, fish will die from ammonia toxicity. However, nitrifying bacteria (in the grow bed of media-based systems and in the filtration area of the raft system) convert poisonous ammonia into nitrites, then nitrates. This keeps the fish happy and converts the ammonia into a form that the vegetables can absorb. Chlorinated water should not be added to an aquaponic system as this will kill the nitrifying bacteria.

Red wiggler worms (see page 70) can be added to aquaponic systems (to the grow bed of media-based systems or to the filtration area of the raft system). They effectively break down the solid fish excreta, excess roots and other debris and convert them into fertile nutrition for the plants. They also reduce the amount of maintenance as the beds do not require as much cleaning. As they breed, they can be fed to the fish, creating a self-sustaining cycle.

The most commonly used fish in aquaponics are tilapia because they are easy to breed, are not too fussy about their water and convert feed very efficiently into body mass. The fish need to be fed regularly with a balanced fish food. At Valverde Eco Hotel in Johannesburg, a large aquaponics system provides vegetables for their restaurant. Here they grow masses of comfrey, which the fish love. They are also fed water hyacinth, an alien plant that is infesting our rivers.

Most vegetables will grow in an aquaponic system, but root vegetables such as carrots, potatoes or sweet potatoes are not suitable. Companion planting also applies, so include some nasturtiums and other beneficial plants. Vertical supports can be added, allowing tomatoes, cucumbers, beans and other rambling plants to grow upwards.

RIGHT: A local company Cibio has developed a home aquaponic system that is simple to set up and run. It is ideal for small spaces.

OPPOSITE: Microgreens growing in the Valverde Eco Hotel's aquaponics system. These are cultivated for their restaurant – they grow quickly and need to be harvested often.

URBAN CHICKENS

I first came across the concept of a 'chicken tractor' in *Mother Earth* magazine, an American publication with great information about living lightly on the earth. Chickens are housed in a moveable hutch that is transported regularly to different areas of farmland. There they scratch out and eat all the greens, weeds and bugs, loosening the soil and fertilising it. The chicken tractor mimics the birds' natural foraging habits, where they move on from one area to another once they have finished eating. The hens need little supplementary feeding and they live a free range, happy hen life.

I loved the idea of it, even if I didn't live on a farm. It took a few years between reading about it and making it a reality, but one winter we built the chicken tractor. Well, Keith hammered and sawed it together, with a bit of "hold this" and "pull that" help from me. After looking at plenty of designs we decided on an A-frame shape, with a covered double-storey section on one side for egg laying. This would maximise the amount of ground space the chooks would have. We decided to make it using as much recycled material as possible. We had solid wood from a fence we had taken down a few years before, although it was more difficult to work with than purchased wood, as it was quite uneven, making it harder to fit all the bits together. In the end the only things we bought were staples for the staple gun and a little bit of chicken wire to add to the scavenged sections. The end result is a lovely, rustic-looking hen house. The space is big enough for two happy hens, Itchy and Scratchy, who provide us with about 12 large eggs a week.

My plans of moving the hutch and using it as a proper chicken tractor didn't materialise. We landed up making quite a bulky and big hen house, which proved to be too unwieldy to move regularly. They now live permanently under the bay tree. I let them out every day for a supervised scratch around the garden, while I clean out their run. They can be very destructive and can decimate an entire bed of newly germinated seedlings in a few seconds, so I do keep an eye on them.

ABOUT HENS

Hens are forest dwellers, spending their days scratching through thick undergrowth or having a dust bath in a dappled sunny glade. They lay their eggs in a dark spot, hidden under a bush, using dried leaves and undergrowth to create a comfy nest for their chicks. At night they fly up into the lower branches of trees to roost, safe from predators.

Hens are social creatures, congregating naturally in groups and communicating to one another with a range of noises. You will learn to recognise a hen's distinctive language quickly, from the excited, "I laid an egg! I laid an egg! I laid an egg!" announcement, to the enticing chuckle

of, "Come, come, come, come," inviting her friends to share in a juicy find. It helps to replicate these noises if you want to communicate with your hens, especially if you want to cajole them back into their run.

The phrase 'pecking order' originates from hens. This is a natural process where hens work out a hierarchy among themselves. It is not so obvious with only a pair of hens, but as soon as you have a flock, you will see the stronger hens being more dominant. Most often hens will work it out themselves. It can involve a bit of bickering and fighting. If a bird is injured and bleeding, it is best to remove it until it heals. Hens are drawn to blood and will keep pecking at another hen's injury. When introducing new hens to your flock, separate them but keep them adjacent to the others for one or two weeks. This way they can see and smell one another, without risk of injury. When you let the new hens out, provide some hiding places for them, and add a couple of feeding and watering stations, and some extra roosting spots.

HEN HOUSE

In a chicken coop we need to replicate hens' natural environment as much as we can. There are many creative solutions to providing a home for them: an old car, a child's unused jungle gym or an abandoned dog kennel can all be converted into hutches. Whichever design you choose, you need to include the following.

A nesting area
This needs to be a darkish area filled with a deep bed of hay and herbs (artemisia, catnip and feverfew all repel mites in hens' bedding).

A ramp ladder
This should extend from the ground to the second level. A wooden plank with evenly spaced horizontal slats screwed into it works well. Don't make it too steep otherwise larger hens will battle to climb up.

Roosting poles
These should be round and about as thick as a broomstick. Branches work best, as these replicate a hen's natural perch of low hanging tree limbs. Position them securely about a metre above ground. These need to be in a warm spot that is sheltered from the wind. Hens don't mind getting wet, but they dislike wind and cold.

Space for them to move around
Allow at least a square metre per hen.

Comfortable access
You will need to clean out the coop regularly so make it as easy for yourself as possible. On our hutch we have two access points. One is on the nesting area (for collecting eggs and cleaning) and the other provides easy access to the ground level for cleaning, feeding and watering.

Shade from the sun
Hens are forest birds and will overheat quickly if they are in full sun for too long.

A chicken coop keeps the hens inside but also protects them from being eaten by predators. Depending on where you live, these can include baboons, eagles, monkeys, genets, dogs and cats. Certain dog breeds will co-exist happily with hens, our German shepherds being a good example. The only interest they have in the hens is following them around to see if they can hoover up any droppings! Other breeds, such as terriers, will go for hens naturally, but can be trained not to. Our cats also leave the hens alone – they are large birds with claws that can do a lot of damage. But if a visiting marauder were to get into the run, the hens would come off second best. To prevent your hens from becoming a chicken dinner for a

predator, batten the coop down securely so they can't get in underneath. Keep the doors securely latched at all times.

FEEDING, CLEANING AND CARING

My daily routine with the hens is quite simple. After letting them out I clean their run, removing fresh manure with a rake and evening out the remaining compost and leaves. This maintains their forest floor environment. The manure is piled into a bucket and dumped into one compost pile. I then fill the bucket with a combination of compost from another pile (they prefer it when it is half decomposed as there are more insects), fresh vegetables, greens and a selection of whatever insects I find on a walk around the garden. Depending on the time of year, these include snails, slugs, grubs, wood lice, termites, aphids and worms. I get to know the hiding places of these and have become a very efficient *gogga* gatherer. The fresh ingredients are seasonal and include Asian

greens, carrot tops, comfrey, beetroot leaves, bulbine, grass clippings, ice plant (sour fig), leaves of broccoli and cauliflower plants that have been harvested, lettuce that has gone to seed, mustard, Swiss chard, sunflower heads, weeds, wild strawberries and other fruit.

Once the bucket is full, I call the hens by making clucking noises and banging the bucket. They come running and flapping to see what I have brought them and go back into their run happily. The compost and greens provide them with plenty to scratch through for the rest of the day. I supplement their greens and grubs diet with kitchen scraps and non-GMO seed mix (see page 40). They love scraps like pawpaw and melon pips, egg shells, vegetable peels and stale bread – the more variety the better. If I am going to be in the garden for a while and can keep an eye on them, I let them out for longer, sometimes fencing off an area where I don't mind them scratching for a few hours.

In their run is a water tower, which delivers fresh water on demand. This is checked every day to see if it needs cleaning or refilling. The bottom of the run is open, giving them access to earth. This is essential for hens who love nothing better than a good dust bath to keep their feathers clear of mites. Another thing hens love is wood ash – mites will run a mile when they encounter ash and hens know it. (Don't use ash from briquettes, as they have additives.) I keep all the ash from our winter wood fires and mix it with river sand to prevent it blowing away. I add this regularly to a corner of their run, where they have hollowed out an area for their daily beauty bath.

Their nesting box is piled with thick hay mixed with dried leaves and herbs, such as lavender, rosemary and tansy, to prevent mites. A more recent addition to my hens' nesting box is dried papyrus fronds. After watching the weaver birds harvesting these from my wetland pool, I thought they would work well as nesting material and I was right. The hens twist the papyrus fronds efficiently into a perfect nest circle. Every winter, when the papyrus dries out and needs to be cut back, we harvest about two thirds of the 'heads', leaving the remainder for the weavers. The nesting material is cleaned regularly and replaced when it becomes too soiled. Every evening I cover the top of the coop. Hens don't mind wet weather but they don't like wind. I have two layers of covering – shade cloth to block the wind on summer nights and a large, recycled canvas for cold winter nights. In areas where it goes down below freezing at night, they need a warm, covered shelter.

EGGS

One of the first surprises from my hens was the eggs they produced; the yolks are a dark orange, rather than pale yellow, as a result of all the greens they eat. Each hen lays up to six eggs a week. Production does slow down during winter when the daylight hours are shorter.

BROODY HENS

If you leave eggs in the nesting area, you run the risk of a hen becoming broody. If this happens, it is difficult to change that hen mind-set. Once, when I was away, my house sitter didn't remove the eggs often enough and I arrived back to a broody Itchy. Unfortunately egg production dwindled to a halt. A broody hen doesn't lay eggs and Scratchy went on strike in sympathy for her broody friend. She made a show of going into the nest box, but stopped laying altogether. A duck farmer, who sells her products at the local farmer's market, suggested I dunk Itchy, head and all, in icy water. I'd read that chilling the nest box down might break a broody hen and had tried putting frozen cooler box blocks in her nest. (It didn't work – she just gathered them under her until they warmed up.) So this ice-water-dunking idea sounded like it might work. However, I couldn't do it. It just seemed so mean. I mentioned it to my gardener Hlonipani, hoping he might be able to do the deed, but his response of, "Oh, the poor hen," suggested otherwise.

So I followed other advice, kicking her off her nest as often as possible and closing off access to it. This meant having the hens running loose in the garden – not a great idea as they can be destructive blighters, eating young seedlings and uprooting plants. The other animals weren't happy with this arrangement either. A broody hen can be a terrifying creature. The dogs quickly learned to give way after a few sharp pecks on their noses. The cats learned the lesson too. I saw white cat Mao tearing across the garden with Itchy, puffed double her size, in hot pursuit. Having eyes only for Mao she tripped and tumbled head first down a bank, a feathery ball of anger.

One morning, after I chased her off the nest, she fluffed herself up and made a cluck-clucking beeline for the wetland pool. She squatted down next to it and drank deeply. She had never done this before. I discovered that Hlonipani had attempted the water bath treatment using the pool. But he just couldn't bring himself to dunk her entire body and had only dipped her feet in the water – hence her newfound drinking knowledge. I realised that hens do not learn by observation – Scratchy followed Itchy to the pool each morning but just watched as she drank her fill.

A few mornings later I was in the bedroom when both dogs suddenly looked up at the window. I stuck my head out and saw water splashed out onto the side of the pool. Dashing out I saw it was Itchy – floating on the pool looking just like a duck, except that she couldn't paddle or get herself out. Her wings were not strong enough to lift her fat body up the side. Keith fished her out with much splashing and squawking and that was the last time we ever saw her drink from the pool. And within a few days she began to lay eggs again.

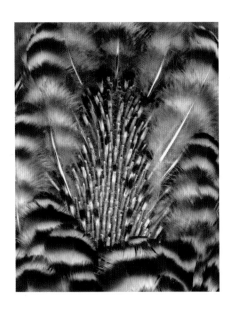

The new feathers that grow through after moulting are called pin feathers. It can be painful for a bird to be handled while this is happening.

Eggs should be removed from the nest every day, otherwise the hens may become broody (see page 211).

When a hen lays an egg, the last stage after the shell is formed is to 'spray paint' it with a protective covering. In a hen's natural cycle, the eggs would stay in the nest for a week or so until she has laid enough to begin sitting on them. The shell is porous and any faeces in the nest could be absorbed, hence the protective covering. (Sometimes you will find an egg with tiny balls clustered on one side of the shell. This is when the covering didn't spread properly.) As long as eggs are unwashed, they do not need to be refrigerated and can keep at room temperature for a few weeks.

As soon as an egg is washed or refrigerated the protective layer is compromised and it will need to be kept in the fridge. I keep my eggs in a bowl on the counter and every day, when I collect the new eggs, I pencil the date on the shell to keep track.

MOULTING

Hens will shed some or all of their feathers periodically. This can be quite shocking for a new hen owner, but moulting is part of their natural process. It usually happens in autumn and takes about six weeks to two months for the new feathers to grow back. (This can be painful for the hen, so be gentle when handling her.) During this time, they stop laying. Feathers are mostly protein and it takes too much out of them to produce both eggs and feathers. You can boost a hen's protein by giving her some cat pellets every week while moulting.

TYPES OF HENS

Bantams were an integral part of my childhood. The many incarnations of Henny Penny followed me from my toddler years to my teens. When troops of cheeping chicks were trailing Henny Penny, Taffy, our German shepherd cross, would herd them through the garden and help them down steep stairs. Her fluffy tail waving above a flowerbed was an indicator of where the mom and chicks might be found.

It is a cute idea to buy chicks, but they will require good care and attention until they reach laying age. With most breeds it is difficult to tell whether they are roosters or hens when they are babies, so you might land up with mostly roosters and few egg-laying hens. In urban areas it is preferable to have only hens, as the roosters start crowing loudly, very early in the morning. This does not make for happy neighbours. Hens do not need a rooster to lay eggs. It is best to buy young hens about 18 to 19 weeks old. These are called point-of-lay pullets. Look on the internet to find suppliers near you and also check with your nearest animal rescue organisation. They often have hens looking for good homes.

When I was deciding on what hens to get, I considered bantams. They are far less destructive than large hens, are very efficient insect eaters and can be left to run free around the garden. However, they have very small eggs. And I wanted big eggs. So I chose larger breeds: an Australorp and a Koekoek. The Australorp, as its name suggests, originates from Australia. With black feathers that shine almost purple in the sun, it is docile and hardy, laying large eggs. The Potchefstroom Koekoek is a hardy South African breed. With speckled black and white feathers they are a handsome birds and good layers, with eggs slightly smaller than the Australorp's.

Other breeds to consider are:
- **Boschveld:** This hardy indigenous breed developed from crossing three other local varieties. The hens have russet feathers with variations of white splotchy patterns and are good layers.
- **Rhode Island Red:** A handsome, dark russet red, this is an American breed. They are good layers, but they can be a bit aggressive to other hens and will quickly become top of the flock.
- **Venda:** Another indigenous breed, this pretty hen has speckled black, white and brown feathers. They are good layers and hardy hens.
- **Hyline:** These hybrid hens are one of the top layers. Hardy and sociable, they do well in an urban run.
- **Buff Orpington:** These large friendly hens, with caramel coloured feathers, are very adaptable and lay large eggs. They can do a lot of damage to the garden though, so keep them contained.
- **White Leghorn:** These pure white intelligent hens make good pets. There are many types of leghorns, but the white is the best layer and hardly ever goes broody.

Free-range bantams are a good choice for vegetable gardens as they are far less destructive than their larger relatives.

COMMON AILMENTS

By keeping the chicken run clean and uncrowded, the risk of disease is minimised. Sniffles and sneezing can be treated by adding a few drops of eucalyptus essential oil to their water. Mites are repelled by the hens having regular dust baths and by adding herbs such as artemisia and tansy to their bedding. If mites do become a problem, diatomaceous earth (see page 56) will sort them out.

An Alternative Approach

Jacques Damhuis installs biodynamic edible gardens and teaches people about nutrient cycles and sustainable food gardens. His business is aptly named Positive Cycle. He lives across the valley from me and in his productive garden is a permanent hen house with mostly hybrid Hyline layer hens.

In their multi-layered run, Jacques has created an ingenious balanced ecosystem. "The hens' perch has been placed above a ring wormery, where the worms process the droppings that are deposited in and around the area. The manure is raked up into the wormery every day, keeping it filled as the chickens scratch through it constantly. It is also watered daily to keep the worms happy, as they need the moisture to process the manure. This also ensures that there are no bad odours because the worms deal with the microbes that create odours and replace them with beneficial microbes that make everything smell like a forest. The chickens do eat some of the worms, but not all. The worms lay their eggs in the wormery and the chickens eat these too, but again not all of them, thank goodness."

The hens are in a multi-layered area with one layer consisting of a tray of barley grass, re-seeded regularly so that the chickens always have fresh grass to eat. "They love this dearly and watch it sprout. As soon as they can reach the blades, they start to nibble. This process lasts about three weeks, until there is not much left."

Jacques provides a natural forest floor environment for his birds, which they love. "The floor area is most important, as the hens spend most of their day here. You need to pretend you are in the forest and provide leaves and other garden waste for the chickens to scratch in. Watering it each day ensures that the beneficial microbes can deal with any chicken droppings." This creates a natural cycle, where the microbes help to control the waste naturally. Fungus and bacteria will use the dry leaves and the nitrogen-rich chicken manure to turn the garden litter into compost quickly. Little insects and worms are attracted to decomposing matter and help make compost and then they become lunch for the hens during their daily scratch and find.

Jacques feeds his hens with a non-GMO chicken feed that he mixes. The selection is based on a scientific formula, choosing seeds with a high nutritional value to meet the needs of hens that are laying daily. He adds additional beneficial microbes to the feed. "Probiotics are crucial in everyone's diet, and keep the intestinal flora in peak performance to assist digestion. To supplement their nutritional needs I also add minerals for both the chickens and the microbes."

Jacques' final bit of advice for hen owners? "They do love fresh vegetables and weeds, so share your salad with them. And love your chickens. They are affectionate and respond well to petting."

URBAN BEEKEEPING

Bees and their magical sweet honey have featured prominently in myth and storytelling from the beginning of humankind. Bees might have had a long relationship with humans, but in the last decade their numbers have been diminishing at a frightening rate. In South Africa, bees are facing a threat called American Foul Brood Disease, a bacterial infection that decimates a hive and can easily spread to other hives. In the United States, bees are disappearing due to an unexplained condition known as Colony Collapse Disorder. Whether these bees are dying due to pesticides, cell phone signals or disease has yet to be determined, the reality is that they are disappearing. Although we could survive without their honey, we cannot survive without the bees themselves. Albert Einstein supposedly said, "If the bee disappears off the surface of the globe, then man will have only four years of life left. No more bees, no more pollination, no more plants, no more animals, no more man."

So where does that place us as gardeners? Simple – we should do as much as we can to ensure that we provide happy homes for bees.

A LESSON IN BEEKEEPING

My friend Duncan Guy encouraged me to start keeping bees in a proper beehive. A swarm of bees had set up home in a pillar in my garden, a little too close to my back door for comfort. Duncan's father Robin had been one of the first professional beekeepers in South Africa and Duncan had some of his old beehives in storage. We positioned one of these next to the pillar, with some honey as incentive. But the bees refused to budge. It was my first lesson in beekeeping – if bees are happy in a home, they dig in their heels. And even if they are evicted by being smoked out, they prefer to choose a new home themselves. The forced removal to their new beehive home lasted a few days before they swirled away in a buzzing mass.

A few weeks later we tried again. This time with a swarm that had set up home in my yoga teacher's electricity box. Duncan suited up and smoked them out, making sure he had the queen. This swarm of bees settled into their new home and lived in my garden for a few years. Then we had builders in and while they worked, we moved the hive outside. It was only for a couple of days but it was long enough for someone to spot and steal the hive – even though we had hidden it under branches.

I purchased a brand new hive, set it up and waited. And a few months later – on my birthday – a new swarm moved in and has lived happily in my garden since.

ABOUT BEES

Approximately twenty to eighty thousand bees live in one hive, working and living together in a complex, harmonious and ordered social group. At the heart of the hive is a single queen who spends her life laying eggs. There are a few hundred drones, the male bees, whose sole purpose is to try to mate with the queen on her maiden flight. Unfortunately for the ones that succeed, they die in the process. The queen stores the sperm from her single flight and ekes it out over the next two to three years of her existence, laying fertilised eggs and keeping the hive supplied with bees. The bulk of the hive is made up of worker bees; infertile females who divide up the work of foraging, creating honey and wax comb, feeding the queen, protecting the hive and nursing the brood.

The foragers are the ones we see most often in our gardens, busily collecting pollen and nectar. On its return to the hive, a forager passes the nectar over to a household bee who places it in her honey stomach. She spends about twenty minutes regurgitating and swallowing droplets of nectar, slowly drying it in the process. The honey stomach also contains enzymes that change the chemical composition of the nectar. When it is ready, she deposits the honey into a wax cell and it is fanned by worker bees until its moisture is further decreased, preventing fermentation. Once it reaches the correct consistency the cell is sealed with a wax cap. These hexagonal cells fill up steadily to make honeycomb, a waterproof and airtight storage area of food for the honey bees during cold, wet or dry times when they can't access nectar. It takes eight bees their whole life span of about six weeks to make a single teaspoon of honey.

One of the worker bees' jobs is to keep the hive waterproof and secure. To do this they seal any gaps with propolis, made from a mixture of resins collected from trees and buds.

BEE TALK

Bees have a complex system of communication, using pheromones to convey messages of alarm, stimulate and co-ordinate activity, regulate the population and guide foraging bees back to the hive.

In addition, they have a fascinating ability to communicate using dance moves. When a foraging bee discovers a good source of nectar or pollen, she is able to tell her sisters exactly where and what the food source is by performing a series of precisely choreographed dance patterns on the honey comb.

BECOMING A BEEKEEPER

Beekeeping is a fascinating hobby and is easy to learn. In main urban areas there are courses available, covering the basics of how to maintain a beehive and harvest your own honey. If you are wary about donning a bee suit and doing it yourself, there are many hobbyist beekeepers who will manage your hive in exchange for a share of the honey (see page 251).

Setting Up an Urban Beehive

There are urban bylaws that apply to different areas, so read up on these beforehand. The first step is to install a hive. Although bees can never be tamed, a hive is a way of containing them in a man-made structure, allowing easier access for the beekeeper to harvest honey. A hive mimics a wild hive, making bees comfortable and encouraging them to set up home and begin making their honey.

There are many different types of beehives used around the world but the most common is a design that was developed by an American reverend in the 1800s called the Langstroth beehive. It consists of a number of stacked rectangular boxes with a lid.

The largest box at the base is the brood box, where the queen lives and lays her eggs, and where the babies are born and fed. Above this are two or three shallower boxes, called supers. The supers are filled with removable frames that the worker bees fill steadily with wax honeycomb and honey. Separating the brood box from the layers above is a mesh grid called an excluder. This prevents the queen (who is larger than the other bees) moving from the lower brood box up into the supers and laying eggs in the frames there. This ensures that the honeycomb in the supers remains free of bee larvae, as it is this clean honey that we harvest.

A new colony of bees will need at least a season to build up a large enough population to start producing surplus honey. Once this happens, you can begin harvesting. How often you harvest depends on various factors – the size of your brood, the amount of nectar nearby and the weather can all influence how much surplus honey will be available.

Bee Gear and Equipment

When you become a beekeeper, you will find that there are a few pieces of equipment that will make your life easier.

- **Clothing.** The first essential item you need is a bee veil. Don't try using a makeshift mosquito net tucked over a hat – it doesn't work. And I speak from bitter experience. Next, depending on your budget, you can buy a full bee suit, a specially designed bee jacket, or simply use an overall. Finally, gloves and boots. When working with bees, you will soon discover that they will find any open gaps and it is vital that you seal off your neck, wrists and ankles. A full bee suit is a great option as it comes with a detachable veil plus wrist and ankle bands. If using an overall, seal your wrists and ankles well with rubber bands.

- **A hive tool** is an all-purpose tool that is used for opening hives. Bees seal the lids that close their hives extremely well and these need to be pried off with the hive tool. It is also useful for lifting frames and scraping off propolis. If you have the option, buy a brightly-coloured one. You are usually working with bees in dim conditions and it is easier to see if you drop it.
- **A bee smoker.** Every time you work with bees – either to inspect the hive, or to harvest honey – you need to smoke the hive (see below). A bee smoker is a simple but effective tool to create and direct smoke where you need it.
- **A soft brush** – to remove bees from the frames.
- **An uncapping fork.** This looks a little like an afro comb but is a tool used to scratch the dry wax cap open, exposing the honey inside so it can be spun out.
- **A honey extractor** spins the frames, using centrifugal force to remove the honey from the uncapped cells. Extractors range from small manual units to large electric ones. An extractor is probably the most expensive part of a beekeeper's kit and is only worth buying if you have a number of hives and intend to process quite a bit of honey. A better option is to make friends with a beekeeper and borrow an extractor for a weekend in exchange for some honey.

Harvesting Honey

A frame is ready to be harvested when more than 90 per cent of its cells have been filled with ripe honey and have been capped. Much as we want to harvest the honey – so the bees want it to remain in the hive. They will protest most strongly if you simply open the roof and remove a frame. This is where a smoker comes in.

Smoke has been used for thousands of years to control bees. However, it is only recently that we are beginning to understand why. Firstly, if a beehive is threatened, the guard bees communicate this to the other bees using pheromones. However, when cool smoke is blown in, it dulls the guard bees' receptors, preventing them from sounding the alarm. Secondly, smoke signals a fire and the bees' instinctive reaction is to gorge themselves on honey in case they have to flee. This makes them sluggish. Plus, with fat tummies, it is more difficult for them to curve their abdomens into the stinging position.

The fuel used inside the smoker varies. You want to use material that will burn slowly and create cool, non-toxic smoke. We have used hessian or pine cones, both of which work well. It is preferable to work with bees after sunset – this is when they are all back in the hive and are more settled and docile.

BENEFITS OF HAVING A BEEHIVE

'Making a beeline' is a phrase that was coined by someone who knew bees well. There are certain areas of my garden where I need to move quickly – if I stand still in the regular flight path of the bees, they become tangled in my hair. The closer to the hive, the more obvious the buzzing line of bees becomes. When bees find a source of nectar or good pollen, they don't mess around and will head straight for it.

One of the first benefits of having a beehive is knowing that I am providing a home to insects that are beneficial, not just to my garden but to the greater neighbourhood. Bees are crucial to our food chain, pollinating plants while they forage for nectar and pollen. One bee can visit up to 5000 flowers in a day. If you watch a bee next time you see one in the garden, you might notice fat yellow or orange balls on her hind legs. These are cleverly designed pollen baskets, made from long curved hair. When she heads inside a flower, a static charge causes pollen to jump from the flower onto her body. As she hovers above the next flower, she uses her front legs to push the pollen into the baskets. But some remains on her body and this pollen will be transferred to the next flower, pollinating it in the process. We can thank bees for pollinating at least a third of our food plants.

Secondly, there is the honey. One beehive can produce more than twelve litres of honey during the summer. Honey's therapeutic properties have been known for thousands of years. Externally its anti-inflammatory and antimicrobial abilities help heal wounds, burns and fungal conditions. Internally its cleansing and antioxidant properties heal colds, flu, coughs and sore throats. It is particularly effective in treating pollen-related allergies – especially if treated with locally produced honey. My bad spring hay fever was vastly reduced after I began eating a daily teaspoon of honey produced from my own garden. Honey is a beneficial addition to bitter herbal teas, not only sweetening them, but also adding to their healing power.

And finally there's beeswax. A by-product from the honey harvest, beeswax was one of the earliest products utilised by humans. It was used as a sealing and waterproofing agent for houses and boats; to make candles for lighting; for coating wooden writing tablets; in cosmetics and herbal preparations; and as a modelling agent for everything from sculpture and jewellery moulds to dentistry. It is a healthy natural moisturiser, used in body lotions, lip balms and face creams. It works well in skin products because it contains compounds called wax esters, which also exist in human skin. Its healing and antiseptic qualities benefit the skin too.

When mixed with borax, beeswax is an emulsifying agent used to mix oils and water together into a smooth cream. Its melting point is 62 to 65 °Celsius. It should be melted using a double boiler, or a bowl set over a pan of simmering water. It is ideal for making candles, as it is very slow-burning and gives off a lovely honey scent.

Dos and Don'ts Around Bees

- If attacked by a swarm of bees, don't jump into water – they will wait for you to surface and sting you on your head. If you do jump into water, surface with your shirt held over your head. Or find the nearest bushy shrub and push your way into it, brushing the bees off yourself.
- Don't attempt to move a swarm without expert help. Call someone as soon as you find a swarm – the longer you leave them to settle, the more difficult they will be to relocate.

- Avoid use of perfume or scented body lotions around bees. Strong scents attract them and incite stinging. This includes the smell of perspiration, so avoid going near your hive when you are hot and sweaty.
- Be careful of using lawn mowers, weed eaters and cell phones near a hive, especially in the height of summer. The frequency and vibrations can make the bees think they are under attack and they could become aggressive.

- Always work with bees after dark, when they are more docile.
- If you are stung, remove the sting as quickly as possible as it will continue to pump venom into your system even after the bee has flown off. Don't pull a bee sting out – this will just squeeze more venom into your skin. Rather scrape it off using a finger nail, a blunt knife or a hive tool.

CREATING A BEE-FRIENDLY GARDEN

Bees can forage up to eight kilometres from their hive, but their lives are made much easier if we provide food for them closer to home by creating a bee-friendly garden. Even if you don't have a beehive, there are some simple things you can do to attract bees to your garden.

- Never use toxic chemical pesticides – they kill bees!
- Reduce hybrid flowers. These have been bred to encourage features such as larger flowers or disease resistance, but often hybridisation results in a reduction of nectar and pollen – which is what bees eat.
- Grow a wide range of plants offering a succession of flowers and therefore nectar and pollen throughout the year.
- Leave herbs and vegetables to flower.
- If you live in a particularly windy area, provide a sheltered spot with flowers for bees.
- A bee-friendly garden is not neat and manicured – it is rambling and haphazard with variation in height and types of flowers.
- Plant similar flowers together in large clusters as this will provide bees with a one-stop shop.
- Bees prefer to sip from moist soil. During dry weather create a 'drinking hole' by filling a saucer with wet sand and sinking it into the ground near the hive.
- Provide plenty of nectar flowers in winter, such as aloes and red hot pokers.

Plants Bees Love

If you can see the middle of a flower easily, it is a good bee attractor. Single-petal flowers, such as marigolds and daisies, provide easy nectar. Aloes, alyssum, borage, bottlebrush, coneflowers, coreopsis, cosmos, fruit trees, lavender, moonflower, poppies, purple ribbon bush, sage, salvia, squash flowers, sunflower, verbena, Virginia creeper and zinnia are a few of the plants bees love. Another favourite tree is the gum tree, or eucalyptus. Many of these have been removed as they were identified as invasive aliens. However, more recently, the regulations have changed to acknowledge the importance of gum trees for honeybees. There are now provisions for gum trees to be demarcated as 'bee-foraging zones'.

HONEY TRIVIA

- A hive of bees will collectively travel over 170 000 km to gather 1 kg of honey.
- Honey takes its flavour from the nectar that it's made from and ranges widely in colour and taste.
- Farmers pay commercial beekeepers to bring hives onto their farms to pollinate flowering crops. The resulting honey takes its essence from the crop, producing flavoured honeys, such as apple blossom or lavender.
- Honey, as long as it is kept in an airtight container, never goes bad. Two-thousand-year-old honey found in Egyptian tombs still tasted delicious.

URBAN ECO
CONVERSIONS

There are many ways inventive urban farmers can create, utilise and maximise both their space and time. Effective eco conversions can contribute significantly to reducing our carbon footprint and increasing our self-sufficiency. Here follow some examples of how to do this. Although not limited to the city, these methods and ideas are particularly suited to urban gardeners.

NATURAL SWIMMING POOLS

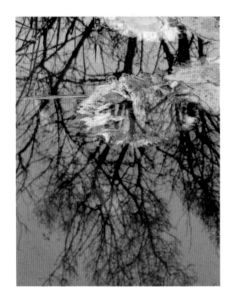

When we moved into our house, there was a sparkling blue pool. With the first summer storms it turned green almost instantly. So began an ongoing battle involving pool testers, chemicals with scary warnings in their fine print, and endless visits to the pool shop to have the water assessed. I have always been sensitive to chlorine. As a child who loved swimming, my eyes would stay an impressive tomato colour almost all summer long. As an adult, this has worsened. I don't even need to dunk my head under water for my eyes to go red; just standing in a chlorinated pool will make them sting. A salt pool isn't a solution as it still produces the chemical chlorine. When, at the end of one summer, our pool developed yet another leak in its buried pipes, we covered it up, and it remained under wraps for three or four years.

Summers seemed to flash by and we were always too busy travelling or doing other things to start digging up paving. Until Tosca arrived. A cute bundle of white puppy fur, who soon spotted the puddle in the middle of the trampoline-like pool covering. It took her about two seconds to bite her way through the netting cover to explore the trampoline further. And the games were on. She would romp through the puddle from one side to the other, splashing and biting the water. And it wasn't good enough to have one entry point. She soon chewed three or four holes so she could hop in and out wherever she chose. This was all fine while she was a pup – but 30 kg of fully grown German shepherd began wearing the edges of the trampoline away. We had visions of the cover tearing and our Tosca floundering and drowning. We uncovered the pool immediately. Surprisingly, the water was crystal clear. The sides were covered with black growth, but the water itself was lovely and fresh. And so the idea of a natural pool began to germinate.

At first I simply turned the pool into a pond by adding large pots of papyrus, bulrushes and other water plants. Four goldfish quickly multiplied into dozens. The pool became a beautiful reflecting pond, with the natural water attracting birds and other wildlife. But it wasn't brilliant for swimming. The plants kept the water semi-clear, but in hot weather algae would grow. And with the plants and fish, a mucky pond floor began to develop. If I wanted a clean swimming area it needed a bit more work. It needed to change into a natural wetland filtered pool.

HOW A WETLAND POOL WORKS

As more and more people are realising, harsh pool chemicals are unhealthy for us and for the environment. These chemicals are costly, especially when added to the rising electricity cost of the large pumps needed to maintain a chemical pool. A natural pool requires far less electricity, and all harmful chemicals are eliminated. Providing a pool of

fresh drinking water attracts wildlife, bringing nature into our gardens.

Wetland pools work hand-in-hand with nature to create clean, healthy water. Water is circulated between the swimming area of the pool and a wetland. The wetland, with plants, animals and substrate, filters and cleans the water, returning it to the swimming pool so clean and pristine that you can drink it. The mass of roots and substrate in the wetland section breaks down complex elements to more simple nutrients. These feed the plants, maintaining a natural cycle and creating a balanced ecosystem.

Architect Anthony Philbrick began exploring natural pools in 2007 when he wanted to build a pool for his four-year-old daughter. "A friend's daughter was allergic to chlorine and was battling because she loved swimming. I thought there must be some alternative. I was very into permaculture at the time and in Bill Mollison's book *Permaculture, a Designer's Handbook* there was a small section on a naturally cleaning pool. And this sparked the idea."

The first wetland pool Anthony built was his own. "I tinkered with it until the balance was perfect." Then a friend wanted one and then a friend of a friend. And so wetlandPOOLS began. It was a steep learning curve, as much of the information available was geared towards the northern hemisphere. Natural pools originated in Austria in the 1980s and the methods that work in a northern European climate do not work as well in our much harsher South African conditions. "We have thunderstorms on the Highveld that add nitrates to the water," explains Anthony, "and in the Cape, the water is much more acidic." Anthony has since created over 200 wetland pools, perfecting the art of using nature to purify the water.

WETLAND POOL DESIGN

When I first met Anthony he said, "A natural pool is much more of a gardening exercise than a chemical one." This resonated with me, as did the idea of emulating a natural rock pool. A wetland pool is divided into two areas – the swimming area and the wetland, with the water circulating continually between the two. The pool and the wetland can be the same body of water, or they can be partially or entirely separate. This creates wonderful design options as the two areas can be joined by streams or waterfalls on different levels, also aerating the water. The resulting water is so fresh, frogs and fish live happily in it. A natural pool can be built from scratch, with designs ranging from modern rectangles with decking and sheets of water, to natural flowing lines with rock stepping stones and trickling water. Or an existing swimming pool can be converted. These pools either have a separate wetland area added, keeping the original swimming pool shape and size intact, or the existing pool is divided in two, with the wetland being created within the swimming pool itself.

Creating a Pool Within an Existing Pool

Our pool was a standard rectangle, something I have never really liked, as all the shapes in my garden are natural and flowing. Instead of simply dividing the pool, I wanted to create a deep splash pool inspired by the rock pools in the rivers of the Magaliesberg, with a wide step for lounging in the water and flat rocks to bask on after a swim. Anthony, with his imaginative architect brain, jumped at the opportunity to create something different. He suggested we create an elliptically-shaped pool rising out of the shallow end, with a seat running all the way around the inside. Water would flow from the ellipse into the wetland below, which would be created in the remaining area of the pool. This would completely change the shape of the old rectangle and create a new and exciting shape and space. So we began.

1.

3.

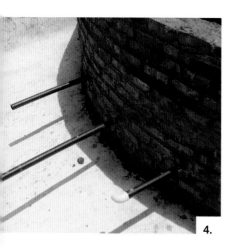

4.

THE CONVERSION

1. The pool was emptied and all the fish were caught and placed in a holding tank. (I make that sound a lot easier than it actually was.)

2. Anthony used ancient Euclidian geometric techniques to design a perfect ellipse in the shallow end of the existing pool.

3. The outer walls of the ellipse were built using bricks, with the inner step created with concrete and bricks. The walls rise 65 cm up above the edge of the existing pool, a good height for sitting on from the outside of the pool. In its centre, the ellipse is 1.8 m deep, ideal for dunking.

4. Three inlet pipes were laid into one of the lower courses.

5. When the ellipse was complete, the interior was plastered smooth. Two overflow gaps were left on the top rim – a larger one, where the bulk of the water would flow over into the wetland, and a smaller one to trickle over the opposite side. These were made as shallow as possible so the level of the water would be very close to the top, creating a feeling of abundance.

6. Cracks were fixed and the interior of the pool and the ellipse were acid washed and painted charcoal with waterproofing Hydro-Seal. We also covered up the existing blue tiles with Hydro-Seal, with the aim of removing as many traces of the original 'blue pool' as possible.

7. Suction pipes were laid out. These are large perforated black pipes lying at the bottom of the gravel to suck the water through the wetland. Large debris is filtered out by the gravel before it gets to the pipes. The pipes have tiny suction slits with parallel fins running the length of the pipes, preventing any smaller debris from entering them.

8. A 200 Watt high-flow submersible pump was installed inside a barrel, and a power cable was connected through the existing weir to electricity in the original pool pump housing. All the pipes were connected to the pump through holes in the wall of the barrel.

9. Anthony designed the pipe layout using a series of valves. By opening and closing these, we can adjust the level of the water in the ellipse. In summer we can have it full to the top, but in winter, when we don't want to swim, we can drop the level below the step creating a sunny, sheltered nook, with the water still circulating below.

10. Gravel was added to one half of the remaining area of the existing pool. Using sand bags filled with gravel, a bank was built to retain the gravel on one side. This created different levels, ranging from the original depth of the deep end, to a few centimetres deep, providing suitable environments for various wetland plants (see page 238). As the gravel was added, the pump barrel was positioned so its cover was level with the top of the gravel for maintenance access. Included in the gravel mix were pine

bark and calcium stones to maintain the pH levels of the water. Water lily soil was added to the deepest section of the wetland.

11. The original steps and gaps between the walls of the original shallow end and the ellipse were filled with gravel. All exposed pool wall area above the gravel and the interior of the ellipse were given a second and final coat of Hydro-Seal.

12. The exterior of the ellipse was clad in Latitude Stone's Autumn cladding to create the impression of a natural stone wall rising out of the water. Larger pieces of the same stone were laid on top of the ellipse. The final level of the two overflows from the ellipse were checked to make sure they were both the same height. We didn't want water flowing from one and not the other. The pool was filled with water using rainwater from my JoJo Tanks and municipal water. The entire system was tested.

13. Stepping stones and plants were added and the fish were returned to their pool after their holding tank sojourn. Although the water was murky in the beginning, within a few weeks it cleared. After a month it was crystal clear and has remained so ever since.

14. Having a natural pool is not just about the joy of swimming in fresh clear water. It has revitalised that area of the garden too, with birds splashing and drinking, dragonflies constantly hovering and dipping, and frogs croaking under the moonlight.

6.

10.

12.

13.

14.

Dividing an Existing Pool into Half Wetland, Half Pool

Instead of building a separate pool, you can divide your existing pool into a wetland and swimming area, using a wall. The principle is much the same. Water is sucked through the wetland via a weir built into the wall. This keeps the water surface clear of debris. Clean water is pumped back into the swimming area. Many of the details are similar to the previous method, but construction differs.

THE CONVERSION

1. Empty the pool and construct a dividing wall using stones inside gabions. This will separate the wetland from the swimming area, while allowing water to pass between the two. The design of the dividing wall can be curved or geometric, but must divide the pool in half.

2. Acid wash and paint the interior of the pool with either Hydro-Seal (for gunite pools) or cover fibreglass with a darker-coloured gel coat.
   Be warned: fibreglass often cracks when you drain the pool and all cracks need to be repaired before you continue.

3. Insert pipes through the lower levels of the gabion wall, to pump water into the swimming area. Install weirs in the top of the gabions. The gabion can be clad with rock with stepping stones on top of it.

4. Lay suction pipes in the bottom of the wetland area and connect all pipes to the pump in the pump barrel.

5. Divide the wetland into deep and shallow areas using a bank of gravel-filled bags or a gabion wall. Fill the shallow side with gravel, and place water lily soil in the deep area.

6. Paint a second coat of Hydro-Seal or gel on all exposed areas.

7. Position stepping stones along the top of the gabion wall.

8. Fill the pool with water and test the system. Plant with suitable wetland plants (see page 238 for some ideas).

1.

3.

5.

Retaining a Pool and Building a Separate Wetland

This option allows for many creative designs, as the wetland does not have to be adjacent or even near the pool. The only limit is that the wetland has to be the equivalent size of the swimming area for optimum cleaning. The best option is to place the wetland on the same level or below the pool, with a waterfall flowing from the pool into the wetland. Clean water is pumped back into the pool. If the property is on a slope, the wetland can be placed above the pool, with waterfalls and streams connecting the two. The water is pumped from the pool up to the wetland. Once it has filtered through, gravity returns clean water to the pool. Putting the wetland above the pool is more challenging. The process varies depending on the design, but the basic principles and materials are the same as the first two options.

Building a Wetland Pool from Scratch

Creating a new wetland pool provides even wider scope for creative design. Remember – the wetland must be the same size as the swimming area. When designing a wetland pool, bear in mind you don't need to place paving around it. The only reason for paving around traditional pools is because chlorinated water will kill grass or plants.

ADD SOME FISH

Fish are a wonderful addition to a wetland pool, helping keep it clean by eating algae and adding a meditative, calming element to the garden. Goldfish are hardy and can grow much bigger than their small-tank cousins once they are given more space. Koi are beautiful but are troublesome as they eat the plants, which reduces the functionality of the wetland. Tilapia are hardy and quick growing and, if you are so inclined, you can fish for your Sunday lunch when they grow big enough.

MAINTENANCE

Once the pool is established, the maintenance is much simpler than for a chemical one. It becomes more of an extension of gardening.

- Water is lost due to evaporation, so keep the pool topped up regularly.
- The above-water wetland plants need to be cut back annually.
- Leaves and debris that fall into the pool need to be removed.
- The bottom of the swimming area can be vacuumed once a month to remove dust, if necessary.

WETLAND PLANTS

The plant selection is a vital component of a successful natural pool. The wetland must provide a range of growing conditions allowing many different types of plants to flourish. A successful wetland is designed to accommodate a wide variety of plants, with a deeper water garden for surface-floating plants and underwater plants, plus a marshy area of above-surface plants. There are three broadly defined groups of plants utilised in natural pools, each having its own niche habitat and distinct function in the system. It is important to include all three groups for the wetland to function efficiently (see chart below for suitable plants in each group). Anthony recommends planting "a broad range of plant species, each having a slightly different nutrient requirement and growing in different ecological niches, broadening the ecosystem and making it more stable."

SUITABLE WETLAND PLANTS

TYPE	FUNCTION	PLANTS
Submerged, oxygenating plants (either rooted in the bottom of the water garden or free floating)	• First line of defence, competing directly with algae for water-borne nutrients • Add oxygen to water during daytime	• *Potamogeton schweinfurthii* (broad-leaved pondweed) • *Vallisneria spiralis* (tape grass)
Plants rooted in the bottom of the water garden (with leaves floating on the surface)	• Best suited for deeper sections of water garden • Create a microclimate for zooplankton	• *Aponogeton distachyos* (Cape waterblommetjie) • *Nymphaea* spp. (water lily) • *Nymphoides thunbergiana* (yellow water snowflake)
Plants rooted in the wetland (with leaves above water)	• Most comprehensive group • Occupies largest section of wetland and performs the bulk of the cleaning • It is advisable to include a wide range of plants in this area as they differ in what their roots take out of the water	• *Berula erecta* (water parsnip) • *Cotula coronopifolia* (golden buttons) • *Crinum bulbispermum* (orange river lily) • *Crinum campanulatum* (marsh lily) • *Cyperus alternifolius* (umbrella sedge) • *Cyperus papyrus* (giant Egyptian papyrus) • *Cyperus prolifer* (dwarf papyrus) • *Cyrtanthus breviflorus* (yellow fire lily) • *Gomphostigma virgatum* (river stars) • *Juncus glaucus* (blue rush – *J. effuses* and *J. kraussii*) • *Lobelia anceps* (swamp lobelia) • *Marsilea schelpiana* (cut-leaved water clover) • *Typha capensis* (cattail or bulrush) • *Zantedeschia aethiopica* (arum lily)

Yellow water snowflake

Water lily

Cape waterblommetjie

Marsh lily

Giant Egyptian papyrus and dwarf papyrus

Dwarf papyrus and water parsnip

HARNESSING SOLAR POWER

anging in the window of my office is a rainbow-maker. A small solar panel powers cogs that connect to a Swarovski crystal hanging below. As it revolves, it refracts sunlight slowly in all directions, creating rainbows dancing throughout the room. It is but a tiny example of the immense energy of the sun.

We humans have used the power of the sun for millennia, for heating, cooking and energy. Nearly 10 000 years ago, someone discovered that the heat of the sun was magnified when refracted through water or a crystal. And the heat created was strong enough to start a fire. Egyptians used mirrors to illuminate tombs and solar power to heat water. Legend has it that Archimedes used reflected heat from curved bronze shields to set Roman ships alight. Today, although we use more sophisticated technology, the principle is still much the same – the sun's heat and light are harnessed to produce energy for generating electricity and heating water.

Most of South Africa's electricity comes from coal-fired power stations. These pollute our air and use massive amounts of clean water to create electricity – in a country that experiences droughts and severe water shortages. Our existing power stations fail to supply electricity to all South Africans and struggle to maintain the supply to those who are on the grid. The solution is to switch to a renewable energy source such as solar.

The amount of solar radiation reaching Earth is enormous. In South Africa, we receive a high level of solar radiation, which is one of the most stable supplies in the world. Harnessing just eight seconds of solar radiation could provide South Africa with energy equal to our annual electricity consumption. In one hour alone, the sun provides sufficient energy to power the whole planet for one year. The sun produces far more energy than we will ever need – yet we are not using it. Solar energy is a renewable source that is freely available. It is durable and eco-friendly. By converting to solar, we reduce electricity costs and increase our self-reliance.

Harnessing the sun's power can range from simply placing coils of hosepipe in the sun, to using complex systems that convert the sun's rays into energy to power an entire house. From solar panels to pool heating, pumps to solar cookers, there are many forms of solar technology available to householders today. Solar energy is a rapidly developing field, with new technology being introduced constantly. I would recommend that anyone looking at installing solar, does some research into the latest technology.

SOLAR WATER HEATING

Electric geysers are one of the highest energy consumers in our homes and offices. Solar water heating is becoming an increasingly popular alternative. Even though technology has improved and prices are dropping, the installation cost is much higher than for an electric system. However, depending on your usage, this will have a payback period of four to eight years, by cutting up to 40 per cent off your monthly electricity bill.

Solar water heating utilises the sun's energy to heat cold water, using solar collectors usually placed on a north-facing roof. In some instances (such as with thatch roofs) they are free standing on mounting brackets. The solar collectors are connected to a water heating system.

Solar Collectors
There are two types of solar collector: flat plate and evacuated-tube. **Flat-plate solar collector panels** should not be confused with solar electricity panels, which convert the sun's energy into electricity. Flat-plate collectors consist of a heat-absorber plate and pipes circulating above it, enclosed in an insulated metal box with a clear cover. Solar radiation heats the absorber plate and the heat is transferred to the liquid circulating through the pipes. These are very efficient heaters in perfect sunny conditions.

Evacuated-tube collectors make use of newer technology based on the same principle as a hot water flask. Copper pipes, running through glass tubes with vacuum walls, capture and maintain the sun's heat. They are very efficient, with more than 90 per cent of the sunlight hitting the collector being transferred to the circulating water. They also function better in cold and windy weather, as the vacuum reduces heat loss. They are simple to install, need very little maintenance and are frost proof. However, many of the evacuated-tube systems are too efficient for South Africa, as our fierce sun can heat water up to 250 °C, which will damage a system unless safety valves are installed. There are local companies that are adapting these systems to suit our conditions.

Solar Water Heating Systems

There are also two primary types of water heating systems: direct and indirect. In a **direct system** the water that is heated by the solar collector is the same water that comes out of the taps. Heated water is stored in a tank that is connected to the existing water system. The direct system is often used when converting an existing electric geyser to solar, as it requires fewer add-on components and no modifications. It also takes less time to install, making it a cost-effective choice. However, direct systems are not suitable for areas where temperatures drop below zero, as the water in the pipes can freeze, damaging the solar collector. A direct system can be installed in colder areas if an evacuated-tube collector is used, as these are protected from frost because of the vacuum.

Indirect systems use heat transfer instead of direct heating. An anti-freeze solution, usually a mixture of water and glycol, is circulated between the rooftop solar collector (where it heats up from the sun) and a heat exchanger on the water tank (where it transfers its heat to the water in the tank). Some heat exchanges go through the centre of the tank, while others are wrapped around the tank. Indirect systems are used in below-freezing areas.

Solar geysers can be either gravity fed or pressurised. With gravity-fed systems, the tank needs to be placed relatively high up. All solar geyser storage tanks need to be well insulated to keep the water hot overnight or during cloudy weather.

SOLAR ELECTRICITY

Solar electricity generators contain solar cells to capture the energy of the sun and convert it to electricity. Solar generators work only when the sun is shining, and the excess has to be stored in batteries if you want electricity during the night or cloudy weather. Installations range from simple systems, which reduce the amount of municipal electricity consumed, or provide a small amount of back-up for power failures, to complex set-ups where you can be completely off the grid. Installing this type of solar system to power your home is a complicated process and it is best done by someone competent. Although solar power is free, the set-up costs aren't. The more you require, the more expensive it becomes. As technology improves these are becoming increasingly affordable.

Photovoltaic (PV) Panels

'Photo' means light and 'voltaic' means electricity and that's what these panels do: turn sunlight into electricity. Manufactured using pure silicon – a costly material – they are complex and time consuming to manufacture, with a resultant steep price tag. In 2005, after 13 years of research, Professor Vivian Alberts of the University of Johannesburg unveiled solar panels that utilise more efficient technology. Instead of using silicon, these panels make use of a semi-conducting metal alloy that enables the conversion of light into energy at a fraction of the previous cost. The alloy is only a few microns thick – about a quarter the size of a human hair – resulting in ultra-thin panels. CIGS (copper, indium, gallium, sulphur and selenium) panels are more efficient at utilising solar power in low light conditions and perform well in temperatures over 25 °C.

They are set to revolutionise the solar energy industry, as they take up about half the space of silicon panels and cost a quarter of the price to manufacture. A further advantage is that they can be used on both rigid and flexible surfaces, opening up possibilities for many applications.

In February 2014, following on from the successful research phase, a pilot production facility was opened in Stellenbosch to begin manufacture of CIGS thin-film solar panels. This will serve as a research facility to develop commercially viable CIGS modules for the market.

Installation

PV panels are placed on the ground or, for most residential installations, on a north-facing roof. They can be grouped together to create a solar array. The power a system produces is measured in kilowatt peak (kWp). To produce 1 kWp requires 8 m² of PV panels. The average weight of a PV panel is 25 kg/m². Before installing, check that the roof can handle the extra weight.

Converters and Batteries

Once you have installed a panel to capture the solar power, there are a few more steps before you can use it to make yourself a cup of tea. Solar cells create direct current (DC). Most home electrical appliances use alternating current (AC). An inverter needs to be installed to convert the DC to AC. The larger the amount of electricity it can convert, the more expensive it is. Solar power will be generated only as long as there is sunlight. If you want to be completely power independent, or use your solar panels as a back-up when municipal power goes out, the solar power generated needs to be stored in batteries. The more power you need stored, the more expensive the batteries are. The final piece of equipment is a charge controller, which prevents the battery from over-charging and being damaged, and also stops it losing power.

Grid Tied Systems

A solar electricity system can be connected in parallel to the existing municipal system and supplement the municipal supply. In a grid tied system, the electricity generated is converted and fed back into the grid, causing your municipal electricity consumption to slow down. If your system is producing more electricity than you can use, your electricity meter will turn backwards if it continues to be fed into the grid. Or the excess energy can be stored in batteries, but this is an expensive option.

For people with digital or pre-paid meters, the electricity meter cannot read which way the electricity is going and unfortunately sees the excess energy going back into the system as usage and charges you for it! Up until recently the only way to prevent this was to store the excess electricity in batteries. However, grid tie limiters have been developed, which control the power production to match the usage, preventing excess being fed back into the system.

All grid tied systems have to be approved by Eskom as it is illegal to turn meters backwards. The relevant forms can be found on their website. Eskom is working on a framework that will make it easier for small-scale producers to benefit from connecting to the grid.

Grid tied systems (without batteries) are suitable for households and offices that are using most of their electricity during the day, as they only operate when the sun is shining.

OTHER USES FOR SOLAR

Solar technology has many applications. A wide range of waterproof garden solar lighting is now available, from strings of fairy lights to lanterns. Solar water pumps for garden ponds, irrigation and boreholes are energy efficient and easy to install. They have a life span of about 20 years and need very little maintenance. Solar cookers range from small models that function as slow cookers, to exceedingly efficient ones with parabolic domes that can boil water in the same amount of time as an electric kettle.

CONVERTING A TENNIS COURT
INTO A VEGETABLE GARDEN

Flying over some of Johannesburg's gracious older suburbs, you look down on extensive well-established gardens, with huge trees, sparkling blue pools – and the obligatory tennis court. 'One family, one pool and one court' was the norm when they were established. These days, however, clubs offer well-maintained tennis courts and private ones are becoming increasingly neglected, with deteriorating surfaces, rusting fences and decaying nets. The owner of one of these is Cliff Rosen, who instead of maintaining a costly court, has converted his into an urban farm, replete with chickens, a large vegetable garden, a wetland pond and greenhouses.

It all began in 2009 with a simple question that he asked himself, "How do I grow food?" He looked at the court and realised he had the ideal place to find the answer. Tennis courts are perfectly suited for a vegetable garden. They are large, flat and smoothly surfaced areas that are most often in full sun. Instead of digging vegetable beds in a lawn area, and then having to construct pathways to deal with mud, the tennis court surface provides ready-made paths.

The first beds Cliff installed were raised beds placed on the asphalt, but this proved to be too hot. So he decided to cut into it and to dig beds. This was slightly more challenging than expected as he discovered two additional layers of clay court surfacing under the asphalt, all of which had to be dug out. But it was summer and the heat helped make the asphalt soft. With pickaxes, door-sized beds were dug into the court, leaving wide pathways in between. The beds were filled with compost and well-rotted manure, and effective micro-organisms (EM) were added to the soil as well. This is a mixture of cultured micro-organisms, consisting of a range of bacteria and yeast that improve both soil health and yield. "You can feel the energy of these billions of organisms at work. Even if you come down into the garden at night, they are busy." And the results are obvious. The abundance in this garden overflows the beds and literally climbs the walls, with squash plants scrambling up the old fencing and rambling over the top of a large chicken run in one corner. The chickens are let out of their enclosure regularly and fenced in over selected beds, cultivating and fertilising them naturally.

All the dug-up asphalt and clay was piled at one end of the court, and Cliff used this to create sloped walls for a large raised section at the end of the garden. Steps at either side provide access to the fertile beds at the top. This not only recycled the waste, but the elevated level creates interest in the garden. Cliff's 'waste not, want not' attitude is prevalent in this unusual and captivating space. A large bin used to brew fertiliser tea is supported by a recycled wrought-iron table frame – another elegant solution.

A few years into his gardening adventure Cliff had a huge setback when a devastating hail storm wiped out his entire garden. He then decided to put a shade cloth roof above it. The first cover he erected was a disaster. He made a flat roof and when the next big hail storm hit, the stones collected on top of the netting. "It was so heavy it just bent the poles." Luckily he was insured and the next roof was made with an apex and many smaller sections of supporting poles.

Cliff's tennis court conversion proved so successful that a friend asked him to do the same at the Sharp Treatment Centre, a rehabilitation facility in Oaklands. Then someone asked him to install a food garden at a shelter in Yeoville. And another in Soweto. So, after a few seasons, and a couple of permaculture courses, Cliff had not only answered his question of "How do I grow food?", but he realised this was what he wanted to do full time. He sold his business and, together with Jayson Fox, set up the Let it Grow Foundation. The Foundation installs commercial food gardens, with a large portion of the budgets being donated to the non-profit edible gardens they establish throughout Gauteng. Cliff also runs food-growing courses and gives lectures.

DOING IT YOURSELF

The average tennis court is about 200m² – enough room for a well-designed vegetable garden, an orchard and even a greenhouse. The rectangular shape is practical for a vegetable garden and can be enclosed with a fence, providing support for an edible creeper. A bountiful fence could be created using espalier fruit trees (see page 125). The tarmac surface of a tennis court will absorb heat during the day and release it at night, keeping the area warmer overnight than a regular vegetable garden, ideal for many heat-loving vegetables.

Working with an area as large as this can be intimidating and costly. The first step is to draw up a plan. This will include the size and position of the beds, trees and pathways as well as any structures. With the space available, options such as a water feature or a gazebo can be included. Having a well-designed plan will allow you to develop the garden, as time and budget allow.

For beds there are two choices: either cut out the surface to create beds, or place raised beds (see page 90) on top of the hard court surface. Cutting and digging will involve plenty of labour. Using raised beds involves the expense of constructing the beds out of a durable material and filling them with a good-quality growing medium. To reduce heat reflecting off the tarmac, cover the pathways with straw.

> **"This is what we do. We show people how to grow food."**
>
> *Cliff Rosen, Let it Grow Foundation*

CONVERTING LAWN INTO
AN EDIBLE GARDEN

Setting up a vegetable garden can be a daunting prospect, especially if you have never gardened before, or did not grow up in a gardening family. Although I only began growing things when I was in my mid-thirties, I didn't realise just how much information I had absorbed from my mother who has the greenest fingers I know. Converting lawn into an edible garden is a project that can be completed in one weekend and requires nothing more than willing hands and enthusiasm to get them dirty – and green.

When choosing a location for a vegetable garden we are looking for an area that receives at least six to eight hours of sunlight a day, ideally flat or on a slight slope. For most urbanites, this will mean an area with lawn growing on it. This is a good spot for a vegetable garden as grass is not a terrifically hungry feeder, meaning the soil below it will be relatively fertile. Also, when a lawn is mown and the blades of grass are cut, the below ground counterpart of the plant will balance out by sloughing off some roots. As a lawn is mown regularly, the roots are dying back regularly too and being added to the soil, creating a humus-rich environment.

Below are instructions to create a single raised bed. Even if you have space for more than this, rather start with just one if you are a beginner gardener. Once you have learned to manage this one, then expand and add more. I recommend covering the pathways, but you can leave grassed pathways so long as they are regularly maintained. To prevent the grass creeping from the paths into the beds, a barrier can be placed on the inside of the bed to block runners.

You will need
- Plenty of newspaper or cardboard.
- One cubic metre of growing medium (see page 92).
- A raised bed frame (or you can use stones, bricks or logs – see page 90 for more ideas).
- Material to cover the pathway (straw, mulch or gravel).
- A selection of seasonal seedlings.

What to do
- Measure out an area roughly the size of a door frame, 1 m by 2 m.
- Add an additional 90 cm on one side for a pathway.
- On the outside edge of the pathway, slice down with a spade, severing all the runners of grass leading into the area.
- Cut the lawn within the area as short as possible.
- Cover the whole area with layers of cardboard or newspaper, wetting the layers thoroughly as you go, until it is 1.5 cm thick. The aim is to smother the grass, so you want to block the sunlight completely.
- Cover the pathway with weed cloth, and place the raised beds on top of the edges, holding the cloth in place.
- Cover the pathway with straw, mulch or gravel.
- Fill the bed with growing medium, watering it in well.
- Transplant the seedlings and mulch the surface well.

By creating a vegetable garden on top of the grass instead of removing it, you don't lose any valuable topsoil. Earthworms and other organisms will convert the cardboard and grass into friable humus within a few weeks. If any grass does pop up, pull it out immediately. Adding an irrigation system (see page 72) will ensure your new vegetable garden is regularly watered. To maintain fertility, add organic matter such as well-rotted manure and compost to the surface of the beds.

Instead of mowing the lawn every week, that time can now be directed towards producing healthy organic food for you and your family.

BIBLIOGRAPHY AND RECOMMENDED READING

Beardshaw, C. *The Secret Life of the Garden* (Dorling Kindersley, 2009)

Bird, R. *How to Prune Fruiting Plants* (Southwater, 2013)

Bradley, FM (editor) and Ellis, BW (editor). *Rodale's All New Encyclopedia of Organic Gardening* (Rodale Press, 1997)

Collins. *Collins Beekeeper's Bible* (HarperCollins, 2010)

Creasey, R. *The Complete Book of Edible Landscaping* (Sierra Club Books, 1982)

Don, M. *The Complete Gardener* (Dorling Kindersley, 2009)

Flowerdew, B. *Complete Fruit Book* (Kyle Cathie, 2000)

Flowerdew, B. *Organic Bible. Successful Gardening the Natural Way* (Kyle Cathie, 2003)

Flowerdew, B. *The Gourmet Gardener: Everything You Need to Know to Grow and Prepare the Very Finest of Vegetables, Fruits and Flowers* (Kyle Cathie, 2005)

Gerber, J. *The Garden Guardian's Guide to Environmentally-responsible Garden Care* (Aardvark Press, 2006)

Gillman, J. *The Truth about Garden Remedies* (Timber Press, 2008)

Gillman, J. *The Truth about Organic Gardening* (Timber Press, 2008)

Hamilton, G. *Organic Gardening* (Dorling Kindersley, 1987)

Hemenway, T. *Gaia's Garden. A Guide to Home-scale Permaculture* (Chelsea Green Publishing Company, 2000)

Hill, F. *How to Grow Microgreens* (David Bateman, 2010)

Hinshaw Patent, D and Bilderback, DE. *The Book of Garden Secrets* (Firefly Books, 1991)

Houbein, L. *One Magic Square. South African Edition* (Jacana Media, 2011)

Jeavons, J. *How to Grow More Vegetables* (Ten Speed Press, 1974)

Kirsten, K. *Gardening with Keith Kirsten* (Struik Lifestyle, 2011)

Littlewood, M. *The Organic Gardener's Handbook* (The Crowood Press, 2007)

Massingham Hart, R. *Vertical Vegetables and Fruit* (Storey Publishing, 2011)

Mitchell, A. *The Edible Balcony* (Kyle Books, 2013)

Mitchell, A. *The Rurbanite* (Kyle Books, 2011)

Paul, J and Windham, W. *Keeping Pet Chickens* (Interpet Publishing, 2005)

Pleasant, B. *Starter Vegetable Gardens* (Storey Publishing, 2010)

Riotte, L. *Carrots Love Tomatoes* (Storey Communications, 1975)

Roberts, M. *Companion Planting* (Briza, 2007)

Rodale Inc. *Organic Gardening Magazine* (Issues November 2007 – July 2008)

Seymour, J. *The New Complete Book of Self-Sufficiency* (Dorling Kindersley, 1976)

Strawbridge, D and J. *Practical Self Sufficiency* (Dorling Kindersley, 2010)

Taunton Press. *Grow. Fine Gardening's Guide to Vegetable Gardening* (Issues 5 and 6)

Woodrow, L. *The Permaculture Home Garden* (Viking, 2007)

ACKNOWLEDGEMENTS AND RESOURCES

A book like this does not happen without the help of many people. My grateful thanks go to the people, organisations and companies who shared their gardens, time and knowledge. Their names and websites are listed below. In particular I would like to thank:

- Jenny, Mike and Claire Slabber from Talborne Organics, for their knowledge, support and ongoing contribution to increased organic production in South Africa
- All the pioneering heirloom seed companies
- Marc Nel from Eva Group for invaluable rooftop gardening information
- Anthony Philbrick, without whom my wetland pool would never have happened
- Healthy Living Herbs for supplying the seedlings for the front cover shot
- Mzansi Gallery Melville, for supplying the bicycle for the front cover shot

Allison Forgèt-Deyes

AMbush Gardening Collective
    www.ambush-gardening-collective.blogspot.com

Babylonstoren www.babylonstoren.com

Barbara Church www.bedford-gardens.co.za

Bark Unlimited Organics www.barkunlimited.co.za

Beechwood Gardens www.beechwoodgardens.co.za

Ben Getz, Urban Harvest www.urbanharvest.co.za

Bev and Gary Brice www.rynfieldhardware.co.za/Garden.pdf

Biogrow www.biogrow.co.za

Brian Green www.44stanley.co.za

Brian Joffin brian.joffin@gmail.com

Cibio Aquaponics www.cibioap.com

Cliff Rosen, Let It Grow ckaran@iafrica.com

Coco Green www.cocogreen.co.za

Daniella Alexander, REEA www.reea.org.za

Denise O'Callaghan

Dis-Chem www.dischem.co.za/dischem-foundation

Duncan Guy

Earth 2 Earth www.earth2earth.co.za

Earth Probiotic www.earthprobiotic.co.za

Emthunzini Hats www.sunhats.co.za

Eva Group www.evagroup.co.za

Garden Shop www.gardenshop.co.za

Garden World www.gardenworld.co.za

Grant Gove www.glcdesignstudio.com

Healthy Living Herbs www.healthyliving-herbs.co.za

Jacques Damhuis, Positive Cycle jacques@positivecycle.co.za

Jane's Delicious Garden Planner
    www.gardenplanner.janesdeliciousgarden.com

JoJo Tanks www.jojotanks.co.za

Justin Sam www.verticallandscapes.co.za

Kathryn Kure www.plus.google.com/+KathrynKure/posts

Latitude Stone www.latitudedecor.co.za

Living Seeds www.livingseeds.co.za

Liz Dahl and Naude van der Merwe for their beautiful
    wetland pool (Page 224)

Mr Price Foundation www.mrpfoundation.org

Mzansi Gallery Melville www.mzansi.gallery/

Reel Gardening www.reelgardening.co.za

Rob Small, Abalimi www.abalimi.org.za

Rogz Farm www.rogz.com/passion/rogz-farm

SABIO (SA Beekeeping Organisation) www.sabio.org.za

Seeds for Africa www.seedsforafrica.co.za

Sheryl Ozinsky, OZCF www.ozcf.co.za

Shirley Wallington Landscaping www.wallington.co.za

SkALE Greenwall www.skalegreenwall.co.za

Sought After Seedlings www.soughtafterseedlings.co.za

Southerns Beekeeping Association www.beekeepers.co.za

Spier Biodynamic Farm www.farmerangus.co.za

Square Foot Gardening www.sfgsa.co.za

Stargrow www.stargrow.co.za/cultivar_development.asp

Talborne Organics www.talborne.co.za

The Company's Garden www.thecompanysgarden.com

The Gravel Garden www.thegravelgarden.co.za

The Saxon www.saxon.co.za

The Star www.iol.co.za/the-star

The Urban Box
    www.janesdeliciousgarden.com/the_urban_box

Tyisa Nabanye www.tyisanabanye.org

Urban Freedom www.urbanfreedom.co.za

Valverde Eco Hotel www.valverde.co.za

Wetland Pools www.wetlandpools.co.za

INDEX

Sam
梁兆基 Leong

A Wok Through Time

Sam Leong
梁兆基

A Wok Through Time

Marshall Cavendish
Cuisine

Chef: Sam Leong
Chef's Assistants: Chef Krisna B. and Chef Thomas Chai
Photographer: Joyce Choo

First published (cased with jacket) 2004
This limp edition 2009

Copyright © 2004 Marshall Cavendish International (Asia) Private Limited

Published by Marshall Cavendish Cuisine
An imprint of Marshall Cavendish International
1 New Industrial Road, Singapore 536196

Other Marshall Cavendish Offices:
Marshall Cavendish Ltd.5th Floor, 32–38 Saffron Hill, London EC1N 8FH • Marshall Cavendish Corporation.
99 White Plains Road, Tarrytown NY 10591-9001, USA • Marshall Cavendish International (Thailand) Co Ltd.
253 Asoke, 12th Flr, Sukhumvit 21 Road, Klongtoey Nua, Wattana, Bangkok 10110, Thailand
• Marshall Cavendish (Malaysia) Sdn Bhd, Times Subang, Lot 46, Subang Hi-Tech Industrial Park,
Batu Tiga, 40000 Shah Alam, Selangor Darul Ehsan, Malaysia

Marshall Cavendish is a trademark of Times Publishing Limited

National Library Board Singapore Cataloguing in Publication Data

Leong, Sam, 1966-
A wok through time / Sam Leong ; [chef's assistants, Krisna B. and Thomas Chai].
– Singapore : Marshall Cavendish Cuisine, 2009.
p. cm.
ISBN-13 : 978-981-261-671-5 (pbk.)
ISBN-10 : 981-261-671-3 (pbk.)

1. Cookery, Chinese. I. Krisna B. II. Chai, Thomas. III. Title.

TX724.5.C5
641.5951 -- dc22   OCN259866124

Printed in Singapore by Times Graphics Pte Ltd

Contents

MY DAD **THE CHEF**

Contents

COOKING FOR VIPs AND CELEBRITIES

Contents

Foreword

Singapore is a gourmet city. Tourists flock to our shores for spicy food, vegetables cooked Chinese style and seafood fresh from the oceans of our region. As for locals, they love food so much that dinner conversations often focus on the next meal.

Yet, excellent food is not possible without excellent chefs. In this regard, Sam Leong stands tall among the best. Locally, he is recognised as a key creator of New Asian Cuisine as well as a mentor and master to many young chefs. Internationally, he is recognised for his ability to blend the flavours of common and exotic ingredients to create sensational new tastes, showcase Chinese dishes in a way that rivals the elegance of fine French and Japanese cuisine, and create a table that is as magical as a spa experience. This is how I would describe Sam's talent; others may describe it differently, but I am sure all who know Sam will agree that a totally unique quality prevails in the way that he creates and presents traditional Chinese food.

Through the many recipes and beautiful photographs in this book, the genius of this master chef blossoms forth. This book required a lot of hard work to put together, including years of experimentation by Sam in the kitchen. Fortunately, our task as book and food lovers is simply to enjoy the flavours, the romance and the uniqueness of the culinary creations he has showcased here for us.

Mrs Pamelia Lee
International Tourism Consultant

Dedication

To my wife, Forest Leong, whose
love and encouragement has
enabled me to pursue my career
to the utmost.

To Andrew Tjioe,
the CEO of the Tung Lok
Group, who has given me
countless opportunities in the
advancement of my career.

Acknowledgement

I would like to thank all my **friends and guests** who have supported me through the years, helping me to win the Asian Ethnic Chef of the Year title at the World Gourmet Summit Awards of Excellence in 2001, 2002 and 2004.